P9-DHM-950

5/94

THE WAR BETWEEN THE SPIES

THE WAR
BETWEEN
THE SPIES

A History of Espionage
During the
American Civil War

ALAN AXELROD

THE ATLANTIC MONTHLY PRESS
NEW YORK

Library of Congress Cataloging-in-Publication Data

Axelrod, Alan, 1952-
    The war between the spies: a history of espionage during the American Civil War / Alan Axelrod—1st ed.
    Includes bibliographical references (p.   ) and index.
    ISBN 0-87113-482-9
    1. United States—History—Civil War, 1861–1865—Secret service. 2. Spies—United States—History—19th century. I. Title.
E608.A94   1992   973.7'85—dc20   92-13982

Published simultaneously in Canada.
Printed in the United States of America
FIRST EDITION

Produced by Zenda, Inc.

The Atlantic Monthly Press
19 Union Square West
New York, N.Y. 10003

For Anita and Ian

CONTENTS

AUTHOR'S NOTE

I do not pretend to have written an exhaustive scholarly study of espionage and counterespionage in the Civil War. I doubt that such a treatment is even possible; for Civil War spies were amateurs, usually ordinary soldiers and civilians who, on one or more occasions, did some spying. Military and political leaders, whether Union or Confederate, were reticent about discussing their use of spies, few formal appointments were made, and few official records exist. There *are*, however, plenty of fascinating, exciting, moving, and even rather hilarious stories here, and I owe my knowledge of them in large measure to the legion of Civil War scholars and chroniclers, past and present, whose writings are listed in the bibliography at the end of this book. To these writers, a collective thank you.

It is also a pleasure to thank Morgan Entrekin and Anton Mueller of Atlantic Monthly Press for publishing *The War Between the Spies*, and my agent, Bert Holtje of James Peter Associates, for taking the book to them. Civil War researcher Curtis A. Utz skillfully and efficiently tracked down illustrations and original resource materials I requested, and my partners in Zenda, Inc., Charles Phillips and Patricia Hogan, have served my book and me as extraordinary editors. As usual, my wife and son, Anita and Ian, have endured patiently and with understanding a process that, also as usual, has taken more time than any of us expected.

Finally, a note on the various examples of African American dialect the reader will encounter in these pages. Few writers of the nineteenth century possessed Mark Twain's sensitive ear for dialects. Most writers did not so much transcribe what they actually heard, as they wrote what racist convention *told* them they had heard. When I have quoted from original sources that attempt to approximate African American speech, I have quoted verbatim. The result, at best, is uneven and, at worst, grossly inaccurate. To modern ears, of course, it is even offensive. The dialect passages are nevertheless important to the stories I relate precisely because they reflect the beliefs and perceptions of the era that produced them— beliefs and perceptions from which the Civil War, in part, was fought to liberate us.

INTRODUCTION

O ften called the second oldest profession, spying is in fact as old as war itself. No commander has ever liked going into battle without knowing everything he can about his enemy, and intercepted field orders, clandestinely obtained enemy strategies, furtive tabulations of troop strength and disposition, secret reports of overheard conversations, and purloined correspondence have proved now and again as important to a military engagement as inspired leadership, effective arms, and fighting spirit. But it was only during wartime that those sneak-thieves called spies were truly appreciated by anyone other than the officers, nobles, pontiffs, and tyrants who employed them. Throughout most of history, espionage was a disreputable activity undertaken by a seedy arm of the military establishment.

In modern times spying has become more glamorous. The rise of the nation-state gave the spy's addiction to deception and betrayal the patina of patriotism. Espionage became something one could do for God and country instead of for blood money or obsequious advancement or in response to extortion or blackmail. The European nation-state was born amid the incessant intrigues of the decaying Holy Roman Empire, and consequently Europe developed through centuries of constant warfare a system of bewildering, always shifting alliances between popes, dukes, and kings. The great mercantile powers continued the habit as the continent's internecine conflicts grew into wars for empire during the seventeenth and eighteenth centuries and the goal of the shifting alliance system became a balance of power. By the nineteenth century, alliances were so entangling that local conflicts almost necessarily grew into international wars. Every nation-state kept a huge standing army ready at a moment's notice to continue its complicated diplomacy by other means. Under such a system, espionage naturally flourished, becoming recognized not only as a military requisite, but also as an economic and diplomatic necessity.

Britain proved especially adept at using a deeply ingrained nationalist fervor to transform the ancient but not very venerable profession of spying into an honorable pastime, something even gentlemen could take up in the service of a higher calling. By century's end, England would dub the alliance system and the traffic in international intrigue that went along with it the "Great Game." Secret and amoral, the Great Game made a romance out of espionage, one in which those who lied, cheated, and stole for the homeland were heroes, while those who did so for other countries were villains and traitors. Spying no longer attracted merely the desperate and the disgruntled but also the noble and the idealistic.

During the American Revolution, which from the British point of view was the start of yet another of its international wars for empirical hegemony, the fledgling republic also fell prey to the new romance of espionage. Consider, for example, Nathan Hale and Benedict Arnold.

Hale, as every schoolchild knows, is an American hero who coolly quipped to his British executioners, "I only regret that I have but one life to lose for my country." Never mind that Hale was an inept secret agent who arrived in Manhattan to begin his spying only after the British had invaded the island by way of Kip's Bay, sending the Patriots scurrying uptown and making any information about English troop movements on Long Island moot. Never mind that Hale continued to poke about Manhattan when he should have packed up and gone home, and that he secreted on his person extensive written notes, which made their discovery—and his execution—certain when the British arrested him. Finally, never mind that Nathan Hale was only a bit player in—and something of an embarrassment to—the efficiently professional spy network developed by George Washington and his commanders during the Revolution. Being captured and executed for spying by the British on September 22, 1776, was enough to give the Connecticut schoolmaster a permanent place of honor in American history.

Benedict Arnold, on the other hand, has become the schoolchild's quintessential traitor, his name a virtual code-word for betrayal, because he sold out his country for personal and financial gain. A high-living gentleman who had married above his station and chronically short of cash, Arnold was a successful and competent officer in the Revolutionary army who felt that neither General Washington nor Congress appreciated and rewarded his military prowess. In May 1779, he offered to betray the Patriot stronghold under his command at West Point for the lordly sum of twenty thousand pounds, an offer British general Sir Henry Clinton immediately accepted by dispatching his adjutant, Major John André, to handle negotiations. When André was arrested on his way back from West Point, the revolutionaries discovered Arnold's detailed plan hidden in the adjutant's boot and subsequently executed André as a spy. Meanwhile, Arnold had fled to General Clinton, receiving a portion of the cash promised despite the foiled plot and organizing a Loyalist regiment to raid his hometown of New London, Connecticut, and parts of Tidewater Virginia. Though he was commissioned in the British army, Arnold never received the major command he craved since His Majesty's government no more trusted the recent turncoat than the Americans now did.

Neither Nathan Hale, the hopeless romantic, nor Benedict Arnold, the self-absorbed opportunist, had any effect on the outcome of the fighting in the Revolutionary War. The truly effective spies of the period were Benjamin Franklin and Colonel Benjamin Tallmadge. A prominent statesman, Franklin intrigued with policy makers in capitals throughout Europe, presiding over an international ring of secret agents who helped to ensure that the flow of arms from France to revolutionary America was maintained at high volume. Back home, Tallmadge organized the Culper Ring, a group of spies upon which Washington came to rely heavily for information on British activity in and around New York City. Franklin, however, became revered not as a spy but as a benign elder statesmen. Tallmadge achieved no fame whatsoever. Hale and Arnold became two of the best known figures of the Revolutionary era precisely because the struggle was for national identity and it mattered not at all how effective their spying was, only that it played well in the patriotic drama of the birth of a new nation.

In the years following the Revolution, however, the United States turned its back on European balance-of-power machinations and its institutionalized espionage. President George Washington made clear in his Farewell Address the abhorrence with which Americans viewed the Old World alliance system and the cabalistic treaties on which it thrived. The United States refused to keep large standing armies, and early nineteenth-century Americans considered espionage a dirty business, at best a sometimes necessary evil. True, American spies and covert agents regularly intrigued in diplomatic circles. The War of 1812 and the Mexican War of 1846-48 both saw the use of spies on more traditional military missions, though they were never deployed as extensively or successfully as in the Revolution. The United States created no department of intelligence within its tiny military establishment. An ocean away from Europe, America had no need to worry about what some neighboring nation would do tomorrow and, therefore, American policy makers saw little use for a secret service to navigate a course through a world of shifting loyalties and constant betrayal.

Which helps to explain the haphazard nature of espionage in the American Civil War. Unlike Europe, America had no extensive network of professionals experienced in the arts of infiltration, of clandestine communication, and of assessing and analyzing intelligence. Though the Civil War was an ideologically inspired conflict with patriotic fervor on both sides, America's national identity was not being threatened by an outside power but by its own citizens. Therefore, the modern romance of espionage did not take hold and attract the brightest and the best to what remained throughout the war not a higher calling but a distasteful, if often neglected, necessity.

Spying during the Civil War was shaped by the peculiar nature of the conflict itself. It was a war fought not by professional standing armies, but by ordinary citizens, born and raised with no intention of ever taking up arms. Confederate muster rolls enumerate more than a hundred different civilian occupations for its enlistees;

Northern records yield some three hundred, which is not surprising, given the far greater industrial and economic diversity of the North. Farmers, tinkers, and tailors, Civil War soldiers were ordinary people, not specially trained retainers of warlike states. A man fought alongside his neighbor, who yesterday had been a plow boy, factory worker, or clerk, and he fought against a more distant neighbor, no more a soldier than himself. Within days after the fall of Fort Sumter, the awful phrase "brother against brother" had become a cliché.

Generations raised on movies and television think of nineteenth-century youth as naturally skilled in the use of firearms. In fact, few recruits on either side came into the army knowing much about guns, and with ammunition a precious commodity, little of it was "wasted" on training. The result was a standard of prodigiously poor marksmanship. It was not only that the Civil War soldier couldn't shoot straight, he was often so scared and inadequately prepared that he failed to shoot at all, and in the thick of the fight, many a man went through the involved process of priming and loading his musket only to forget at last to fire it. Yet, somehow, these inept soldiers managed to kill almost a half-million of themselves.

On the one hand, fighting in the Civil War was intimate, even claustrophobic: troops advanced upon their enemy in close-rank formations. They opened fire on one another at a range of at most a few hundred yards. When they got even closer together, the order might be given to "club" their muskets, which meant holding the gun by its barrel so that the stock could be used as the weapon familiar to cave men. On the other hand, these tragic tableaus of one man against another were played out on a collective scale unprecedented in the history of war. The Civil War was the first modern war of mass destruction, fueled by the burgeoning technology of the industrial nineteenth century. Arms were mass produced. Artillery was bigger and more destructive. Wooden ships were, in a stroke as of hammer on anvil, made obsolete by the seaborne killing machine known as the "ironclad." Friends, neighbors, farm boys, clerks, brother and brother—all were fed into one great and impersonal killing machine.

The War Between the Spies

For an endeavor of amateurs, the stakes were awfully high. It is well to remember this, as we bear witness to the heroic bumblings of improvised secret agents. For what was true of the soldiers of the Civil War was even more true of the spies; they were even ranker amateurs than the troopers. While both armies had a core, however small, of professional military officers, neither had a formal intelligence division until well into the war. The phrase "secret service" was bandied about freely by both the North and the South even early on, but neither side had an official secret service *department* until the middle year of the conflict. We know the South developed two intelligence arms (the chiefs of which were rivals prone to feuding), at least one of which used official-looking stationery that bore a letterhead proclaiming the "Secret Service Bureau." The North also sprouted poorly coordinated, quasi-official groups, including one grandiosely dubbed the National Detective Police—though it mustered, at maximum, about thirty men.

Despite names and titles, those who manned such bureaus and departments were in no sense trained secret agents. The closest thing to professional espionage the Civil War offered was the famed Allan J. Pinkerton and his "operatives," as he liked to term them. These were detectives, however, the world's first "private eyes," and not military spies. They were quite adept at counterespionage, catching enemy agents, which was rather like tracking down embezzlers, train robbers, and strike organizers, the kind of work to which Pinkerton and his men were accustomed. However, as agents of espionage—spies—they were dutiful and daring, but inefficient and unreliable.

If there was no bona fide espionage organization at the outbreak of the Civil War, there was, however, no shortage of spies. Commanders on both sides took it upon themselves to solicit volunteers for "special service," with the result that intelligence activities were fragmented and uncoordinated, the ad hoc agents often operating without knowledge of one another and even at cross purposes. It was all remarkably casual. At the beginning of the war, Abraham Lincoln, fretting over the dearth of hard intelligence about the enemy, dragooned a traveling businessman into being the Union's first behind-the-lines spy. Lafayette C. Baker, an ambitious ex-Californian with a penchant for vigilante work, wandered into the office of the aged and obese Winfield Scott, the Union army's general-in-chief, and simply volunteered for espionage work. Within a few months he was heading up the aforementioned National Detective Police, an outfit Baker himself named. In Richmond, a birdlike spinster, dismissed by her neighbors as an old maid eccentric to the point of lunacy, became the leader of a highly effective Union underground operating in the heart of the Confederacy.

Neither side knew what to do with all that their amateur spies had gathered. The failures of Civil War espionage were due less to a lack of a trained corps of agents, than to the want of intelligence-processing machinery. Both North and South threw away intelligence as prodigally as their armies consumed lives and materiel. Still, by the end of the war both the North and South had in place rudimentary intelligence services. But in the rush to demobilize following Appomattox, a battle-weary nation quickly undid what little had been done to establish permanent intelligence-gathering and intelligence-processing apparatus, and the Secret Service died aborning.

It was not until 1882 that the U.S. Navy established an Office of Intelligence as part of its Bureau of Navigation, and 1885 that the War Department created the Military Information Division under the army's Adjutant General's Office. Both of these organizations were aimed at acquiring technological rather than strategic information. In the wake of the Civil War, Congress was niggardly with military appropriations even as European nations were continually arming themselves and perfecting the technology of warfare. If the U.S. Navy and Army lacked the funds to participate in such activities, at least the Office of Intelligence and the Military Information Division would let American commanders know what they were missing out on. From this humble beginning, rather than from the improvised and individualist efforts of the Civil War, the U.S. "intelligence community" developed.

And it developed according to a European model. By the end of the nineteenth century, the Great Game was in full swing. The ante was upped by the introduction of increasingly devasatating modern weaponry, the first inkling of which had come during the American Civil War. German unification seriously destabilized the European alliance system. Bismarck's machinations of realpolitik led to a new round of alliances attempting desperately to reestablish a balance of power. At the same time, within the industrialized countries, the first true ideological challenge to the nation-state system was born as disgruntled workers sought to unite under the banner of class rather than state. The nation-states rushed into two immensely destructive world wars, and in their wake socialism gained ground. A fully developed ideological clash between the new bureaucratized workers' states and the old capitalist nation-states became a powerful new fuel driving the engines of espionage.

The romance of espionage reached its apogee as trained intelligence agents spied to change the world or to save it from change. The United States, drawn inexorably if reluctantly into the arena of international alliances since the Spanish-American War of 1898, learned at last to play the Great Game at the feet of British tutors during World War II. The upper-crust spies of MI6 showed the good old boys of the wartime OSS (Office of Strategic Services) how to train and run the teams of agents and analysts required by the huge institutionalized espionage establishments of modern times. After the war, America's own gentlemen spies, whose roots were to be found mostly in big business and international finance, lobbied for and created the Central Intelligence Agency.

Only American counter-intelligence could trace its lineage back to the Civil War. After Appomattox, Allan Pinkerton's detective agency grew into something approaching a privately funded national police force, which specialized in class warfare against an American work force whose ranks were being filled by masses of new immigrants, many of them steeped in a proud European socialist heritage. Finding subversive plots wherever he sent the thugs he hired as strikebreakers, Pinkerton created a network of operatives that worked not merely as a contemporary agency for ideological repression but also served as the historical model for what in time would become the Federal Bureau of Investigation. And the FBI, in turn, became America's primary counter-intelligence organization, comparable to England's MI5 (MI6 focuses exclusively on foreign intelligence; MI5 is Britain's spy-catching agency) and responsible— as Pinkerton had been during the Civil War—for seeking out and capturing secret agents operating within the borders of the United States.

In truth, America's twentieth-century spies were neither more heroic nor more talented than their Civil War-era counterparts. They were, however, *trained*, and, even more important, they worked within the context of a greater "intelligence community," as the system of U.S. intelligence organizations has come to be called. With the electronic revolution of the last few decades, the business of spying has become increasingly a matter of technology, of communications and computer-stored and computer-manipulated data, of electronic monitoring of electronic phenomena, in short of intelligence gathered by remote control. Nevertheless, the romance of espionage still flourished at least through the collapse of the USSR and the end of the Cold War. If nothing else, the millions of readers addicted to the legion of modern spy novels and popular histories of twentieth-century espionage testify to its continuing power.

Such readers will not find that kind of romance here. For this is a book about espionage prior to the Great Game and outside its historical tradition, a book about *amateur* spies in a nation suspicious of official secrets. Many of these men and women were extraordinarily skilled, very daring, and spectacularly ambitious. Some were bent on nothing less than singlehandedly overthrowing the government they opposed. But none of them had any experience of the endemic duplicity of European diplomacy and its attendant espionage system, and certainly none of them could even imagine the wilderness of mirrors that characterizes the modern intelligence community.

Nevertheless, their stories are filled with courage, suspense, and sheer inventiveness. Neither side, after all, was in a position to issue the equivalent of a CIA or KGB handbook to their operatives, who were compelled, therefore, to make up the rules as they went along. Sometimes the results of such enforced spontaneity were surprisingly effective; sometimes they were catastrophic; frequently they were just plain funny. Readers looking to discover nineteenth-century adumbrations of James Bond will have more often to content themselves with prototypes of Maxwell Smart.

The War Between the Spies

Yes, the spies of the Civil War bumbled; they improvised; sometimes they suffered and died. Yet in a long and melancholy war that strains the word *tragedy,* the tragedy of a their fate pales beside the windrows of blanched and bloodied corpses, a half-million of them, that were once men and brothers. In that horrible context, the fate of spies, especially amateurs, may well seem comic. But it is precisely here that their story seems strikingly modern, an absurd comedy, suited more to the twentieth century than the nineteenth, a black comedy made blacker by the cruel irony that so much of what they did and risked was done and risked in vain, wasted on armies that felt the need for spies but—ignorant of the ways of a profession as old as war itself—rarely knew how to use them or the information they so dearly bought.

CHAPTER ONE

INAUGURAL JOURNEY

In the opening weeks of 1861, Mr. Samuel H. Felton, president of the Philadelphia, Wilmington and Baltimore Railroad, was hearing disturbing rumors concerning the "roughs and secessionists of Maryland." It seems they meant to sink the ferry boats that carried the trains—*his* trains—across the Susquehanna at Havre de Grace or to blow up the bridges over the Gunpowder River and other streams. Felton owed it to his road—and, in these troubled times, to the great federal Union—to get the best man on the case. He fired off a letter to Allan J. Pinkerton, the nation's first professional private investigator, asking him to come to the railroad's offices in Philadelphia.

The man whose name, by the 1860s, was virtually a synonym for detective had fallen into his profession by chance. He had been born on August 25, 1819, to an impoverished Glasgow family. At the age of eight, he was apprenticed to a cooper and, soon after completing his apprenticeship, came to the United States, where he settled on the Fox River near Chicago, setting up a business in his trade. He was on an island in the river one day, cutting barrel wood, when he accidentally discovered the hideout of a band of counterfeiters. Pinkerton was moved to organize a raid on the malefactors, which proved so successful that he was soon hired to do other odd jobs of detection, nabbing horse thieves and the like. His reputation grew so rapidly that he was appointed Chicago's first police detective in 1849, but, after a year of that city's corrupt politics, he left office to open his own agency. His reputation and clientele grew exponentially.

Pinkerton consulted with railroad president Felton and H. F. Kenney, superintendent of the Philadelphia, Wilmington and Baltimore, obtaining what information they had gleaned concerning the "Maryland secessionists." Determining to plant agents at strategic points along the railroad, Pinkerton made a preparatory tour of investigation. He found Wilmington, Delaware, unsettled but essentially loyal. Perryville, Maryland, was more agitated, but Pinkerton judged that the town offered little threat at present. "At Havre de Grace, however, the lines were more clearly drawn and the popular feeling more bitter." The village was strategically located at a ferry point across the Susquehanna, "where serious damage might be done to the company." Pinkerton deposited one agent at Havre de Grace, instructing him to observe and report on conditions there, infiltrating whatever subversive organizations might come into being. The next stop, Perrymansville (present-day Perryman), proved even more seditious. "Loud threats were uttered against the railroad company; and it was boastfully asserted that 'no d____d abolitionist should be allowed to pass through the town alive.' " Here Pinkerton placed his best agent, an ex-New York police officer named Timothy Webster.

The closer Pinkerton drew to Baltimore, the more intense he found the spirit of rebellion. At nearby Magnolia he left John Seaford, and in Baltimore proper he ensconced himself. From a room in the Howard House, Pinkerton began to probe an extensive network of conspiracy. When he heard that the chief of police, Marshal George P. Kane, was a secessionist—as, apparently, were the men he commanded—Pinkerton established a permanent headquarters in a building on South Street, sent for additional operatives, and deployed them "among the people of all grades and conditions of life." He had chosen his building as carefully as he had selected his men. It had entrances on all four sides, including concealed alleyways, through which his agents could enter and exit unobserved. He received reports daily.

Allan Pinkerton knew what to do to head off the railroad sabotage. He'd policed many a railroad strike before, and he had put down the infamous Molly Maguires. But now his men were bringing him news of a much more sinister nature than mere sabotage. The Maryland secessionists intended to prevent the inauguration of President-elect Abraham Lincoln, and the only way to do that, they believed, was to kill him.

On February 11, 1861, Lincoln boarded a train at the Great Western Railroad station in Springfield, Illinois, and began the long journey to Washington. He was scheduled to make stops at Indianapolis, Cincinnati, Columbus, Pittsburgh, Cleveland, Erie, Buffalo, Albany, New York City, Trenton, Newark, Philadelphia, and Harrisburg. At Baltimore, he was not only to stop, but to change trains, going by carriage from the Calvert Street depot to Camden Station. The day before the president-elect left Springfield, Pinkerton received a letter from the master mechanic of Felton's railroad:

> I am informed that a son of a distinguished citizen of Maryland said that he had taken an oath with others to assassinate Mr. Lincoln before he gets to Washington, and they may attempt to do it while he is passing over our road. I think you had better look after this man, if possible. This information is perfectly reliable. I have nothing more to say at this time, but will try to see you in a few days.

Together with his best operatives, Pinkerton set about penetrating the Baltimore cabals of assassination. One of those "ops," whom Pinkerton called Joseph Howard, was of French descent and admirably suited to clandestine activity, so Pinkerton reasoned, because he had been trained as a Jesuit priest. He had also spent several years in New Orleans and other cities of the South, so he was well acquainted with Southern customs and culture. His mission was to register in one of Baltimore's best hotels, pass himself off as a prominent citizen of New Orleans, and make his ultrasecessionist sentiments widely known.

Howard quickly discovered that Barnum's Hotel was the "favorite resort of the Southern element. The visitors from all portions of the South located at this house, and in the evenings the corridors and parlors would be thronged by the tall, lank forms of the long-haired gentlemen who represented the aristocracy of the slaveholding interests." They spoke volubly and violently, these "fire-eaters," and among them Howard cut a romantic figure, especially in the eyes of the Baltimore belles. Soon he entered into the circle of Marshal George P. Kane and confirmed Pinkerton's intelligence that the entire police force of Baltimore was secessionist. Through Kane he gained admittance to the city's chief secret secessionist society, an assemblage of those lanky, long-haired, aristocratic young men Pinkerton had noted thronging the streets of Baltimore. They were led, incongruously enough, by an Italian immigrant who had until recently served as the Hotel Barnum's barber. Captain Fernandina, as he was called, stirred his men to action with a speech, "his black eyes flashing . . . his sallow face pale and colorless and his long hair brushed fiercely back from his low forehead":

> This hireling Lincoln shall never, never be President. My life is of no consequence in a cause like this, and I am willing to give it for his. As Orsini gave his life for Italy, I am ready to die for the rights of the South and to crush out the abolitionist.

Howard reported it all to Pinkerton, who was sufficiently impressed to want to see this barber-assassin for himself. At three o'clock on the afternoon following Fernandina's speech, Pinkerton and Howard casually wandered into the saloon of Guy's Restaurant, where the captain was holding court. Howard introduced Pinkerton as a Georgian, whereupon the Italian cordially took his hand—as Pinkerton recounted in his memoir, *The Spy of the Rebellion*—and the conversation turned to assassination.

"Are there no other means of saving the South except by assassination?" someone asked.

"No," replied Fernandina, "as well might you attempt to move the Washington Monument yonder with your breath, as to change our purpose. He must die—and die he shall. And, if necessary, we will die together."

Howard played his role to the hilt: "There seems to be no other way, and while bloodshed is to be regretted, it will be done in a noble cause."

"Yes," replied Fernandina, "the cause is a noble one, and on that day every captain will prove himself a hero. With the first shot the chief traitor, Lincoln, will die, then all Maryland will be with us, and the South will be forever free."

Pinkerton, the newcomer, was appropriately skeptical: "But have all the plans been matured, and are there no fears of failure? A misstep in so important a direction would be fatal to the South and ought to be well considered."

"Our plans are fully arranged," replied the former barber, "and they cannot fail; and if I alone must strike the blow, I shall not hesitate or shrink from the task. Lincoln shall certainly not depart from this city alive."

Another conspirator, a Captain Trichot, piped up: "Yes, it is determined that this G___d d____d Lincoln shall never pass through here alive, and no d____d abolitionist shall ever set foot upon Southern soil except to find a grave."

"But about the authorities"—Pinkerton was still feigning incredulity—"is there no danger to be apprehended from them?"

"Oh, no," Fernandina answered, "they are all with us. I have seen Col. Kane, the Chief Marshal of Police, and he is all right. In a week from to-day the North shall want another President, for Lincoln will be a corpse."

Allan Pinkerton heard the applause that greeted Captain Fernandina's reply, but, like the good detective that he was, took special note of the single man who remained undemonstrative. He was, Pinkerton soon learned, "one of the fast 'bloods' of the city." A lieutenant in the Palmetto Guards, a secret military organization, he wore a gold palmetto badge on his breast, but his face betrayed a "doubtful, troubled expression." Pinkerton and Howard left the saloon of Guy's Hotel with this man, Lieutenant Hill, and had a long talk. Of "a weak nature and having been reared in the lap of luxury, he had entered into this movement more from a temporary burst of enthusiasm and because it was fashionable, than from any other cause." Pinkerton knew he had found the weak link in the chain of conspiracy and instructed Howard to become his close comrade.

As Pinkerton had hoped, the aristocratic Hill introduced Howard to the cream of Baltimore secessionist society, at last disclosing to him the details of the plot against Abraham Lincoln.

The conspirators' first step was to agitate and arouse public feeling against the president-elect. The itinerary of the inaugural train had been widely published: Lincoln would reach Baltimore from Harrisburg on February 23 at midday. A crowd would greet him at the Calvert Street Depot, from which he would be taken in an open carriage a half-mile to Camden Station. There only a small force of policemen would be positioned, who were, in any case, of secessionist stamp. A disturbance would be staged to attract their attention, and the fatal shots fired. Nor did the conspirators rely solely on the published itinerary. They had dispatched agents to all the Northern cities along the inaugural route, who reported on the progress of the presidential train and, using a prearranged cipher, stood ready to telegraph any change in plan. The actual assassin was to be determined by lot.

As the fatal day drew near, Pinkerton and Howard observed that Lieutenant Hill grew by turns increasingly melancholy and manic. He drank heavily and depended upon the constant companionship of Howard. He would launch into extravagant rhapsodies: "I am destined to die, shrouded with glory. I shall immortalize myself by plunging a knife into Lincoln's heart. . . . Rome had her Brutus, why should not we? I swear to you, Howard, if it falls to me I will kill Lincoln before he reaches the Washington depot [Camden Station], not that I love Lincoln less, but my country more."

While Pinkerton and Howard infiltrated the Baltimore cabal, Timothy Webster was still at Perrymansville, piecing together additional components of the conspiracy. Having joined a local company of cavalry rallying to the cause of the South, he drilled daily with the men and gradually gained the confidence of the officers. After drill one day, the captain summoned Webster to his home. A group of men had gathered in an upstairs room, its curtains closed and heavy quilts hung over the windows so that not even a glimmer of light would escape to the outside. Three of those gathered were Baltimoreans, and they were meeting to discuss how best to capitalize on the impending assassination. Merely to kill the president-elect, they reasoned, would have little effect; indeed, the North "would rise as one man to avenge the death of their leader." No, the assassination was to be only the opening shot in a lightning campaign of chaos. News of the deed was to be telegraphed along the line of the railroad, whereupon agents were to cut the wires to the capital and destroy the bridges and right-of-way leading north. In the confusion and paralysis that would result, Washington itself might be invaded before reinforcements could arrive. Demoralized, the North would abandon its scheme to enforce its will upon the South, and the Civil War would be won even before it was fought.

Pinkerton dispatched a message to Norman B. Judd, who was accompanying the inaugural party, informing him of the plot against the president-elect's life. That note reached Judd at Cincinnati: Pinkerton provided an update at Buffalo. And he decided that he needed to communicate definitive information to Judd by the time the train arrived in New York City. He determined to put another operative on the case, Mrs. Kate Warne, the "lady superintendent" of the Pinkerton Detective Agency. Ingratiating and of a "commanding person," her job was to cultivate the wives and daughters of the conspirators. She supplied Pinkerton with a good deal of information, but the identity of the assassin or assassins was yet to be determined. Pinkerton decided to push Howard's connection with Hill to the limit. Howard was to persuade the young conspirator to take him to the meeting where the actual lots would be drawn, ostensibly so that Howard would have, with the others, a chance to kill Abraham Lincoln.

The pair entered a darkened chamber in which many of the conspirators were already gathered, hushed, as if in awe of the task they were about to perform. First, Howard was ceremoniously inducted into the cabal. A contemporary engraving, most likely fanciful, shows him on bended knee, being anointed with a sword as if he were a candidate for knighthood. Second, came the details of the assassination plans and, third, the drawing of lots. It was decided at last that the killing should take place at the Calvert Street Depot, where a crowd of secessionists would effectively choke off all passages leading to the street and Lincoln's carriage. The president-elect would have to thread his way through the throng, a diversionary disturbance would be staged, and Lincoln would be shot. A fast steamer waiting in the harbor would carry the assassin to the South. Lots were prepared and placed in a box. To the man who drew the red lot would fall the role of assassin. The leaders of the conspiracy took two precautions: they darkened the room, so that no one could see the color of the drawn lots, and they stuffed the box with eight red lots, thereby insuring that *someone* would carry out the deed—"each man [nevertheless] believing that upon him, his courage, strength and devotion, depended the cause of the South."

With matters carried so far, Pinkerton dispatched Warne from Baltimore to New York, where she conveyed the details of the conspiracy to Norman Judd. In the meantime, Pinkerton reported to his original client, railroad president Felton, and secured carte blanche from Colonel E. S. Sandford, president of the American Telegraph Company, to use the lines as he saw fit. At last, on February 20, it was decided to lay all the facts before President-elect Lincoln when he arrived in Philadelphia on the twenty-first.

Lincoln was mobbed in the City of Brotherly Love, and the police struggled to keep the enthusiastic crowd at a distance. At the corner of Broad and Chestnut streets, however, young George H. Burns, Sandford's confidential agent, plunged through police lines and handed Norman Judd a slip of paper: *"St. Louis Hotel, ask for J. H. Hutchinson."* J. H. Hutchinson, Judd knew, was the name under which Allan Pinkerton had registered at the St. Louis Hotel, and he met with the detective there immediately. Pinkerton related all that he learned, concluding with the advice that "Mr. Lincoln [should] proceed to Washington this evening by the eleven o'clock train, and then once safe at the capital, General Scott and his soldiery will afford him ample protection."

Judd expressed doubt that Lincoln would agree to so precipitant a flight, "but as the President is an old acquaintance and friend of yours," he remarked to Pinkerton, "suppose you accompany me to the Continental Hotel, and we can lay this information before him in person and abide by his decision."

Enthusiastic throngs prevented the two men from going into the Continental by the main entrance, so they entered through the servants' doorway. Lincoln's private secretary, John G. Nicolay, was sent to fetch the president-elect, who heard for the first time of the plot against him.

Lincoln was less fearful than saddened. Disbelieving, wanting not to believe, he made Pinkerton repeat every point of his report. The detective concluded by advising Lincoln to curtail his preinaugural itinerary and proceed directly to Washington that very night. Judd pointed out that "the proofs that have just been laid before you cannot be published, as it will involve the lives of several devoted men now on Mr. Pinkerton's force, especially that of Timothy Webster, who is now serving in a rebel cavalry company under drill at Perrymansville in Maryland."

Lincoln was now convinced that he was in danger, but he was unsure how best to proceed.

"You will therefore perceive," Norman Judd continued, "that if you follow the course suggested—that of proceeding to Washington to-night—you will necessarily be subjected to the scoffs and sneers of your enemies, and the disapproval of your friends who cannot be made to believe in the existence of so desperate a plot."

At last the president-elect became resolute: "I fully appreciate these suggestions, and I can stand anything that is necessary, but I cannot go to-night. I have promised to raise the flag over Independence Hall to-morrow morning, and to visit the legislature at Harrisburg in the afternoon—beyond that I have no engagements. Any plan that may be adopted that will enable me to fulfill these promises I will accede to, and you can inform me what is concluded upon to-morrow."

With Lincoln's mind made up, Pinkerton quickly formulated a contingency plan. He left the Continental Hotel in search of Thomas A. Scott, vice-president of the Pennsylvania Central Railroad. Failing to locate him, he called on G. C. Franciscus, the railroad's general manager, at midnight. Pinkerton, Franciscus, Sandford, and Judd met until dawn. They decided that, after the ceremonies at Harrisburg were concluded, a special train consisting of a baggage car and one passenger coach would carry Lincoln back to Philadelphia. Franciscus and railroad General Superintendent Enoch Lewis would see to it that all track between Harrisburg and Philadelphia was cleared of traffic. In the meantime, Felton would hold the eleven o'clock Baltimore train until Lincoln's train arrived from Harrisburg. Allan Pinkerton would personally escort Lincoln from one depot to the other in Philadelphia. The Baltimore conspirators were expecting Lincoln to arrive from Harrisburg on the Northern Central Railroad, but Pinkerton knew that it was not sufficient merely to change the city of departure and the rail line because Baltimore agents had been planted all along the inaugural route. George H. Burns, the American Telegraph Company confidential agent, was sent to company manager H.E. Thayer, who agreed to intercept telegraph traffic between Harrisburg and Baltimore, delivering any messages to Pinkerton. In the meantime, W. P. Westervelt, American Telegraph superintendent, and Andrew Wynne, lineman, went to Harrisburg to "fix" the telegraph lines shorting them out with fine copper grounding wire, by temporarily cutting off Harrisburg from Baltimore and the rest of the nation.

If Abraham Lincoln had any lingering reservations about the cloak-and-dagger preparations surrounding the final phase of his journey, they were dispelled by a visit from Frederick H. Seward, son of William H. Seward, the man who would soon be appointed Lincoln's secretary of state. Young Seward had been sent by his father and General Winfield Scott's inspector-general, Charles P. Stone, to warn the president-elect of the danger afoot in Baltimore. With the plot thus independently confirmed, Lincoln was able to overcome the objections of those who thought he would suffer ridicule for "sneaking" into Washington. "I have thought over this matter considerably since I went over the ground with Mr. Pinkerton last night," Lincoln declared to Judge David Davis, one of the inaugural party, "and the appearance of Mr. Frederick Seward, with warning from another source, confirms my belief in Mr. Pinkerton's statement; therefore, unless there are some other reasons than a fear of ridicule, I am disposed to carry out Mr. Judd's plan."

In Philadelphia, Warne engaged the rear half of a sleeping car bound for Baltimore. It was "for her invalid brother" and was to be separated from the rest of the car by a curtain. The conductor of the train was told not to depart until he received personal instructions from Superintendent H. F. Kinney, who would hand him an important parcel from President Felton to Mr. E. J. Allen, Willard's Hotel, Washington. E. J. Allen was an alias Pinkerton frequently employed when he was on a case, and the parcel contained nothing more than some carefully wrapped newspapers.

At 5:45 p.m. Nicolay handed Abraham Lincoln a note while he and his traveling party were at a table in the dining room of a Harrisburg hotel. The men abruptly rose, the president-elect changed out of his dinner clothes and into a traveling suit, a shawl upon one arm and a soft felt hat tucked into his coat pocket. Escorted by

Pennsylvania Governor Andrew G. Curtin, Ward H. Lamon, Judd, and Colonel Edwin V. Sumner, Lincoln climbed into a waiting carriage. Judd whispered to Lamon, "As soon as Mr. Lincoln is in the carriage, drive off." Colonel Sumner, a stalwart but bumbling and aged officer, stubbornly insisted on accompanying Lincoln to Washington. Judd laid a gentle hand on the old man's shoulder, he turned around to see what Judd wanted, and the carriage bearing the president-elect drove off without him.

Accompanied now only by Lamon and railroad officials, Lincoln boarded the train for Philadelphia. He arrived in that city shortly after ten, where Pinkerton and Kinney were waiting with a carriage. Wordlessly, Lincoln, Lamon, and Pinkerton boarded the carriage and proceeded to the depot of the Philadelphia, Wilmington and Baltimore Railroad. At Carpenter Street, in the shadow of a tall fence, the carriage stopped, and Lincoln and the others alighted. Near the train, Warne approached them, enthusiastically greeting Lincoln—who still carried the invalid shawl over one arm—as her brother. Together with Pinkerton and Lamon, they entered the sleeping car by its rear door. The "important" parcel was delivered to the conductor, and the train started for Baltimore.

Even with all the secrecy, Pinkerton left nothing to chance. He planted his agents all along the right-of-way to Baltimore, having arranged a series of lantern signals against the possibility of track sabotage. At Havre de Grace, the first hotbed of conspiracy, Pinkerton nervously mounted the rear observation platform and strained to see the lantern, which finally flashed its "All's Well." The signal was repeated at every bridge crossing, all the way to Baltimore.

It was a chill 3:30 a.m. when the train pulled into Baltimore. A railroad official entered the sleeping car, took Pinkerton aside, and whispered to him, "All's well." The eight conspirators who had drawn the red lots were presumably in their beds, sleeping—or not.

President-elect Lincoln did not leave the sleeping car, which was drawn by horses over the horsecar tracks from the Philadelphia, Wilmington and Baltimore depot to the Camden Station. Here the first hitch occurred, as Lincoln and his party had to wait two hours for the arrival of the train that would take their car to Washington.

Lincoln remained in his berth, joking easily with the nervous men around him. The depot was hardly deserted, even so early in the morning, as passengers waited for various trains. Lincoln and the others caught snatches of rebel tunes—"My Maryland" and "Dixie"—and when a drunkard belted out the latter, Lincoln observed, "No doubt there will be a great time in Dixie by and by."

The belated train arrived at last and left for Washington, reaching the capital at about six in the morning. Lincoln wrapped his shawl around his shoulders and left the sleeping car with Lamon and Pinkerton. The crowd outside did not recognize him, but, suddenly, an acquaintance from Illinois stepped up and clasped the president-elect's hand. Pinkerton rudely intruded. "No talking here!" he whispered loudly. The man from Illinois glared at the detective, but before he could utter a word, Lincoln interposed: "That is Mr. Pinkerton, and everything is all right." The party was bundled into a carriage, which set off for Willard's Hotel, where Lincoln would be lodged prior to his inauguration.

It was at this point that Inspector-General Charles P. Stone took over the protection of Abraham Lincoln. The nation's capital was scarcely more secure than Baltimore.

On the afternoon of March 3, General Winfield Scott conferred with his staff, including Stone, on plans for escorting President Buchanan and President-elect Lincoln from Willard's to the Capitol. The two men were to ride in a single carriage between double files of a squadron of the District of Columbia cavalry. A company of sappers and miners would precede the carriage, and infantry and riflemen would follow it. Sharpshooters were to be positioned on commanding rooftops along Pennsylvania Avenue. Their orders were to watch for threatening movements in windows along the route and to be prepared to open fire. A small force of regular cavalry was to be dispatched to guard side-street intersections along the avenue, a battalion of District of Columbia troops would be stationed near the U. S. Capitol steps, and riflemen were positioned in the windows of the Capitol's wings. That same night, Stone received word that an attempt would be made to blow up the platform on which Lincoln was to take the oath of office. The inspector-general decided to station men under the platform and would form a battalion in a semicircle around it. Plainclothes policemen were also to be distributed among the gathering crowd.

James Buchanan, the courtly bachelor president who had done virtually nothing to avert the crisis now facing the nation, called on Abraham Lincoln at Willard's. Stone personally saw to the formation of a company of mounted marshals around the carriage, *within* the cavalry escort. As the procession started, Stone rode near the presidential carriage, spurring his mount with deliberate clumsiness in order to keep the cavalry horses agitated. It would be very difficult, Stone reasoned, for an assassin to get a clean shot through a screen of prancing horses.

Lincoln and Buchanan survived the inauguration and were escorted from the Capitol to the White House, where the former president walked the president to the door, welcomed him to his new home, and bade him good morning, doubtless relieved to be rid of the reins of so troubled a government. If Lincoln contemplated the site of his inauguration from a window of his new residence, surely he would have reflected on the Capitol dome, just beginning construction at the time and giving the building an all-too-symbolic air of decapitation. The city on which the president now gazed was, as it were, without head, and its feet trod quicksand.

Loyalties?

On the very night following General Scott's March 3 staff meeting, his military secretary, a lieutenant colonel who had taken the minutes of the meeting and who had written up for Inspector-General Stone full instructions regarding the disposition of the troops who were to guard the president-elect, resigned his commission, headed south, and subsequently joined the Confederate army.

Charles P. Stone himself would be arrested on February 8, 1862, for treason, charged with having deliberately slaughtered his men at Ball's Bluff on October 21, 1861. Imprisoned, no indictment was forthcoming, and he was released on August 16.

Leaving Washington, James Buchanan may have thought about Rose O'Neal Greenhow, the attractive—some would have said beguiling—widow of a State Department official. The bachelor president was a frequent late-night visitor to her Sixteenth Street home. She would soon be known as the Rebel Rose, a Confederate spy avidly pursued by Allan J. Pinkerton.

And Lincoln? He survived the inauguration, but, as several who had made the inaugural journey predicted, his clandestine entrance into Washington did earn him much ridicule. For many years, a story circulated that Pinkerton had disguised the president as an old woman in Scotch cap and shawl.

CHAPTER TWO

THE RELUCTANT SPY

He was a perfectly ordinary man. True, he was making his way through the dusty July streets of Washington, D.C., to see President Lincoln on a personal matter—but, in the troubled spring and summer of 1861, plenty of perfectly ordinary men called on the president. Office seekers, aspirants to postmasterships, to consular posts, to Indian agencies and the like clogged the halls of the White House, lined the stairways, and poured out onto the lawns. Lincoln's office was located in three rooms on the east end of the second floor, at the head of the principal stairway. The president's bedroom was at the other end of that very hall, as were the bedrooms of Mrs. Lincoln and their two sons. If the president left his bedroom for his office or even for the dining room, he had to ply a sea of petitioners. There was a single doorkeeper outside the president's office, but, really, anyone could gain access to the chief executive—office seekers, politicians, assassins, madmen, and ordinary men like William Alvin Lloyd.

The fall of Fort Sumter, which signaled the start of the great rebellion that April, had hardly been a momentous battle. Confederate General P. G. T. Beauregard sent two men rowing under a flag of truce out to the fort in Charleston Harbor. They presented commandant Major Robert Anderson with a chivalrous note demanding surrender of the fort: "All proper facilities will be afforded for the removal of yourself and command, together with company arms and property, and all private property, to any post in the United States which you may select. The flag which you have upheld so long and with so much fortitude, under the most trying circumstances, may be saluted by you on taking it down." About to fight in a war between brother and brother, Anderson had been Beauregard's artillery instructor at West Point. Lincoln had earlier sent Anderson a dispatch informing him that Sumter would be relieved, that he should endeavor to hold the fort. "We shall strive to do our duty," Anderson replied in a message Beauregard's agents intercepted, "though I frankly say that my heart is not in the war, which I see is thus to be commenced." To Beauregard's surrender demand, Anderson replied in a similar vein: it was "a demand with which I regret that my sense of honor, and of my obligations to my government, prevent my compliance." Handing the two rowboat-borne soldiers this latter note, he declared to them: "Gentlemen, if you do not batter us to pieces, we shall be starved out in a few days."

The fall of the fort was a foregone conclusion, but Anderson meant to play out the game of honor to a respectable end. When four more rowboatmen called on him after midnight on April 12, 1861, with a warning that bombardment was about to commence, he replied that, barring further orders or supply from "my government," he would, indeed, evacuate the fort by April 15. No, Beauregard's men declared, commence evacuation now, for the bombardment would begin in one hour. Sixty-seven-year-old Edmund Ruffin, a rural Virginia newspaper editor, fired the first shot at 4:30 a.m. Some four thousand rounds followed through Friday and into Saturday.

Yet, remarkably, no one had been hurt when Anderson, content that honor had been satisfied by enduring the two-day cannonade, at last surrendered. The first casualties of civil war came after the battle proper. Roger Pryor, a Virginia fire-eater who had exhorted South Carolinians to "strike a blow," acted as one of Beauregard's emissaries presiding over the surrender of the fort. He was seated at a table in Sumter's empty hospital, waiting while the surrender terms were put in writing. He became thirsty, seized a bottle that was close to hand, slugged it down, then read the label: iodine of potassium. Having poisoned himself, Pryor sought the fort's surgeon, who hauled him outside, pumped his stomach, and saved his life. The next day, Sunday, the rebels lived up to the terms they had offered Anderson, permitting him to salute the flag he had served. The commandant ordered a fifty-gun volley. A stray ember touched off some powder, which exploded, injuring five and killing one. Union Private Daniel Hough was the first to fall in the American Civil War.

There would be others. Though surprisingly few people had any inkling of just how many.

An Indiana farm boy named Theodore Upson recorded how his father had greeted the commencement of war with horror:

> Father and I were husking out some corn. We could not finish before it wintered up. When William Cory came across the field (he had been down after the Mail) he was excited and said, "Jonathan the Rebs have fired upon and taken Fort Sumter." Father got white and couldn't say a word.
>
> William said, "The President will soon fix them. He has called for 75,000 men and is going to blockade their ports, and just as soon as those fellows find out that the North means business they will get down off their high horse."
>
> Father said little. We did not finish the corn and drove to the barn. Father left me to unload and put out the team and went to the house. After I had finished I went in to dinner. Mother said, "What is the matter with Father?" He had gone right upstairs. I told her what we had heard. She went to him. After a while they came down. Father looked ten years older. We sat down to the table. Grandma wanted to know what was the trouble. Father told her and she began to cry. "Oh my poor children in the South! How they will suffer! God knows how they will suffer! I knew it would come! Jonathan I told you it would come!"
>
> "They can come here and stay," said Father.
>
> "No they will not do that. There is their home. There they will stay. Oh to think that I should have lived to see the day when Brother should rise against Brother!"

And then there was William Tecumseh Sherman. Having left the army because he saw no future in it, he accepted a position as superintendent of the Louisiana State Military Academy. On Christmas Eve 1860, when news reached him that South Carolina had seceded from the Union, Sherman declared to the academy's classics professor, with whom he was having supper, that "this country will be drenched in blood, and God only knows how it will end. It is all folly, madness, a crime against civilization! You people speak so lightly of war; you don't know what you're talking about. War is a terrible thing!"

For most Southerners, the prospect of war was not terrible at all, but exhilarating. For many Northerners, the ardent abolitionists aside, it loomed neither as an exhilarating nor as a terrible thing, but as an occasion of enervation or, at least, inconvenience. Even President Lincoln seemed to be in a trance. Sherman resigned from the academy in February 1861 and, at the urging of his brother, a U.S. senator, came to Washington to see the president and report on the situation in the South.

"Ah," Lincoln asked him, "how are they getting along down there?"

"They think they are getting along swimmingly. They are preparing for war."

"Oh, well," the president replied, "I guess we'll manage to keep house."

Whereupon Sherman went to St. Louis to head up a streetcar company, returning to Washington and military command only after the fall of Fort Sumter.

By July 1861, as William Alvin Lloyd walked to his appointment with the president, emotions were at last running high in the capital. The city was ringed by the rebellion. The passage of his inaugural train through conspiratorial Baltimore in February had given President Lincoln all the proof he needed of hostile sentiment in Maryland, and the talk in the public parlors of Willard's Hotel was that an army was massing in Virginia for an assault on Washington. On Saturday, April 20, the city awoke to find itself cut off from the North. Rioters in Baltimore had blockaded railroad traffic and had seized the telegraph office. Hundreds, even thousands, deserted the capital. Shops and homes were boarded up. The Prussian attache, eager to identify his legation as a diplomatic agency, placed a large sign over the doorway to his building. He wanted a Prussian flag, too, but couldn't get one because of the disruption in rail service. At the U. S. Treasury, workers were installing iron bars on doors and windows. There were rumors that the building was also being mined with explosive charges. Additional rumor had it that old Ben McCulloch of the Texas Rangers was assembling a force of five hundred men in Richmond to make a lightning raid on Washington, kidnap the president and his cabinet, and carry them to the South. Summoned to Washington by President Lincoln, Allan J. Pinkerton

found a condition of affairs at once peculiar and embarrassing, and the city contained a strange admixture of humanity, both patriotic and dangerous. Here were gathered the rulers of the nation and those who were seeking its destruction. . . . Here . . . lurked the secret enemy, who was conveying beyond the lines the coveted information of every movement made or contemplated. Men who formerly occupied places of dignity, power and trust were now regarded as objects of suspicion, whose loyalty was impeached and whose actions it was necessary to watch. Aristocratic ladies, who had previously opened the doors of their luxurious residences to those high in office and who had hospitably entertained the dignitaries of the land, were now believed to be in sympathy with the attempt to overthrow the country, and engaged in clandestine correspondence with Southern leaders. The criminal classes poured in from all quarters, and almost every avenue of society was penetrated by these lawless and unscrupulous hordes.

At the U. S. War Department, General Winfield Scott, the superannuated hero of the Mexican War—known since that time as Old Fuss and Feathers—responded to a situation report issued by the District of Columbia's freshly appointed inspector-general, Colonel Charles P. Stone. "They are closing their coils around us, sir!" Scott gasped.

On the eve of the war, the only regular troops near Washington were three or four hundred marines at the marine barracks and about one hundred enlisted men at the Washington arsenal. Armed volunteer groups included the Potomac Light Infantry (one company), the National Rifles (one company), the Washington Light Infantry (a skeleton battalion of 160 men), and the National Guard Battalion. Other local militia companies were hurriedly cobbled together. But it would be very easy to lose a war with such companies. Men older than General Scott, veterans of the War of

1812, formed themselves into the Silver Grays' Home Guard. And when Stone complimented Captain Schaeffer on the readiness of his National Rifles, the commander, evidently unaware of Stone's appointment to inspector-general, replied:

> "Yes, it is a good company, and I suppose I shall soon have to lead it to the banks of the Susquehanna!"
> "Why so?" [Stone] asked.
> "Why! To guard the frontier of Maryland and help to keep the Yankees from coming down to coerce the South!"

"It must be admitted," Stone recalled of the exchange, "that this was not a very cheerful beginning."

No more "cheerful" was the case of the Georgetown-based Potomac Light Infantry, whose members took an emergency vote to *disband* until peace was restored. A disgruntled corpsman proposed a toast: "The P.L.I., invincible in peace; invisible in war."

Worse, Stone learned, "the great hall over Beach's livery stable was nightly filled with men, who were actively drilled. Doctor B____, of well-known secession tendencies, was the moving spirit of these men, and he was assisted by other citizens of high standing, among whom was a connection of the Governor of Virginia." Stone was able to infiltrate the National Volunteers, as they called themselves, by means of a "skillful New York detective officer"—probably Pinkerton's operative Timothy Webster—and discovered that they planned to pass themselves off as a militia loyal to the Union in order to obtain arms. Dr. B____ presented himself at Inspector-General Stone's office, seeking just that. Stone responded that he needed the company's muster roll, which the doctor furnished the next day. "I looked him full in the face," Stone later recalled, "smiled, and locked the muster-roll in a drawer of my desk, saying: 'Doctor B____, I am very happy to have obtained this list, and I wish you good morning.' The gallant doctor evidently understood me. He smiled, bowed, and left the office, to which he never returned." The doctor went south, and his National Volunteers disbanded.

By the end of April, however, when the Seventh New York marched in to garrison the city, Washington was becoming increasingly better defended from external enemies. Security within the city was an altogether different matter. Not only could people of any stripe gain access to the president, but, it seemed, could get almost anything else they wanted. One day, Lincoln heard what sounded like cannon fire. He walked outside to investigate, strolling to the south. He never did discover the source of the explosion, but he did find out that the city's arsenal was entirely without sentry protection, its doors wide open.

The doors of government were likewise ajar. With army officers and federal officials defecting to the South daily, everyone was a potential spy. Samuel Cooper, U.S. Army adjutant-general, joined the Confederate cause in March. The quartermaster general, Joseph E. Johnston, did the same soon afterward. The acting commander of the Army Medical Bureau, Robert C. Wood, was the brother of Jefferson Davis's first wife. Captain John Magruder (not to be confused with the soon-to-be celebrated Confederate commander "Prince John" Bankhead Magruder), charged with command of the First U.S. Artillery and brought to Washington with that unit specifically to see to the defense of the capital, was openly disloyal. The commander of the Washington Navy Yard, Marylander Franklin Buchanan, was a rebel sympathizer. He resigned in April, protesting that his loyalties lay with Maryland, but honorably admonishing his men to remain faithful to their government. Shortly after Buchanan's departure, it was discovered that many of the bombshells manufactured at the Navy Yard had been filled with sand and sawdust instead of black powder. In the civil government, from bureau clerks to Supreme Court Justice John A. Campbell—who carried on a correspondence with Confederate officials at Montgomery—rebellion was also rife.

Nor did Abraham Lincoln have to walk as far as the arsenal, the War Department, the Supreme Court, or any other government office to find breaches in security. John Watt, a gardener employed at the White House, admitted that he had sold official secrets, not directly to the Confederates, but to a newspaper—which came to about the same thing. The breach was revealed on November 16, 1861, when *New York Herald* reporter Henry Wikoff published the contents of Lincoln's message to Congress concerning the capture of two Confederate diplomats, James Murray Mason and John Slidell, *before* Lincoln delivered the message. This was a potentially disastrous leak, as Mason and Slidell, returning from a clandestine mission to England, had been taken from a British steamer, the *Trent*, flying British colors. The Confederates might well have been able to exploit their advance knowledge of the incident to overcome Britain's official policy of neutrality and strike up an Anglo-Confederate alliance against the North. Watt had been particularly trusted, since he was a great favorite of the president's wife, Mary Todd. But, then, even *she* was a security risk. A Kentuckian with a brother and three half-brothers enlisted in the Confederate army, Mary Todd Lincoln had a half-sister, Mrs. Clement White of Alabama, recently a guest at the president's inauguration, who was an ardent and outspoken secessionist. At the commencement of hostilities, Lincoln gave her a pass to return to the South. What secrets—if any—she took with her is not known, but she did transport "her weight almost" in quinine, a drug sorely needed by the Confederacy.

It was just such a pass William Alvin Lloyd now sought from the president. He was a highly respected businessman, "long and intimately acquainted with President Lincoln," whom he hoped would help him now. For while the war was greeted by some with horror, by others with exultation, and by others still with numbed indifference, to Lloyd it threatened personal disaster. His was a perfectly ordinary business. But these were extraordinary times. Based in New York and Baltimore, William Alvin Lloyd was a publisher of railroad and steamboat guides and maps—of the Southern states. To continue conducting his business, Lloyd needed to travel freely into those states, and for that, in order to get by Union border pickets, he needed a pass endorsed by no less than the president.

Doubtless, Lloyd felt no little self-satisfaction at having received from Lincoln, obviously burdened by the affairs of war, so prompt a reply to his request for an audience. For his part, the president saw much more than an opportunity for doing an acquaintance a favor. One fairly tripped over rebel spies in Washington, but what agents did the Union have in the centers of the rebellion?

None.

As late as the end of 1862, General Daniel Butterfield, chief of staff under General Joseph E.—"Fighting Joe"—Hooker, complained that the Union army was "almost as ignorant of the enemy as if they had been in China." In July 1861, that ignorance was even more profound. To President Lincoln, William Alvin Lloyd seemed descended as from a *deus ex machina.* He was a well-known businessman, widely respected in the South. His business was travel and transportation, and, since he had spent his professional life looking at and asking questions about steamboats and railroads, it would strike no one as odd if he continued to do so. Moreover, he was as apolitical as anyone and was associated neither with the army nor the civil government. He had no training as a spy, of course, but nevertheless he seemed to Lincoln the ideal secret agent.

The only snag was that Lloyd hadn't the least inclination to become a spy. To risk his life in "difficult and hazardous service" for the sake of obtaining a pass through the Union lines was not, he reasoned, good business. But Lincoln did not give up. During the next few days, he had further meetings with Lloyd and his employee, Thomas H. S. Boyd, as well as with a friend of Lloyd's, F. J. Bonfanti, a language teacher and a New York courtroom translator. Bonfanti desperately wanted to go to New Orleans to look after some property he had there.

Whatever motives of patriotism Abraham Lincoln may have suggested to Lloyd, Boyd, and Bonfanti, it was the offer of a two-hundred-dollar monthly salary that prompted the most serious thought from Lloyd. In an age when unskilled labor earned a dollar a day, two hundred dollars a month was inviting—though Bonfanti insisted that it was scant compensation for risking one's life. But, Lloyd again reasoned, it was two hundred dollars *added* to the income from his publishing business, which the espionage assignment would allow him to continue. And it wasn't as if he had to do a lot of extra work to obtain the information Lincoln sought. Really, he just had to do what he had always done: collect timetables, study rail and shipping facilities, look into centers of transportation, engage in conversation with his Southern business cronies, the owners and managers of railroads and steamboat lines, who, doubtless, would enjoy passing the day in gossip about troop movement, supply, and the like. The war, after all, was very good business for them. He took the job.

When Bonfanti and Boyd agreed to work with Lloyd to gather information, Lincoln wrote out passes for them as well. Then there was Mrs. Lloyd and her maid, Helen R. ("Nelly") Dooley. They would require passes, too. These the president also furnished, figuring, perhaps, that no one would expect a spy to encumber himself with wife and chambermaid. Beyond this fortunate stroke, however, neither Lincoln nor Lloyd can be credited with much aplomb. To begin with, it occurred to neither that gathering information was all well and good, but the information also had to be communicated. They formulated no plan for couriers or any other line of communications, which meant that Lloyd would have to carry on his person whatever he gathered—maps, reports, notes—none of which would even be encrypted, since neither Lincoln nor Lloyd knew anything about ciphers.

As if this weren't bad enough, Lloyd, his wife, and her chambermaid, as well as Boyd and Bonfanti each carried a pass signed by the president of the United States. These were fine for getting past the Union pickets, but, if discovered behind Confederate lines, they were as good as death warrants. Most incredible, however, was the fact that Lloyd also carried with him at all times the contract he and Lincoln had drawn up officially appointing him a secret agent. Not that Lincoln had ever implied that such an arrangement was best kept secret. The president had handed the contract to Lloyd in the presence of witnesses, and, for his part, Lloyd proudly displayed it to a number of friends, as well as Boyd and Boyd's brother Charles, who was a child. Lloyd also announced to his seventeen-year-old wife that "he was to go South on secret service, or something of that kind."

About July 18, 1861, Lloyd and Bonfanti left for Cincinnati, whence Lloyd continued on to Nashville. Boyd temporarily remained in Washington. From Nashville, Lloyd traveled to Grand Junction, Tennessee. There three Confederate officials arrested him. Lloyd had the presence of mind to remember the contract and slipped it to his friend Charles T. Moore, who had met him en route and was traveling with him at the time of his arrest. The officials searched Lloyd's baggage, and though, of course, they did not find the contract, sent him to jail in Memphis anyway. Moore secured a pair of lawyers for a fee of two hundred dollars in gold, paid a jailer incredibly named Captain Clink another one hundred dollars in gold, and gained his friend's release.

In the meantime, apprised of her husband's arrest, Mrs. Lloyd (and Nelly) took a train from New York, bringing with her twelve hundred dollars in gold against this and future emergencies. She joined Lloyd in Clarksville, Tennessee, around October 1, and the trio—he, she, and Nelly—returned to Nashville, apparently in company with Bonfanti, who then went on to New Orleans.

None of Lloyd's documents or notes survives, so it is impossible to determine everything he was doing during his early days among the Confederates. It is clear that he aroused considerable suspicion, particularly from Brigadier General John Henry Winder, provost marshal at Richmond. Lloyd plied the general with groceries and cash. He even spent twelve hundred dollars on a custom-tailored dress uniform for him. Boyd was present when Winder was being measured for it. Was this blatant bribery? Yes. But it is unlikely that Winder, greatly feared and respected as a provost marshal, thought he was taking bribes to ignore espionage. Lloyd, after all, was a businessman, whose ostensible occupation required freedom of movement and the cooperation of those in command. Winder probably thought he was granting harmless favors. Indeed, although he was in charge of counterespionage in the Confederate capital, General Winder was at first about as adroit in matters of security as Lincoln had been in dealing with Lloyd. Winder kept a current roster of regiments defending Richmond, complete with commanders and strength, on a chalkboard in his office, which was open to the public. Thus Lloyd could have sent President Lincoln considerably more than information on the provost marshal's suit size.

We do know that between August and October 1861, Lloyd and Boyd, who had left Washington to join his employer late in July, toured Harpers Ferry, the Shenandoah Valley, Lynchburg, and Petersburg, ending up in Norfolk and Portsmouth, where they gathered a great deal of information on fortifications and the strength of General Benjamin Huger's troops. They also drew a map of the harbor. Lloyd gave the documents to the engineer on a transport vessel that ran between Norfolk and Craney Island. From Craney Island, the engineer-turned-courier followed the Elizabeth

River to Hampton Roads. He rowed across the Roads to Fort Monroe, a Union stronghold, and handed over the map and other information.

Having completed this mission, Lloyd left Boyd in Norfolk toward the end of November 1861 and went on to Savannah, Georgia. He was to collect a sum of money there—not, apparently, the fruits of his spying, but earnings from his civilian business. He was also seizing the main chance to speculate on cotton or tobacco prices, both of which were destined to rise as battles and a Union blockade impeded export. But, true to his commission, Lloyd did not neglect espionage, which he went about with his customary indiscretion. A local actress, a Miss Jordan, reported to Savannah authorities that she "had overheard conversation between Lloyd and other parties in which Lloyd was sending information to the United States Government, in regard to the plan of fortifications surrounding Savannah." Either before or after they were tipped off by Miss Jordan, Confederate officials intercepted one of Lloyd's messages, and he was arrested in November or December. Lieutenant Colonel William S. Rockwell, First Georgia Volunteers, reported the matter to Secretary of War Judah P. Benjamin, specifically noting that Lloyd had been arrested as a spy.

Lloyd avoided summary action by producing two Confederate passes. Where he had secreted his pass from Lincoln and his espionage contract is not known. Lieutenant Colonel Rockwell still had his doubts, though he believed Lloyd was a New York journalist rather than a Federal spy. That might have been bad enough. Newspapers published what should have been top secret information every day. Early in the war, Confederate General P. G. T. Beauregard found the press such a valuable source of military information that he arranged to have Northern newspapers regularly delivered to him from Washington.

As Lloyd cooled his heels in Savannah's Ogelthorpe Barracks, his case was reviewed by the War Department, who passed it on to Brigadier General Winder. Perhaps the provost marshal did not dare let himself believe that the man from whom he had accepted groceries, cash, and a uniform could be a Federal agent. He said that he agreed with Lieutenant Colonel Rockwell: Lloyd was doubtless a journalist, though "he ought to be viewed with great suspicion." The matter did not end with Winder. Lloyd's name percolated through the Confederate bureaucracy to Jefferson Davis himself, a man who took an avid interest in matters of espionage and counterespionage. The Confederate president reviewed the case and turned it over to Brigadier General A. R. Lawton, who had been president of a railroad and was acquainted with Lloyd and his business. Lawton made inquiries of various railroads in an effort to ascertain the nature of the prisoner's activities.

In the meantime, absent an indictment, Lloyd demanded a writ of habeas corpus. In the North, this basic right, inherited from English common law, was now virtually suspended. As early as April 1862, Lincoln had personally denied habeas corpus—even writs issued by the Supreme Court—in the case of individuals held on far less evidence than the Confederates were holding Lloyd. The spy may, in fact, have obtained a writ, since Lawton reported to President Davis that his investigations had turned up no incriminating evidence. Nevertheless, Lloyd was held for six weeks in solitary confinement. This so damaged his health that he was sent in June 1862 to Macon, Georgia, where he lived in the home of his jailer because he was now suffering from partial paralysis of the legs.

Still, he got around. He was not *confined* to the jailer's house, just domiciled there. He gave his word not to attempt an escape and was therefore allowed to roam, collecting military information in the process. President Davis himself issued a pass, and various Confederate officers conversed freely—all too freely—with him. Lloyd was apparently arrested again and held in Richmond's Libby Prison—a converted warehouse that would rapidly become infamous as an overcrowded hellhole for federal prisoners of war—but was soon released.

While Lloyd was incarcerated in Richmond, Thomas Boyd used his position as Lloyd's employee to persuade Robert E. Lee, at the time Jefferson Davis's personal military advisor, to grant permission for him to call on Brigadier General William Nelson Pendleton, who was chief of artillery. Lloyd, it seems, was released in time to accompany Boyd on their officially authorized visit to Pendleton's headquarters between batteries four and five of the Richmond defenses. Astoundingly, Pendleton led the pair on a tour of the

Richmond defenses and proudly replied to Lloyd's questions concerning the number of batteries positioned around the Confederate capital.

During this period—just before the series of bloody battles fought between July 1–7, 1862, within ten miles of Richmond that came to be called the Seven Days—detailed information concerning the Confederate capital's artillery and entrenchments would have been tremendously valuable. Well aware of what he had obtained, Lloyd nevertheless played it cool. Deciding that it would be foolhardy to try to get off a dispatch from well-guarded Richmond, he returned to Macon, reunited with Boyd, passed the papers on to him, and sent him back North. It was already the end of the month—or early August—when Boyd handed the packet to President Lincoln. By then the Seven Days had been fought, with the result that Major General George P. McClellan had failed to take Richmond, but, even now, new plans were being made for an assault on the Confederate capital. Yet Abraham Lincoln appears to have done nothing with the information he received. Certainly, he did not convey it to McClellan, nor to any other commander. He did, however, award Boyd a salary of a hundred dollars a month.

By late summer 1862, Lloyd had moved to Lynchburg, Tennessee, with his wife and maid. In October he sent Boyd back to Lincoln with information concerning fortifications and the strength of Lee's forces. Boyd quickly returned to Lynchburg. Then, on November 8, 1862, Confederate detectives raided Lloyd's house. Since Lloyd had so recently transmitted information to Lincoln, the only incriminating item in the house was his espionage contract—which, of course, was incriminating enough. Lloyd had passed the document to his wife for safekeeping some time before, and she, in turn, had given it to Nelly, who sewed it into her dress.

While the Confederates searched Mr. and Mrs. Lloyd, they left Boyd and Nelly alone in a room. Nelly took the opportunity to remove the contract from her dress and tear it into little pieces, which she scattered. It occurred to Boyd that even detectives stupid enough to leave two suspects alone in a room would not be so obtuse as to overlook torn-up scraps of paper littering the floor. The room had a fire in the fireplace, and Boyd deftly gathered up the scraps and tossed them in. Indeed, Boyd even had time to burn a few other papers.

Although the detectives found little or nothing, they deposited Lloyd in the local jail. His incarceration was brief, but his health was bad, and he was running out of money. He had pawned his wife's jewelry and furs in order to borrow five hundred dollars in gold. He wanted to quit—to quit his business, to quit spying, and, above all, to quit the South. But he discovered that he was trapped. He was under constant surveillance and, burdened with wife and maid as he was, would never be able to slip across the Confederate lines. There was nothing to do but resume being a spy.

Lloyd returned to Richmond toward the end of 1862, collecting material on Confederate forces in the Gulf states. In the meantime, Boyd toured southwestern Virginia, returned to Washington, set out for Richmond again, and reunited with Lloyd in Salem, Virginia. The two continued their spying in North Carolina, then split up, Lloyd going to Augusta, Georgia, and Boyd going back to Richmond. There, much to his surprise, Boyd was arrested in March 1863 and sent to Castle Thunder, a military prison that often accommodated suspected and convicted spies. It was at Castle Thunder that Boyd stumbled on just the channel of communications Lincoln and Lloyd had failed to establish. During roughly the first half of the war, the North and South routinely exchanged prisoners, and Boyd began regularly giving dispatches to prisoners about to be exchanged. Such men were ideal couriers since they were never searched. After all, they had been thoroughly examined upon capture and had been under lock and key since. Nor did Boyd lack for information to send out. Confederate authorities obligingly allowed Lloyd to visit his employee in prison. Lloyd unburdened himself of his most recent information, and Boyd passed it to the next outward-bound prisoner. And he continued doing so until his release a month later in April 1863.

Although President Lincoln as always received a steady stream of office seekers and other petitioners in the White House, the new-found "couriers" were not among them. Once they arrived in the North, the redeemed prisoners sent the documents entrusted to them through the regular mail to Boyd's family. Boyd's young brother, Charles, was probably the one who delivered the documents. Not only did the family ignore all security measures, they often handed envelopes to Lincoln unsealed. Clearly, the Boyds enjoyed reading the dispatches before passing them on.

In December 1863, Lloyd gave Boyd a comprehensive map detailing forts and encampments throughout the Confederacy. With his usual good luck, Boyd made his way north and delivered this valuable document directly into Lincoln's hands. Early in 1864, Lloyd attempted to use the faithful Nelly as courier, but she was turned back by Confederate pickets and returned the documents to her employer. Lloyd decided next to try a blockade runner.

It is surprising that the spy had not employed blockade runners—a term applied to the vessels as well as to their commanders and crews—before this. They were a mixed bunch, blockade runners, some motivated by Confederate patriotism, to be sure, but most driven by cash. At the outset of the war, General Winfield Scott, the Union commander in chief, proposed a massive blockade of the Southern seaboard—about five thousand miles, when one stopped to figure it out, taking into account rivers and an irregular coastline—a project quickly dubbed "Scott's Anaconda." At the end of the first year of war, the Union navy had increased in strength from the forty-two ships, 555 guns, and seventy-six hundred sailors to 264 ships, 2,557 guns, and twenty-two thousand sailors. But even these augmented numbers were grossly inadequate to patrol so much land and water. However, if the Union's navy was small, the Confederate's was almost nonexistent. Jefferson Davis issued letters of marque to privateers, thereby commissioning private vessels into an irregular navy. In many cases, blockade runners did not even hold such letters, but were simply illegal traders. Abraham Lincoln refused to distinguish among any of them and vowed to treat all blockade runners as pirates. Thus the work of evading Scott's Anaconda carried with it the possibility of being hanged. When the *Savannah*, a privateer, was captured in June 1861, the crew stood trial on piracy charges, and the Northern public cried out for blood, but a New York jury could not reach a verdict. Jefferson Davis threatened to execute one Union prisoner for each privateer hanged. Later in 1861, the *Jeff Davis* was taken, its crew tried, and, this time, convicted and sentenced to death. In view of Davis's threat, however, Lincoln overturned the sentence of the court.

If the life of a blockade runner was perilous, the lives of those charged with maintaining the blockade were tedious almost beyond endurance. Weeks and months would pass without sighting a runner. One sailor wrote to his mother that she could get an idea of what the duty was like if she would "go to the roof on a hot summer day, talk to a half dozen degenerates, descend to the basement, drink tepid water full of iron rust, climb to the roof again, and repeat the process at intervals until she was fagged out, then go to bed with everything shut tight."

For the balance of the war, Lloyd seems to have used blockade runners frequently as couriers. By this time, the Confederates, war weary and in retreat, had stopped arresting Lloyd, who continued to gather information on Lee's army and on the gunboats, batteries, and water defenses of the important port of Wilmington, North Carolina. In March 1865, by way of "a blockade runner named Anderson," he sent a report on Lee's strength, garnered from a free-talking staff officer. Lloyd was living in Richmond when word came that the city was to be evacuated. This man, who had been under continual scrutiny and suspicion and who had been jailed off and on, though never tried, for a total of almost two years, now called on President Davis and his final secretary of war, John C. Breckenridge. Not only was Lloyd given permission to leave the city with his wife, Nelly, and Boyd, but he was invited to travel on the very train that carried Davis and his cabinet out of the capital.

It must have been abundantly clear to Lloyd that the war was rapidly nearing an end, yet, weary and ill, he continued to spy, filing a report from Greensboro, North Carolina, on Joseph E. Johnston's army. He sent it to Petersburg via a black man.

Lloyd, his wife, Nelly, and Boyd were in Danville, Virginia, the town to which Davis and his cabinet had fled, when federal troops arrived. Major General Horatio G. Wright saw to it that the faithful spies were provided transportation back to Washington. But it was hardly a triumphal homecoming. Lloyd had become a chronic invalid and would die three years after war's end, in 1868. Although he and his family were reimbursed for expenses to the tune of $2,380, the government refused to pay him the four years' salary he had earned—$9,753.32. Although Mr. and Mrs. Lloyd, Boyd, and Nelly could literally recite the contents of the contract with Lincoln, the document itself, preserved so carefully (and foolishly) through the early days of the war, had been torn to bits and then burned. The only other party to the contract, President Abraham Lincoln, had been assassinated by John Wilkes Booth. Following Lloyd's death, his family unsuccessfully filed suit in the United States Court of Claims, and subsequently appealed to the Supreme Court. The appeal was denied in an 1875 decision (92 U.S. 105) that established the precedent that an intelligence agent cannot sue the government to recover compensation for secret services rendered: "Agents . . . must look for their compensation to the contingent fund of the department employing them, and to such allowance from it as those who dispense the fund may award." Lloyd had been hired not by a department, but by the president, an individual, deceased. Contract? No trace of it existed. And of his four harrowing years behind Confederate lines not a scrap of written record was to be found.

CHAPTER THREE

THE REBEL ROSE

Spies have found work for as long as armies have found reasons to fight. During the American Revolution, General Washington put spies to brilliant use, and secret agents were active as well during the War of 1812 and the Mexican War. But even as late as the Civil War, neither the North nor the South had a department devoted to what today would be called intelligence. The gathering of information was an ad hoc and erratic process, the province of a president, perhaps, or of individual commanding officers. Lincoln hired William Alvin Lloyd, but his was never an official government appointment. Major General George McClellan hired Allan Pinkerton, and Lieutenant General Winfield Scott hired Lafayette C. Baker; both men thought of themselves as directors of a "secret service," but neither cooperated with the other. Indeed, on at least two occasions, members of one organization arrested members of the other. During the Civil War, the United States government never had an official body known as *the* Secret Service.

The Confederates, at least early in the war, had more spies than the Union, but this was not the result of any plan, let alone the function of an official intelligence organization. Washington, D.C., more a Southern than a Northern city, was virtually brimming over with Confederate sympathizers willing to supply intelligence to the South. The Confederate Congress established the first formally organized military signal corps on April 19, 1862. Headed by a

Marylander named William Norris, the Signal Bureau was sometimes referred to as the Signal and Secret Service Bureau or even
the Secret Service Bureau and was official enough to warrant its
own stationery. A requisition dated February 23, 1864, carries the
following letterhead:

> War Department,
>   SECRET SERVICE BUREAU,
>   Richmond, Va.

However, Confederate espionage and counterespionage were never
wholly centralized in this or any other "bureau," but for the most
part remained the province of numerous commanders, provost
marshals, and even President Jefferson Davis, who on numerous
occasions interrogated suspected spies personally. At the outbreak of the war, nevertheless, one man, Thomas Jordan, took it
upon himself to harvest the bumper crop of spies Washington
yielded.

In actuality, much of that crop proved unworthy of harvest.
Informants were willing and abundant, but their information was
often little more than unreliable rumor. Jordan's great service to
the Confederacy was in separating the wheat from the chaff—or,
more to the point, in finding the rose among the thorns.

Thomas Jordan, a West Point roommate of William Tecumseh
Sherman, is variously reported to have been a lieutenant or a
captain serving on the staff of General Winfield Scott. While most
U.S. Army officers with Confederate leanings resigned their com-
missions at the outbreak of the war, Jordan lingered in the capital
city and on Scott's staff for a month after the fall of Fort Sumter.
This not only gave him an opportunity to study the general's war
plans, but also to organize a Washington-based spy ring. Among
Jordan's acquaintances was a popular Washington hostess—who
some say was his lover—Rose O'Neal Greenhow, a woman with
many friends, most of them male and of considerable consequence
in the government.

Through her husband, Dr. Robert Greenhow, a scholarly Virginia
lawyer and State Department official, Rose had gotten to know
virtually everyone of importance in Washington. Daughter of an

aristocratic Maryland family, kin of the Lees, Randolphs, and Calverts, Greenhow reserved her greatest admiration, even idolatry, for one of her husband's particular friends, South Carolina Senator John C. Calhoun, the architect of the doctrine of states' rights. "I am a Southern woman," she later wrote, "born with revolutionary blood in my veins, and my first crude ideas on State and Federal matters received consistency and shape from the best and wisest man of this century." Greenhow nursed Calhoun through his final illness in 1850, when he lodged in a boarding-house run by her aunt. The building, on A Street, was called the Old Capitol, for it had been built in 1815 to house Congress while the original Capitol, burned by the British during the War of 1812, was being repaired. By and by, Greenhow would become an unwilling inmate of the Old Capitol herself, after the building had been converted into a prison during the Civil War. Through a remarkable coincidence, she and her young daughter would be confined in the very room in which John C. Calhoun had died.

Robert Greenhow died in 1854. His widow was no longer a young woman, but many men found her irresistible. James Buchanan, the nation's only bachelor president, was a frequent nocturnal caller at the house on Sixteenth Street, as was Senator William Seward of New York. Greenhow's Southern sympathies were long and well known, but even after the outbreak of war, she continued to receive Union army officers and Seward, now secretary of state, whom she found "convivially loquacious after supper." She vowed to make herself useful to the South: "To this end," she later wrote, "I employed every capacity with which God had endowed me, and the result was far more successful than my hopes could have flattered me to expect."

The Washingtonian who may have been most captivated by that "with which God had endowed" her was the U. S. Senator from Massachusetts, Henry Wilson, chairman of the Senate's military affairs committee. Of humble origin, Wilson had been a farm laborer and then a shoemaker before he entered politics. Frowning and rotund, he was not a handsome man, but Rose, while she destroyed much of her correspondence before she was arrested, preserved a packet of love letters, each signed with the initial H. The letters now reside in the National Archives and Records Administration, accompanied by a fragment of an envelope on which Greenhow had written, "letters from H. Not to be opened—but burnt in case of accident or death." "You will know that I love you," reads one letter, "and I will sacrifice anything. You know that I *do love* you. I am suffering this morning, in fact I am sick physically and mentally, and you know that nothing would soothe me so much as an hour with you. And tonight, at whatever cost I will see you. . . ." Although the letters are written on official stationery bearing the letterhead of the Thirty-sixth Congress, manuscript experts have judged them not to be in Wilson's hand. Moreover, after her arrest, Wilson was one of a very small number of Greenhow's friends who visited her, and he certainly did not do so surreptitiously. Federal authorities were in possession of the letters, yet no harm came to Wilson, who continued to serve on the Senate Committee on Military Affairs and who, in 1872, became vice-president of the United States. Nevertheless, in 1870, President Grant's secretary of state, Hamilton Fish, reported having heard from his friend James Watson Webb, a newspaper owner and diplomat, that Thomas Jordan had revealed to him that he had been Rose Greenhow's lover and had learned that she had also established "an intimacy" with Senator Wilson. Jordan, according to Webb, persuaded Greenhow to exploit the relationship in order to "get from Wilson all the information she could."

Just before he left Washington to join the staff of Confederate General P. G. T. Beauregard, Jordan provided Greenhow with a rudimentary cipher for encoding dispatches, which he instructed her to send via courier to Thomas J. Rayford, an alias for himself. Her first dispatches were valuable indeed. According to Beauregard, on July 10, 1861, he received from her the information that federal forces were advancing on Manassas. The courier in this instance seems to have stepped out of the magnolia-steeped pages of a romantic novel. Pretty Betty Duvall, a youthful Washingtonian, crossed the Chain Bridge over the Potomac in a farm wagon on July 9. She exchanged the "peasant dress" she had selected as appropriate to a farm girl for a more fashionable and becoming riding habit at the house of a Virginia friend, former U.S. Navy lieutenant Catesby ap R. Jones (he would later serve as executive officer aboard the ironclad *Virginia*—better known by its original name,

Merrimack). Though pausing to change costume meant a day's delay in delivering Greenhow's dispatch, one had, after all, to look one's most attractive when calling on a general. Betty rode off on a borrowed horse and was admitted into Fairfax County Court House, headquarters of South Carolinian General M. L. Bonham. She removed the comb that held her dark, glossy hair in place, shook her tresses free—"the longest and most beautiful roll of hair I have ever seen," recalled the general—and withdrew a silver-dollar-size package sewn up in a silk pouch as black as her hair. It contained a terse message:

> McDowell has certainly been ordered to advance on the sixteenth.
> R.O.G.

The substance of this intelligence was corroborated by newspaper stories and by a Union soldier, captured on July 4, 1861, who had been attached to Major General Irvin McDowell's headquarters. Accordingly, Beauregard decided to deploy his troops behind Bull Run Creek.

Rose Greenhow had provided a date for the advance, and the captured soldier as well as the newspaper stories gave a good picture of troop strength. But the Confederate commander wanted even more current information as the situation continued to develop. On July 15, from a point just below Alexandria, he secretly ferried a Washingtonian, a former Land Office employee named George Donellan, across the Potomac. Donellan called on Rose Greenhow, whose home, Beauregard had told him, was "within easy rifle-range of the White House." He handed her a scrap of paper on which was written, in Thomas Jordan's cipher, "Trust bearer." Greenhow hurriedly wrote, using the same cipher, "Order issued for McDowell to march upon Manassas tonight." Donellan hid the message in the specially hollowed-out heel of his boot and, traveling by buggy and a relay of horses, made his way down the eastern shore of the Potomac to a ferry in Charles County, Maryland. He delivered the message to a cavalry officer on the Virginia side of the river, who sent it by relays to Manassas. Beauregard, who had originally contemplated an attack on Washington, was confirmed in his decision to make instead a stand at Manassas and telegraphed Richmond, requesting General Joseph E. Johnston's twelve thousand troops—who were sixty miles away, in the Shenandoah Valley—as reinforcements.

If Rose Greenhow's account is to be believed, the speed with which the dispatch reached Beauregard was remarkable. She claimed that on July 17 she received a reply from Thomas Jordan: "Yours was received at eight o'clock at night. Let them come; we are ready for them. We rely upon you for precise information. Be particular as to description and destination of forces, quantity of artillery, etc." Obligingly, on the same day, Greenhow sent another dispatch, this one warning that McDowell's troops intended to destroy the railroad from Winchester to Manassas to prevent the arrival of Johnston's troops.

The information Greenhow sent was further augmented by a July 19 report from the young and apparently quite beautiful daughter of E. R. Ford, a merchant, whose house was situated midway between Washington and Fairfax. Antonia Ford walked six miles from her father's house to that of her grandfather in order to borrow a horse. She rode with an aunt to Beauregard's headquarters and apprised the general of the progress of the federal advance. Alas, Ford was not accorded the same reception as Betty Duvall. Suspecting that Ford might be a double agent, Beauregard had her and her aunt placed under genteel arrest until a Confederate officer serving under J. E. B. Stuart corroborated her information. Ford sporadically engaged in further espionage over the next three years. Finally arrested, she ended up marrying the Union major who had charge of her.

Beauregard was able not only to thwart the attack on the Winchester-Manassas railroad, thereby ensuring that Johnston and his men would arrive in good time, he managed to turn what had seemed like a sure victory for the North at Bull Run into a Confederate triumph.

Rose Greenhow's own account of her contribution to the first Battle of Bull Run reported that she had in her possession the map used by the Senate Committee on Military Affairs. It bore red dotted lines showing the planned route to Manassas. The implication, of course, was that Henry Wilson had delivered it into her hands. She also claimed that she supplied Jordan with a steady stream of "verbatim" cabinet reports. Whether Greenhow was exaggerating or not, on July 23, she received from Jordan a note reading, "Our President and our General direct me to thank you. The Confederacy owes you a debt." And it is true that, by any measure, the information Rose Greenhow supplied on the eve of Bull Run was as remarkable as it was devastating. Yet equally remarkable is the fact that Beauregard was able to corroborate her intelligence simply by reading Northern newspapers.

Indeed, throughout the war, the press constantly published detailed accounts of troop movements, strategies, and orders of battle. One modern scholar has observed that "had the Confederate commander at the first Bull Run battle had a personal representative on the staff of the Union commander, he scarcely could have had better information than what was furnished him by the Northern press." Braxton Bragg, commanding in the West in 1862, subscribed to several Northern papers in the name of a Confederate sympathizer who lived in Elizabethtown, Kentucky. A line of couriers carried the papers from Elizabethtown to him daily. Likewise, Robert E. Lee regularly read the New York and Philadelphia papers and was seriously shaken when Union army activity temporarily interrupted delivery. Major William Norris, chief of the Confederate Signal Bureau, personally delivered Northern papers to Jefferson Davis each morning. Northern commanders also made use of Southern newspapers, but not so extensively and routinely as Southern leaders studied the Northern press. Every day, couriers brought Northern and Canadian newspapers into Richmond.

Certainly, the Bull Run campaign had been widely publicized. On Saturday, July 20, the day before the battle, Washingtonians rushed to obtain passes to Virginia in order to view the fighting. William Howard Russell, a correspondent for the London *Times*, reported a great demand for picnic lunches. The city's "French cooks and hotel-keepers," he wrote, have tripled the prices of "wines and of the hampers of provisions which the Washington people are ordering to comfort themselves at their bloody Derby." Similarly inflated was the price of carriage transportation to Centreville, overlooking Bull Run. At first, the picnickers were treated to what seemed a Union victory. Some who left Centreville by the early afternoon returned to Washington to report the good news. But the

War Department was receiving a series of telegrams from the field: McDowell would hold Centreville; McDowell would hold Fairfax; McDowell was falling back on the Potomac. Secretary of State Seward reported the contents of the final telegram personally to President Lincoln: "General McDowell's army in full retreat through Centreville. The day is lost. Save Washington and the remnants of the army." By sundown, the retreating, then routed, soldiers were stumbling over frantic picnickers, whose expensively hired carriages jammed the roadways and bridges back to the capital.

Directly after the battle, Rose Greenhow left Washington for Manhattan to put her second daughter, Leila, on a ship bound for California, where she would join her older sister. Greenhow's youngest, eight-year-old "Little Rose," would remain with her mother. When word of the Union defeat reached New York, the spy made no attempt to conceal her jubilation. She returned to Washington on July 23 and set herself to work ministering to Confederate prisoners taken in the battle, who were being held in the Old Capitol. She also worked with Mrs. Philip Phillips, the wife of a former Alabama congressman who was now a Washington attorney, to raise money to feed and clothe them.

Greenhow resumed meetings with the circle of spies that had by now clustered around her. Among them was George Donellan, the courier; Colonel Michael Thompson (who code-named himself Colonel Empty, phoneticizing his initials); Dr. Aaron Van Camp, a dentist; and Lewis Linn McArthur, clerk to Colonel Empty. Betty Duvall, Mrs. F. A. (Bettie) Hassler, and Lily Mackall served as couriers. There was also Samuel Applegate, a Union soldier who was either a double agent from the beginning or was later persuaded to turn against Greenhow. Together, they intended no less than to ripen Washington for the Confederate invasion they believed imminent. Mostly, the spies reported on troop disposition and strength in and around the capital. The few dispatches that survive are fragmentary, as indicated by the ellipses:

July 31, 1861
. . . the panic is great and the attack hourly expected. They believe that the attack will be simultaneous from Edward's Ferry. . . .

Baltimore. . . . A troupe of Cavalry will start from here this morning
to Harper's Ferry. Don't give time for re-organizing.

7 P.M., August 10, 1861
McClellan is very active and very discreet. McDowell moved toward
Fairfax yesterday at 9 A.M. with 20,000 men. Every order is being
executed without attracting attention. Activity pervades McClellan's
forces.—It is reliably stated that 45,000 occupy the Va. side
and 15,000 the approaches from the District side of the City. An
attack is apprehended by McClellan. Judging McClellan's movements
indicate apprehension of an attack. Banks has 35,000 men more or
less. So the reliable rumor says. It is doubt . . . a combined force of
100,000 . . .

Another dispatch records the prospect of fifth-column activities: "to
effect an organization here in order to take advantage of emergencies. If possible their telegraph wires will . . . all be simultaneously
cut, and their guns spiked along the Va. side."

An agent engaged in such activities best keep a low profile. But
such behavior was not in Greenhow's nature. Soon, federal authorities explicitly barred her from visiting Confederate prisoners. It is
also possible that one of Greenhow's lesser conquests, a Washington
clerk named Doolittle—perhaps Anson O. Doolittle, the son of
Wisconsin Senator James R. Doolittle—was actually a double agent
working for General McClellan. It is equally possible that Greenhow
finally became suspicious of Doolittle. When he asked her to
forward a letter to a Colonel Corcoran in Richmond, she accepted
the document but made no attempt to send it on, as if to demonstrate that she was not in communication with the Confederacy.
However, with or without a double agent, Rose Greenhow's boasting
furnished the federals with more than enough reason for suspicion.
Mrs. Greenhow—it finally dawned upon the powers that were—bore
watching.

The man selected for the mission of surveillance was the nation's
first private detective, the operative who had ushered Abraham
Lincoln safely to his Washington inaugural, Allan J. Pinkerton. On
April 19, three months after the president-elect's perilous passage,
the Sixth Massachusetts Regiment, on its way to garrison the

virtually besieged capital, changed trains in Baltimore. The troops were mobbed by Confederate sympathizers, who hurled stones and bricks at them, killing four of their number. The Sixth Massachusetts opened fire, killing twelve Baltimoreans and wounding others. Three days later, a citizens' committee called on President Lincoln, protesting the "pollution" of Maryland soil. "Our men are not moles, and cannot dig under the earth," Lincoln replied to the committee members. "They are not birds, and cannot fly through the air. There is no way but to march across, and that they must do." In response, Baltimoreans cut telegraph lines, sabotaged railroad tracks, and destroyed bridges. For a time, Washington was cut off from communication with the North.

It was shortly after these events, in an atmosphere of trembling and crisis, that Allan Pinkerton arrived in the capital to speak with the president. It is not clear whether he came on his own initiative or had been summoned. In any case, the detective recalled, "around the executive mansion everything was in a state of activity and bustle. Messengers were running frantically hither and thither . . . there was a crowd of visitors, all anxious, like myself, to obtain an interview with the Chief Executive." Pinkerton "was not required to wait an unusual length of time" but was ushered directly into Lincoln's office, where the president greeted him warmly and introduced him to several cabinet members. Mr. Lincoln told the detective that "the authorities had for some time entertained the idea of organizing a secret-service department of the government, with the view of ascertaining the social, political, and patriotic status of the numerous suspected persons in and around the city." Beyond the decision to make the mission of the secret service counterespionage rather than the positive gathering of intelligence, "no definite plans had been adopted." The president and his advisors asked Pinkerton for his views on the subject and then dismissed him with a promise that he "would receive further communication from them in a few days."

Amid the confusion of a city and nation responding to civil war, Pinkerton believed that more than a few days would pass before he heard anything. He was right. Nor did it help that the War Department at the time was administered by Simon Cameron, an inept and incompetent patronage appointee (as Pennsylvania's

Republican Party boss, Cameron had drummed up support for Lincoln's nomination at the 1860 Republican convention). At last, Pinkerton tried to "obtain satisfying particulars from the heads of several departments," but was repeatedly disappointed. Discouraged, the detective left for Philadelphia. He found there an important letter waiting for him:

Columbus, Ohio,
April 24, 1861

Allan Pinkerton, Esq.,
Dear Sir:—

I wish to see you with the least possible delay, to make arrangements with you of an important nature. I will be either here or in Cincinnati for the next few days—here to-morrow—Cincinnati next day. In this city you will find me at the Capitol, at Cincinnati at my residence.

If you telegraph me, better use your first name alone. Let no one know that you come to see me, and keep as quiet as possible.

Very truly yours,
Geo. B. McClellan,
Maj. Gen'l Comd'g Ohio Vols.

Pinkerton was anxious to get into the action—"to serve the country in this, the hour of her need"—and, leaving the president and his cabinet to their indecision, set out for Ohio.

Pinkerton knew George B. McClellan well. After serving as a captain in the regular army, McClellan became an official of the Illinois Central Railroad and then president of the Ohio and Mississippi line. The detective, whose principal clients were the nation's railroads, had worked for him "upon various important operations." Like the governor of Ohio, who had called McClellan out of private life at the outbreak of the war to command that state's regiments, Pinkerton was impressed with McClellan. Thirty-four years old and boyish in appearance, his dark auburn hair parted on the left and brushed straight across, clean shaven but for a neat goatee and manly mustache, he was five-feet-nine, but his stocky build and muscular neck ("a neck such as not one man in ten thousand possesses," a star-struck admirer wrote) made him appear rather short. Soon, after he had been summoned to Washington to take command of the Army of the Potomac, the Northern press would invoke hopeful comparison with another less-than-statuesque military figure by dubbing him the Young Napoleon.

Pinkerton called on his friend and former client at his house on Ludlow Street in Cincinnati. McClellan, who had been advised that his Ohio troops were now to join soldiers from Indiana and Illinois as part of the regular army's Department of the Ohio and that he was to take command of this department, hired Pinkerton to create a secret service bureau directly answerable to him and him alone. The sphere of Pinkerton's activities was thereby enlarged beyond counterespionage to espionage. What McClellan wanted was observations made from behind the rebel lines. Within six hours of his meeting with McClellan, Pinkerton had dispatched his most trusted agent, Timothy Webster, to Louisville, with instructions to proceed southward from there to Bowling Green, Clarksville, and Memphis. A few days later, McClellan again met with Pinkerton. The general needed to ascertain the mood—the loyalty, the leanings—of the populace south of the Ohio River, in Kentucky, Tennessee, Mississippi, and Louisiana. While Mississippi and Louisiana had voted in January to secede, by the beginning of May, Kentucky and Tennessee were still ostensibly loyal, though anti-Union sentiment ran very high in all the states. The mission would be hazardous. Pinkerton decided to make the tour himself. "I have invariably found," declared the detective, "that a personal knowledge is far more satisfactory than that gleamed [sic] from others. . . ."

Representing himself as a Georgian, Pinkerton traveled through Louisville and Bowling Green, Kentucky, to Nashville, Tennessee. Whereas the detective found a good deal of pro-Union sentiment in Kentucky (indeed, the state would declare itself neutral on May 20), Tennessee was rife with secession, and the Confederate army was already present in Nashville. Pinkerton met one army surgeon who had hatched a scheme to fill a commissary wagon with strychnine-laced whiskey, simulate a breakdown, and abandon the wagon to Union forces. The soldiers would, of course, greedily lap up the liquor and suffer painful deaths.

In Memphis, Pinkerton found the city girding for war as General Gideon Pillow directed construction of earthworks and other fortifications. "Here to be known or suspected as a Union man was to merit certain death. . . . Fearlessly, however, I mingled with these men . . . and . . . obtained a ready passport to the favor and confidence of the most prominent of their leaders." The detective sipped brandy and water with General Pillow, who boasted in detail of the city's defenses.

Valuable as Pillow's information was, Pinkerton found his best sources in "the colored men, who were employed in various capacities of a military nature which entailed hard labor." One of these men saved Pinkerton's life. It was the detective's third night in Memphis, and he was preparing for bed. He heard a faint knock at the door, opened it, and was nearly mowed down by the hotel's black porter.

According to Pinkerton's memoir: "His eyes were fixed wildly upon me, his lips were quivering, and his knees trembled under him, as though unable to sustain the weight of his body."

"What is the matter, Jem? What has happened to frighten you so?"

"'Fore God, Massa Allen"—Pinkerton assumed the alias E. J. Allen for most of his espionage work—"you done can't sleep in this housn to-night, ef ye do, ye'll be a dead man before morning."

"As may be imagined," the detective observed, "this information was not of a very agreeable nature, indefinite as it was."

"Out with it, Jem, and let me know what it is all about."

"I tell you what it is, Massa Allen, and I'se gwan to tell it mighty quick. Ye see, de General hab got a lot of spies up de river at Cairo [Illinois], a watching of the Linkum sogers, and one o' dem fellows jes came in as you were going up stairs. De berry minit dat he seed you he said to de man what was wid him, 'Dat man is 'spicious; I seed him in Cincinnati two weeks ago, and he ain't down here for no good,' and he started right off for de General, to tell him all about it. I kem right up heah, massa, and you must git away as fast as ye can."

Thanks to Jem, Pinkerton made good his escape. He later met the man behind Union lines in Virginia and employed him as an agent.

Pinkerton did not flee northward, but into Mississippi. At Jackson, the detective paused, not only to assess the military situation there, but to catch a self-congratulatory breath. After all, his mission had thus far been very successful. He had plans of the roads, a description of the countryside, and a "pretty correct" estimate of troop strength and deployment. He descended the stairs to the hotel parlor, saw a Confederate officer standing in the doorway, bade him good morning, and invited him to breakfast for a chat. Afterwards, "it occurred to me that . . . I owed it to myself to procure the services of a barber for a much-needed shave. I had been traveling for a number of days, and my face had been a stranger to a razor for a long time."

Pinkerton seated himself in the shop of the hotel's "well-fitted saloon" and waited his turn to submit himself to what he called "the deft fingers of the knight of the razor."

"Next!"

And he took his place in the chair of a dapper little German barber, who seemed "puzzled and speculative" as he lathered the detective. He finished shaving one side of Pinkerton's face when he unaccountably broke into a smile.

"Vy, how do you do, Mr. Bingerdon?"

Though the detective felt as if he had been struck by a thunderbolt, he refused to lose his self-control.

"I am not Mr. Bingerdon, and I don't know the man."

"Oh yes, your name is Bingerdon, and you leev in Geecago."

The barber was obviously so delighted at having recognized Pinkerton, that it was clear he meant no harm. However, it would hardly do for this German, no matter how good naturedly, to blow the detective's cover.

"I tell you," Pinkerton said sternly, "I don't know the man you are speaking of."

"Oy, Mr. Bingerdon, I know you well. Don't you mind me shaving you in the Sherman House in Geecago, you was a customer of mine."

Exasperated by the barber's "pertinacity," Pinkerton jerked the towel from around his neck, wiped the lather from the unshaven half of his face, rose from the chair, and thundered: "I tell you I know nothing of you[r] Mr. Bingerdon, or any other d____d Yankee abolitionist, and if you say another word to me upon this subject, I'll whip you on the spot!"

A crowd had gathered around the barber and his irate customer.

Pinkerton angrily told them his story. He lived near Augusta, Georgia, had never been to Chicago, and knew nothing of Pinkerton and his gang. Then he invited the assembled gentlemen to have a drink.

That won them over. By the time they had all drained their glasses and returned to the barber shop, one of the men proposed hanging the little German barber on the spot. Pinkerton pleaded on his behalf, he was let go, and the men once again retired for another drink. Afterward, Pinkerton "procured a razor and shaving materials, and performed that operation for myself, as I did not care to excite curiosity by exhibiting my half-shaved face to any more inquisitive barbers."

After this, Pinkerton returned to Cincinnati and continued to direct covert operations in the war's western theater. It was about this time that the debacle at Bull Run shook Union command. On Monday, July 22, 1861, the day after the battle, George McClellan received a telegram from Abraham Lincoln: "Circumstances make your presence here necessary. Charge Rosecrans or some other general with your present department and come hither without delay." Put in command of the army defending the capital, the Young Napoleon summoned Pinkerton to Washington. He was to enlarge his secret service operations, both espionage and counterespionage. The latter was concentrated chiefly in the capital itself, which was placed under martial law and administered by Provost Marshal Colonel Andrew Porter. "In operating my detective force," Pinkerton wrote in a letter to General McClellan:

> I shall endeavor to test all suspected persons in various ways. I shall seek access to their houses, clubs, and places of resort, managing that among the members of my force shall be ostensible representatives of every grade of society, from the highest to the most menial. Some shall have the *entree* to the gilded saloon of the suspected aristocratic traitors, and be their honored guests, while others will act in the capacity of valets, or domestics of various kinds, and try the efficacy of such relations with the household to gain evidence. Other suspected ones will be tracked by the "shadow" detective, who will follow their every foot-step, and note their every action.

It was as just such a "shadow" that Pinkerton first functioned in

Washington. Pennsylvanian Thomas A. Scott, acting assistant secretary of war, commissioned Pinkerton and his brand-new secret service to observe the activities of Rose Greenhow. Note was to be made of every person entering or leaving her house, and of any suspicious persons with whom these visitors might communicate. Any of her visitors who attempted to cross Union lines was to be arrested and searched immediately.

Pinkerton was eager to begin his mission and set off at once with two of his men. Largely unfamiliar with the streets of Washington, Pinkerton thought it best to begin his operation by the light of day. Storm clouds gathered and a slight shower commenced as Pinkerton took up a position near the house. It consisted of two stories and a basement, the parlors elevated several feet above ground level, and the entrance at the top of a flight of steps. The blinds were closed. Apparently, no one was home. Pinkerton went back to his office to get three more agents. When he returned to Greenhow's house, a violent storm blew up, the rain fell in torrents, and the sky, approaching evening, blackened. Pinkerton sent the first two men back, posted the others, and moved closer to the house. The storm was miserable, to be sure, but at least it kept the curious away and allowed the detectives free range to prowl.

In the gathering darkness, the detective glimpsed a light between the slats of the closed blinds. The parlor windows were too high up to permit Pinkerton to look inside, so he summoned two of his men and had them hunker down below the window while he pulled off his boots and climbed up on their shoulders. Level with the windows now, he gingerly raised the sash and noiselessly turned the slats of the blinds. What he saw was a luxuriously appointed room—but an empty one.

"I was about to give expression to my chagrin at this discovery, when a warning 'Sh!' from one of my sturdy supporters induced me to be silent."

A figure approached the house. The three operatives dashed under the front stoop, heard the visitor's footsteps ascending the stairs, heard him ring the bell, and heard him enter. The human pyramid was again formed under the window. Now Pinkerton saw the visitor seated in the parlor, waiting for the lady of the house. He was in the uniform of the regular army, a captain of infantry whom

Pinkerton recognized as one of the commanding officers of a provost marshal station.

Out of delicacy of feeling, Pinkerton referred to him as Captain Ellison. A number of historians believe this was John Elwood of the Fifth Infantry, who was appointed provost marshal of Washington on May 1, 1861. Elwood, however, was arrested on October 26, 1862, quite some time after the confrontation with Pinkerton; the charge against him was corruption rather than espionage. Tall, handsome, about forty, "Ellison" appeared to be a model officer. The detective's eye, however, discerned a troubled, restless look about him. He shifted nervously in his chair until Greenhow walked into the room. The captain bowed, his face no longer troubled, but aglow with pleasure.

At this critical juncture, one of Pinkerton's "supporters" warned him that some people were coming. The three detectives hid themselves again until the passersby were at a safe distance. Then Pinkerton climbed atop his men once more and saw the captain and Greenhow in conversation across a table. He could catch fragments of sentences—enough to satisfy himself that the talk was treasonous. Captain Ellison was discussing the disposition of troops. Next, he took from his coat pocket a map. Pinkerton thought that it looked like a plan of the fortifications around Washington and even seemed to show a "contemplated plan of attack." The pair fell to discussing the map while, at intervals, Pinkerton and his men were compelled to dash under the stoop to avoid an encounter with this or that pedestrian.

When the detective finally resumed his position, the room was again empty. After an hour, the "delectable couple," as Pinkerton referred to them, reappeared, arm in arm, and took their seats. Yet again, Pinkerton's man warned of an approaching passerby. From under the stoop, the three detectives heard the captain's footsteps, a pause at the doorway, a whispered goodnight, "and something that sounded very much like a kiss."

It was past midnight as the captain descended the stairs. In his excitement and, doubtless, exhaustion, Pinkerton took off after him without pausing to put on his boots. The secret agent, in his stocking feet, shadowed the captain through the pelting storm, following closely, because, unfamiliar with the city, he was afraid of losing him. As his man reached Pennsylvania and Fifteenth, Pinkerton thought he saw him draw a revolver—but, no. Then, suddenly, the captain passed a sentry and ducked into a building. Instantly, four armed soldiers rushed out of the building, pointed their bayoneted rifles at Pinkerton's breast, and the officer of the guard called out: "Halt, or I fire!"

Pinkerton knew he could not escape, and certainly it would be foolish to resist four armed men. He tried to explain the situation: he had been out late and had lost his way—but they weren't listening. Doubtless, his lack of footgear on this sodden night did not add to his credibility. The detective was taken to the guard house, where he waited about half an hour before being ushered upstairs to the office of the very man he had been following.

The captain, pacing excitedly, glared at the soggy operative and demanded: "What is your name?"

"E. J. Allen."

"What is your business?"

"I have nothing further to say, and I decline to answer any further questions."

"Ah! So you are not going to speak. Very well, sir, we will see what time will bring forth."

The captain fingered the handles of two revolvers that lay on the table before him. "Take this man to the guard-house," he ordered, "but allow no one whatever to converse with him; we will attend further to this case in the morning."

Pinkerton bowed deeply to the officer, who swore at him, and the sentries took him downstairs among the other prisoners, most of whom were drunk and disorderly. One of the detective's two "supporters" had also been arrested and was profiting from his incarceration by impersonating a rebel sympathizer in order to pump information from the genuine articles.

Cold and miserable, his teeth chattering "like castanets," Pinkerton pondered his next move. Prevented by the captain's order from conversing with his fellow prisoners, Pinkerton commenced ingratiating himself with his guard by telling him humorous stories. Finally, he asked if the man would deliver a note in return for suitable payment and dashed off a message to the assistant secretary of war. It was six in the morning before the changing of the guard, at which time Pinkerton's friendly turnkey left on his errand. He returned at seven.

"How is the weather outside?" Pinkerton called to him.

"All right, sir!" came the reply with a sly wink, and the detective knew the message had been safely delivered.

At 8:30 the sergeant of the guard called out: "E. J. Allen and William Ascot"—the latter being the name of Pinkerton's operative. The pair were taken to the captain's office. "The Secretary of War has been informed of your arrest," Ellison/Ellwood declared, "and you will be conducted to him at once, and then we shall see whether you will remain silent any longer."

With four guards, Pinkerton, Ascot, and the captain marched to assistant secretary Scott's house. Pinkerton was summoned into the Assistant Secretary's chamber and proceeded to detail all he had seen and heard the night before.

"Mrs. Greenhow," said Scott, "must be attended to. She is becoming a dangerous character. You will therefore maintain your watch upon her, and should she be detected attempting to convey any information outside of the lines, she must be arrested at once."

Next, Scott summoned the captain into the room.

"Did you see any one last evening who is inimical to the cause of the government?"

"No, sir," the captain replied in a faltering voice. "I have seen no person of that character."

"Are you quite sure of that?"

"I am, sir."

"In that case, Captain, you will please consider yourself under arrest, and you will at once surrender your sword to Captain Mehaffy."

"Ellison" sank into a chair and sobbed. A search of his home revealed more incriminating evidence, and Pinkerton claimed he was confined for more than a year at Fort McHenry and died soon after his release. Captain John *Elwood* was sent to the Old Capitol Prison, where he committed suicide before his release. This may mean that "Ellison" and Elwood are not one and the same, or that Pinkerton does not quite have the facts right—judging from his later, notorious record of misjudging enemy troop strength, the latter is a distinct possibility.

To his great relief, Pinkerton's men had recovered his boots before daybreak. "I was afraid [they] would be found by some one connected with the house," he wrote, "and thus lead to the suspicion that the premises were the object of espionage." He and his men continued their surveillance, witnessing a steady stream of "prominent gentlemen" pour in and out, including senators and representatives. One, an attorney, appeared night after night, and it was he that Pinkerton shadowed most tenaciously. At last, he was caught transmitting information south by courier. He was arrested and, eight days later, so was Rose Greenhow.

She certainly could not have been unaware that she was being watched. Indeed, it is as if she had *wanted* to be arrested. On August 23, about 11 A.M., Greenhow was strolling with "a distinguished member of the diplomatic corps," when an unnamed individual warned her that her house was being watched. She hardly needed the warning, for she had noticed two men clumsily following her. If Greenhow's account is to be believed—and here, as elsewhere, she stretches the limits of credibility—one of her circle happened to come up the street just at this time. Greenhow whispered to this agent, "Those men will probably arrest me. Wait at Corcoran's Corner, and see. If I raise my handkerchief to my face, give information." Then she *ate* a "very important note" she was carrying.

At this point, as she was mounting her front stairs, the two men who had been following accosted her.

"Is this Mrs. Greenhow?" asked the one who wore a major's uniform. (It was Allan Pinkerton.)

"Yes. Who are you, and what do you want?"

"I come to arrest you."

"By what authority?"

"By sufficient authority."

Then Greenhow demanded a warrant. Pinkerton, who called himself Major E. J. Allen, could only explain that he had verbal authority from the departments of war and state.

"I have no power to resist you. But had I been inside of my house, I would have killed one of you before I submitted to this illegal process."

Pinkerton's reply was unaccountably lame: "That would have been wrong."

Soon the house was filled with men searching beds, drawers, the books in her library, her furniture, her armoires. They worked carefully and quietly, hoping not to discourage any rebel spies who might come calling and obligingly walk into their hands. But "Little Rose"—Mrs. Greenhow's eight-year-old daughter—ran out, shinnied up a tree in the garden, and shouted to the neighborhood, "Mother has been arrested!" The detectives climbed after her and dragged the sobbing little girl down. Despite the alarm she had sounded, a number of rebel sympathizers did, indeed, call at the house and were taken into custody. That same day, Mrs. Philip Phillips, the Alabama congressman's wife who fed and clothed rebel prisoners of war, was also arrested, and that night the mayor of Washington, James G. Berret, was taken into the custody of the provost guard. An ex-officio member of the Metropolitan Police Board who, in that capacity, had taken a loyalty oath, Berret stubbornly resisted as foolish the exercise of repeating the oath in his capacity as mayor.

Rose Greenhow was placed under house arrest and was subject to continual surveillance. Although Pinkerton had a number of female operatives on his staff, it was principally men who kept the vigil. An operative even sat by her bed at night. In a "most bravely indelicate" letter she sent to friends in South Carolina, a letter that the brilliant diarist Mary Chesnut read on December 5, 1861, Greenhow lavishly detailed the treatment to which she was subjected:

> She wants us to know how her delicacy was shocked and outraged [Chesnut wrote in her diary]. That could be done only by most plain-spoken revelations. For eight days she was kept in full sight of men—her rooms wide open—and sleepless sentinels watching by day and by night. Soldiers tramping—looking in at her leisurely by way of amusement.
>
> Beautiful as she is, at her time of life few women like all the mysteries of their toilette laid bare to the public eye.
>
> She says she was worse used than Marie Antoinette when they snatched a letter from the poor queen's bosom.

At the end of August, Greenhow was not removed *to* a prison, her house was transformed *into* one. Female political prisoners, like herself, were now confined to Fort Greenhow, as the house was dubbed, and Pinkerton's detectives were relieved of guard duty by a detachment of McClellan's personal bodyguard known as the Sturgis Rifles.

During this time, War Department employees sifted through the documents and scraps of papers found in the Sixteenth Street house. Although Greenhow had destroyed the key to Thomas Jordan's cipher, the code was rudimentary enough to yield to a brief analysis of messages written in it. The government had more than enough evidence to keep Rose Greenhow under confinement.

The men of the Sturgis Rifles were more considerate guards than the Pinkerton operatives had been, and Lieutenant N. E. Sheldon, their commanding officer, was an indulgent jailer. In her memoir, *My Imprisonment and the First Year of Abolition Rule in Washington,* Greenhow recorded that this handsome New Yorker had been most obliging in sending on to the rebels the dispatches she continued to write. He also did his best to fend off visits from the brigade surgeon, whom the provost marshal had charged with the daily duty of inspecting her "sanitary condition." When Greenhow objected to taking her meals with a fellow prisoner, a "woman of bad repute" named Mrs. Onderdonk, Lieutenant Sheldon restricted Onderdonk to her own room—even though the lady, like Pinkerton a Chicagoan, was very probably a federal plant whose mission was to pump Rose Greenhow.

A more desirable companion was Mrs. Philip Phillips, consigned to Fort Greenhow with her two eldest daughters, a sister, and the courier Bettie Hassler. But most of the prisoners were women "of the lowest class," in Greenhow's words. Miss Ella (Ellie) M. Poole, first arrested in Wheeling, West Virginia, on October 6, escaped several times until, in Louisville, she realized she was being followed by the interestingly named Delos Thurmon Bligh, a detective acting on General Sherman's orders. Bligh followed her onto a train and finally made the arrest when they reached Vincennes, Indiana. When she was found to be carrying $7,500, Bligh returned her to Louisville for an audience with Sherman himself. The general judged her to be a dangerous spy, and Bligh himself escorted her to Washington for confinement in Fort Greenhow. Many believe that she became a Union informant, reporting on Greenhow's conversations. There is no hard evidence of this, but it is a fact that Greenhow disliked her intensely.

Another inmate, Mrs. Baxley, was fatuous at best and unbalanced at worst. She was overheard boasting that she had gotten a Baltimore doctor named Septimus Brown a commission in the Confederate army. She also claimed to have in her possession nuts from Jefferson Davis's table as well as a letter from Rose Greenhow! Authorities searched Baxley and found sensitive documents sewn into the lining of her bonnet. Arrested and confined, she protested that no one would entrust secret documents to a maniac like herself. She had visited Jefferson Davis out of curiosity only, and the documents were nothing more than friendly letters. These protests notwithstanding, she refused to sleep under blankets stamped "U.S."

Throughout all of this, Rose Greenhow continued to communicate with the Confederacy—and not just by means of Sheldon, but through something she referred to as a "vocabulary of colors" sewn into the "tapestry" work (presumably, needlepoint embroidery) with which she busied herself. Most astonishing was the publication in a Richmond newspaper of a letter she sent to Secretary of State Seward, complaining of mistreatment in prison. In December 1861, she wrote to Thomas Jordan that she expected soon to be sent south. But, to her surprise, she suddenly found the walls closing in. A newspaper story appeared charging that authorities had discovered in a Christmas cake sent to her a letter containing plans for escape from Fort Greenhow. Seventy-eight-year-old Major General John E. Wool telegraphed Secretary Seward on January 7, 1862, advising him that someone in Washington was obtaining "all the information necessary for those who command the rebel army. They know much better than I do what is doing at Washington." Immediately, Greenhow's window was boarded up, and all writing materials were denied her. Soon after, on January 18, Fort Greenhow was closed, and all prisoners—save for Mrs. Baxley and Rose Greenhow—were released.

Those two were transferred to the Old Capitol. It was a tumbledown place harboring a motley assortment of prisoners: rebel soldiers, spies, suspicious persons, Union deserters, and "contrabands"—escaped slaves who, having no means of supporting themselves, were confined here out of charity. D. A. Mahoney, a Confederate prisoner, recalled that the "principal floor" of the building housed the "Halls of the Senate and House of Representatives, which are now divided into five large rooms, numbered respectively from 14 to 18—room 16 being the center and largest. These rooms [are] fitted with similar bunks filled with filth of every imaginable kind, and entirely destitute of any furniture or necessary accommodations indispensable in the humblest cabin." The average size of each room was less than thirty feet square, yet each contained eighteen to twenty-five prisoners. The political prisoners, including Rose Greenhow, were confined to room 16.

Old Capitol Prison was run by William P. Wood, who, before the war, had been a professional model maker. He met Secretary of War Edwin M. Stanton in 1854 when Stanton and the present assistant secretary of war, Peter H. Watson, were law partners defending an inventor named Manny, who was being sued by Cyrus McCormack for infringing on his reaper patents. At the lawyers' behest, Wood surreptitiously altered an early patent model of the reaper in order to support the defendant's case. In fact, McCormack did lose, and while court records indicate that the doctored model played no part in the decision, Wood ever after seemed to exercise a particular influence on Stanton.

A private at the beginning of the war, Wood ended up not only as the superintendent of the Old Capitol, but, in this most sedentary capacity, was commissioned a colonel of cavalry. When Provost Marshal Andrew Porter protested to Stanton that Wood repeatedly flouted or even rescinded his orders, the secretary of war replied that he could either endure Wood's insults or resign. Not only did Wood share a secret with Stanton, he was actually a valuable intelligence asset. He managed a network of detectives and paid informants who regularly reported conversations overheard in the Old Capitol. Wood was himself an effective agent because, though a stern disciplinarian, he won the confidence and respect of his prisoners. Belle Boyd, the teen-aged Confederate spy who celebrated herself in a memoir titled *Belle Boyd in Camp and Prison*, recalled that "Mr. Wood [was] a man of middle height, powerfully built, with brown hair, fair complexion, and keen, bluish-gray eyes."

> Mr. Wood prides himself, I believe, upon his plebeian extraction; but I can safely aver that beneath his rough exterior there beats a warm and generous heart.
>
> "And so this is the celebrated rebel spy," said he [when Belle Boyd first entered Old Capitol Prison]. "I am very glad to see you, and will endeavor to make you as comfortable as possible; so whatever you wish for, ask for it and you shall have it. I am glad I have so distinguished a personage for my guest. Come, let me show you to your room."

The superintendent even furnished Belle with a rocking chair.

Wood's other "guests" were particularly impressed when he seized an informant, a constable of the District marshal's office, and shook him "almost out of his clothes" for having reported directly to Andrew Porter on the Confederate sympathies of another prisoner. The other inmates thought Wood hated a stool pigeon as much as they did. Actually, Wood's objection was to the fact that the constable was trespassing on territory he had reserved for his own stable of informants. For her part, Rose Greenhow was not impressed. And, for his part, Wood was not *quite* as indulgent with her. At her request, he helped her recover her private papers. He wrote her a note asking for power of attorney so that he could secure the documents on her behalf. All too familiar with Greenhow's style, he asked that, in replying, she "be kind enough to dispense with the God and Liberty style in your *pronunciamento.*"

Old Capitol was no Andersonville, to be sure, but it was filthy, and Greenhow certainly suffered physical hardships. Spiritually, however, imprisonment gratified her romantic and aristocratic imagination, and she frequently compared herself to Marie Antoinette. "Greenhow enjoys herself amazingly," Augusta Morris, a fellow prisoner, wrote. Her fame soon spread to the women of Richmond, not all of whom regarded her with unmixed emotions. Diarist Mary Chesnut recorded sardonically on August 29, 1861, that her "party of matrons had their shot at those saints and martyrs and patriots, the imprisoned Greenhow and Phillips." One of the ladies—a Mrs. Lee (perhaps the wife of Robert E. or of his brother, Sydney Smith Lee)—was profane enough to pun "upon the odd expression 'Ladies of their age being confined.'" And there was talk among Chesnut's circle that

> Mrs. Greenhow had herself confined and persecuted, that we might trust her the more. She sees we distrust her after all. The Manassas men swear she was our good angel.
>
> And the Washington women say: up to the highest bidder, always. And they have the money on us.

With Greenhow at all times was her daughter, Little Rose. "My little darling," said mother to daughter, "you must show yourself superior to these Yankees, and not pine."

"O mamma, never fear. I hate them too much."

When Little Rose became ill, Mrs. Greenhow refused the ministrations of the despised brigade surgeon—"At your peril but touch my child. You are a coward and no gentleman, thus to insult a woman"—and Wood sent her a private doctor.

Near the end of March 1862, Rose Greenhow was given a hearing ("tried" is too formal a term to describe the proceeding) in the temporary office of the military governor and provost marshal at Nineteenth and I streets. Judge Edward Pierrepont read the charges of espionage, to which Greenhow replied: "If I gave the information that you say I have, I must have got it from sources that were in the confidence of the government. . . . If Mr. Lincoln's friends will pour into my ear such important information, am I to be held responsible for all that?"

It really was difficult to argue with such reasoning, and the proceedings got nowhere. When Judge Pierrepont raised the prospect of offering the prisoner the opportunity to take an oath of allegiance, Greenhow replied, "You would blush to do that." Exasperated, the judge finally suggested that Mrs. Greenhow's intentions partook less of treason than "mischief." To which Greenhow imperiously responded, "In these war times, you ought to be in some more important business, than holding an inquisition for the examination of women."

Greenhow was not acquitted, but, in June 1862, "paroled," transported beyond the Union lines into Virginia in return for a pledge not to come back North for the duration of the war. In

Richmond, she was generally greeted as a heroine, though, according to Mary Chesnut, "One-half of these ungrateful Confederates say Seward sent her." Chesnut's husband, James, however, "says the Confederacy owes her a debt they can never pay. She warned them at Manassas." After a stay in the South, Greenhow sailed to Europe to generate support for the Confederacy. Louis Napoleon of France received her, as did Queen Victoria, and Greenhow quickly wrote *My Imprisonment and the First Year of Abolition Rule at Washington*, which sold very well abroad. In August 1864, she boarded the British blockade runner *Condor*, out of Greenock, Scotland, bound for the South. The night before *Condor* entered Cape Fear River with the object of putting in at Wilmington, North Carolina, another blockade runner, *Night Hawk*, had run aground at the mouth of the river, was boarded by Union sailors, and set ablaze. *Condor*'s skipper, no less a figure than Admiral Hobart Hampden, eighth Earl of Buckinghamshire, had entrusted the helm to a local pilot, who as he brought the ship into the river through heavy seas, steered sharply to avoid the burned-out hulk of *Night Hawk*. In so doing, he ran *Condor* aground on New Inlet Bar, just two hundred yards from Confederate Fort Fisher. The London *Daily Mail* reported:

At 3 in the morning of [September] 1st . . . the *Condor* [ran] aground in the breakers. . . . After the *Condor* took the ground, a Yankee vessel was seen approaching through the gloom, with a view to shelling the stranger. Mrs. Greenhow, remembering her long former imprisonment in Washington, and apprehensive of its repetition, insisted, against the advice of the captain, upon having a boat lowered, upon trusting herself to the tender mercies of the waves rather than to those of the Yankees. Into this boat she carried with her the mail bags [presumably containing secret dispatches]. . . . To the pilot, who had just run the *Condor* aground, was committed the delicate task of steering Mrs. Greenhow's boat, which was lowered into a raging surf. Directly the boat left the leeside of the vessel she was caught, broadside on, by a huge breaker, and overturned. All the male passengers succeeded in clambering up and clutching the keel of the capsized boat, but in the darkness and amid the deafening thunder of the breakers, nothing was seen or heard of poor Mrs. Greenhow. Her body was subsequently washed ashore near Fort Fisher, and close beside it a heavy leather reticule, containing $2,000 [actually, $3,000] in gold [quite possibly royalties from the well-received British publication of her book], which was believed to have been slung around her neck when the boat was upset. It is a strange proof of the strength of that boisterous sea that such a weighty article as this reticule should not have sunk, but should have been tossed up on the beach like a bit of seaweed. Upon the afternoon of the 2nd Mrs. Greenhow's body was committed to the grave at Wilmington, according to the rites of the Roman Catholic Church.

The "male passengers" to which the article refers included four sailors and James P. Holcomb, a Confederate agent Jefferson Davis sent to Canada as part of a commission bent on smuggling arms, restoring to the South escaped Confederate prisoners of war who, having taken refuge in Canada, were now stranded there, and, most important, fomenting a Copperhead uprising throughout the North. As for the unfortunate Greenhow, the *Daily Mail* failed to detail the full story of the body's recovery. It was first discovered by a Confederate soldier, who took the bag of gold and pushed the corpse back into the waves. When it was washed ashore again, later in the day, and identified as that of Rose Greenhow, the soldier was so affected by his conscience that he surrendered the gold, which, presumably, was put to some use in the service of the Confederate States of America.

CHAPTER FOUR

AUGUSTA AND THE CLEOPATRA OF THE SECESSION

The ladies lodged with Rose Greenhow in the Old Capitol Prison were hardly in her league—not as spies and, as far as Mrs. Greenhow was concerned, not in social standing. Ella—or Ellie—Poole may have turned informant, and the woman known only as Mrs. Baxley was given to vulgar histrionics and staged fainting fits. But at least neither of these women had much in the way of pretensions. Augusta Morris was another story altogether, and Rose Greenhow disliked her as intensely as she detested Poole and Baxley.

Morris said that her people were French, but Major William E. Doster, of the provost marshal's office, discovered nothing beyond the fact that she was the daughter of an Alexandria, Virginia, baker. It was true that this attractive young woman had been married in Paris, to a Virginia physician named J. F. Mason, but the two had separated, and Augusta resumed her maiden name. At the beginning of the war, she came to Washington from Richmond, a pair of young sons in tow, and called at the State Department with an offer to sell the Confederate army signals. The price she threw out to Chief of Staff General Randolph B. Marcy was ten thousand dollars.

Marcy must have alerted his son-in-law, George McClellan, to Morris and her offer, for he promptly put his man Pinkerton on the case. His detectives discovered that she was in regular correspondence with Thomas J. Rayford, alias Lieutenant Colonel Thomas

Jordan, Greenhow's contact and, at the time, the closest thing the Confederates had to a genuine spymaster. Pinkerton detectives even followed her to the cemetery, after one of her infant sons died in February 1862. She was arrested soon afterward, at four in the morning, as she lay in bed with Mansfield T. Walworth, a clerk for the adjutant-general, in a room at Brown's Hotel. Morris wrote to her estranged husband, who was serving in the Confederate army, that, before her arrest, she had gotten McClellan's "plans, as laid before the military committee, from one of the members."

Walworth, the son of New York State Chancellor Reuben H. Walworth, was a married man. His wife's family was prominent in the South, and Walworth, whose appetite for romance and intrigue was evidenced by the potboiler novels he wrote in his spare time, had approached Secretary of State Seward with an offer to exploit his Southern connections by spying for the Union. Walworth believed that Seward failed to act on his proposal because General Marcy intervened. Marcy, Walworth thought, had it in for him because he had told Seward that Marcy was taking too great an interest in Augusta Morris. Denied an official commission as a secret agent, was Walworth sleeping with Morris to get the kind of information that would prove to Seward his value as a spy? Or had *she* seduced secrets from *him?* Or was Walworth sleeping with her simply because she was both pretty and available? Pinkerton inclined to the latter view. He did find a Confederate lieutenant's uniform in Walworth's trunk, but, beyond that, no real evidence of disloyalty, let alone treason. After two months in the Old Capitol, Mansfield T. Walworth was released.

Morris entered Old Capitol Prison with her surviving son, a three-year-old named Frank. Like Little Rose Greenhow, he freely expressed his feelings toward the soldiers who held him and his mother captive: "Let me out, you damned Yankee!" Morris was far more polite than her little boy, though she delighted in toying with Judge Pierrepont and Secretary of War Stanton's other commissioners charged with determining the disposition of her case. Asked if she had been a spy, she replied enigmatically, "Even if I could have committed treason, I don't know as I should have cared to do it." Where, she asked the commissioners, could she, a "poor delicate, fragile woman," have gotten any secret information? The only Union officer she knew was Randolph B. Marcy.

"He didn't give you anything?" asked Judge Pierrepont.

"I shouldn't suppose he would. Do you think he would?"

When the judge reminded her that she had once offered to sell a very important *Confederate* secret, she replied that she was selfish, that she had no particular desire to serve either side, that what she had wanted was ten thousand dollars, period.

Judge Pierrepont offered Augusta Morris what he had offered Rose Greenhow, release in return for an oath of allegiance. She declined. Then, Pierrepont said, she would be sent South. No, the little woman demanded to be returned to Brown's Hotel. The judge promised to speak to President Lincoln about simply setting her free, and Morris bade her interlocutors good morning. "I shall remember you with pleasure." In the end, Augusta Morris was "deported" to Dixie.

The only Old Capitol inmate whose stature as a spy approached that of Rose Greenhow was Belle Boyd. She was nineteen when she arrived at the prison late in July 1862, having been arrested earlier in the month when a Union medical officer attached to the Second Division, I Corps, sent a message directly to Secretary of War Stanton: "The celebrated Belle Boyd the 'Rebel Spy' now in Front Royal has apparently fallen in love or is anxious to make a victim of the Medical Director of the 1st Army Corps (Dr. Rose)."

A "celebrated" spy, one would think, could not be a very effective spy. But, like Rose Greenhow, Belle Boyd had a way with men, especially young Federal officers. David Hunter Strother, a secret agent for the Union, knew the young lady—for he had been a spy in her hometown of Martinsburg, West Virginia—and when he encountered her at Front Royal, Virginia (this time he was attired in the uniform of a Union colonel), she gleefully exhibited to him her "trophies," a large collection of officers' brass buttons from Federal uniforms. She seems even to have solicited a contribution from Colonel Strother.

It would be pleasant to think of Boyd as a latter-day Delilah or a precursor of Mata Hari, a temptress of irresistible beauty. In fact, the most flattering description a New York *Tribune* correspondent could muster was that, "without being beautiful, she is very attractive. Is quite tall, has a superb figure, an intellectual face, and dressed with much taste." Anyone who cares to examine a photograph of Belle Boyd will understand that "intellectual" was a euphemism for "angular." She also had a long nose and buck teeth. That she knew how to flirt is beyond dispute; Northern newspapers went a step further, calling her "an accomplished prostitute." Perhaps. But what must have been most fascinating, most attractive about this girl was her unbounded romantic exuberance. The life of a spy is supposed to be cold and empty. For Boyd, espionage was, in a word, fun. And she seemed capable of getting everyone, federal or rebel, to join in her game.

Actually, it all began with a killing. Boyd was seventeen when the war broke out, the daughter of a storekeeper in Martinsburg. It was a Virginia town at the beginning of the war, but became part of the Union when West Virginia broke away from the Old Dominion and was admitted as a state in June 1863. Despite this, the Boyds were ardent secessionists. Her father served in the Confederate army, and her cousin, Captain William Boyd Compton, Thirty-first Virginia Militia, was a rebel spy. Colonel John E. Boyd, another relative, was also a spy. Both men were eventually captured and sentenced to hang, but both managed to escape. Captain James W. Glenn, an uncle, was a spy and guerrilla, and Lieutenant Colonel William R. Denny, also a spy and the agent to whom Belle often reported, was probably a relative as well. The rest of the family served the Confederacy through their sheer defiance of federal authority.

In July 1861, Confederate General Stonewall Jackson, having suffered a defeat at Falling Water, retreated through Martinsburg, leaving behind two fever-stricken soldiers in the care of Belle Boyd and her maid Eliza. Not far behind Jackson came the federals. As Boyd was ministering to the sick men, a captain and two soldiers entered her house. The captain—according to Belle Boyd's own unabashedly romantic memoir, *Belle Boyd in Camp and Prison*—waved an American flag over the suffering soldiers, cursing them as "___ rebels." Boyd protested that these men, "helpless as infants," had no power to reply to his insults.

"And pray, who may you be, Miss?" asked the captain.

Eliza replied for her: "A rebel lady."

Upon which the captain cursed Boyd as he had the sick men and withdrew.

A short time later, on the Fourth of July, the Union troops occupying Martinsburg observed the holiday with the aid of a liberal ration of liquor. Word spread among the celebrants that the room of Belle Boyd was decorated with rebel flags. According to Boyd's own book, this was, in fact, the case, and there is no reason to doubt her on this point. The New York *Tribune* correspondent who interviewed Boyd in 1862 observed how she decked out her person with tokens of the Confederacy: she wore "a gold palmetto tree [emblem of South Carolina] beneath her beautiful chin, a rebel soldier's belt around her waist, and a velvet band across her forehead, with the seven stars of the Confederacy shedding their pale light therefrom.

"It seemed to me," the correspondent continued, "while listening to her narrative, that the only additional ornament she required to render herself perfectly beautiful was a Yankee halter encircling her neck."

The Yankees decided to go to the Boyd house, tear down the offending banners, and raise the Stars and Stripes. When Eliza saw the soldiers approaching, she took down the flags herself. Somewhat disappointed at finding no banners to capture, the men announced that they would raise the American flag anyway.

"Men," declared Belle Boyd's mother, "every member of my household will die before that flag shall be raised over us."

The soldiers ignored her and set about hoisting the flag.

That's when Belle drew a pistol, fired, and gravely wounded one of the boys, probably Private Frederick Martin, a Pennsylvania volunteer. (If Martin was, in fact, the victim, his wounds ultimately proved fatal; he was buried in Martinsburg on July 7, 1861.) The other Yankees picked up their fallen comrade and retreated, flag unraised.

But it was not quite over. A slave ran in to announce that the federals were piling kindling around the house and were about to light it. The Boyds managed to get a message off to Yankee headquarters, which dispatched a guard detail to stop the arsonists.

At about this time, Boyd began making herself popular with the federal officers, who were all too willing to boast of troop strength and battle plans. Boyd wrote the information down, sometimes in cipher, sometimes in the clear, and either delivered it herself, often to Colonel Denny, or through a courier known only as Sophia B., or by slaves. Reportedly, one old slave transported small, much-folded messages in his pocket watch. Boyd also pilfered officers' sabers and pistols, which she passed on to Confederate forces chronically short of material.

It is not that Boyd was casual about her espionage; she was downright ostentatious. Some time toward the end of 1861, knowledge of her activities penetrated even the thick pates of the local Union command. A captain arrested Boyd and took her to headquarters, where she was confronted by an assemblage of Union officers. They read her the Articles of War, lingering over the prescribed penalty for espionage—death—and then did nothing more than scold her. What, after all, could an eighteen-year-old girl do? They let her go.

After serving for a time as courier for Beauregard and Jackson, Boyd seems to have laid low for the winter of 1861-62. A close call came not during a spy mission, but when she was out riding for pleasure with two young rebel officers. Her horse inexplicably bolted toward the federal outpost line. The two Confederates knew it was useless to give chase: the Yankees were not likely to shoot Boyd, but they were certain to fire upon two uniformed enemy soldiers. One of the federal pickets caught the spooked animal, and all eyes turned toward Boyd. From these young men there was no talk of espionage and hanging. Two officers presented themselves as escorts back through the lines. Just two, and one of them made the embarrassing mistake of dropping a remark about "cowardly rebels."

That was all Boyd needed. Doubtless, without the remark, she would have been grateful enough for the escort. Now she was mad, and she led the boys back to where her two rebel companions were waiting for her.

"Here are two prisoners that I have brought you." To the Yankees she announced, "Here are two of the 'cowardly rebels.'"

Confederate command, obviously abashed at the method of their capture, released the captives within an hour.

In early spring 1862, with the federals again bearing down on Martinsburg, Boyd moved south to Front Royal. In short order, that town was invaded as well, and Boyd decided that she wanted to go home to Martinsburg. She had been issued a pass by Union General James Shields and boarded a train, but before it left the station, a Union officer entered and, indicating that he was armed with a warrant, arrested her. Boyd was put on a Baltimore-bound train, and she waved a small Confederate flag out the window during the entire trip. Arrived in Baltimore, she became the prisoner of General John Dix, who, having no idea what to do with her, lodged Boyd in a fine Baltimore hotel for a week before sending her on a train back to Martinsburg.

She was not totally free. For now, at last, the Union command had decided to place her under surveillance. But when she asked the Martinsburg provost marshal for a pass to Richmond through Winchester and Front Royal, he was only too happy to oblige. For with Belle Boyd there was always the potential for trouble, and he was relieved to have her off his beat for a while. It was en route that she gave an interview to the New York *Tribune* reporter: "she pleads guilty to nearly all the charges made against her, as far as they refer to conveying information to the enemy, carrying letters and parcels from the rebels within our lines to those without, and performing acts of heroic daring worthy of the days of the Revolution." The story was published, and still the federals made no serious move against her.

So, at Front Royal, she began spying again, compromising a "Captain K," identified by one recent scholar as Captain Daniel J. Keily, aide-de-camp to General James Shields. K—or Keily—wrote her verses, gave her flowers, and, Boyd reported, gave her information. Among the tidbits was the news that General Shields would hold a council of war with his officers before his command marched against Jackson. Moreover, the council was to be held in the drawing room of what had been the house of Boyd's own aunt. Boyd, of course, knew the house well and in particular was aware of a bore hole in the floor of a bedroom closet above the drawing room. The girl was able to secret herself in the closet, put her ear to the hole, and listen. What she heard was Shields's plan to take all of his troops, except for the First (Federal) Maryland Infantry, a cavalry squadron, and a battery of field artillery, out of Front Royal to support McClellan in an assault against Richmond. The First (Federal) Maryland was, therefore, vulnerable, and Boyd wrote and enciphered a report, which she delivered herself to General Turner Ashby.

Immediately after, on May 20, 1862, Boyd tried unsuccessfully to obtain from the provost marshal of Front Royal a pass to Winchester. When she was turned down, she persuaded a young Lieutenant H to get her, her cousin, and Eliza through the Union pickets to Winchester. There, on May 22, she was given two packets of papers and a little note. One of the packets, she was told, was of comparatively little importance—it was nothing more than a Northern newspaper, which, however, being a Northern newspaper, had printed the usual compromising quota of strategic information. The other packet was much more important, and the little note most important of all. Her mission was to bring these documents back to Front Royal.

Boyd gave the more important packet to Eliza, reasoning that the slave was less likely to be searched. The newspaper packet and the note she kept herself. On both packets Boyd wrote the phrase "Kindness of Lieutenant H.," hoping that this would get them through the lines with nothing more than a cursory examination. In fact, seeing his name on the packet given to Eliza, Lieutenant H took the parcel himself.

Now Boyd worked her magic on Lieutenant Colonel James S. Fillebrown, provost marshal at Winchester. She sent a request for a pass, accompanying it with a bouquet. The colonel furnished the document, together with a thank you note for the flowers.

But it wasn't to be quite so simple this time. Fillebrown had had his own spy present when Belle Boyd met the "gentleman of high social position," as she described him, who gave her the packets and note. A slave had observed the entire transaction and reported it to Fillebrown. Southerners of the period, who often professed great fear of a mass slave revolt, nevertheless took for granted the loyalty of individual slaves attached to their households. Some, like Belle Boyd's Eliza, were indeed loyal, but many—probably more—were eager to deliver information into Northern hands. Neither the Confederates nor the federals ever fully acknowledged the role of slaves in espionage. It was undoubtedly a major one. Belle Boyd, her cousin, Eliza, and Lieutenant H. were arrested at the Union picket line.

They were taken to the headquarters of the Tenth Maine Infantry and interrogated by Colonel George L. Beale, who asked Boyd if she were carrying any letters. Why, yes, she answered, offering the newspaper packet. The colonel asked her about the inscription, "Kindness of Lieutenant H." It was meaningless, she answered, a "thoughtless act of mine." At this, the lieutenant surrendered his packet. It turned out to contain another newspaper, this one the *Maryland News-sheet,* a radical secessionist publication. Having carried it would mean the lieutenant's court martial.

At last Beale turned his attention to the note Boyd held in her hand.

"What is that you have in your hand?"

"What—this little scrap of paper? You can have it if you wish: it is nothing."

Spies had played a role in the War of 1812 and in the Mexican War, but most Americans, when they thought of espionage, thought of the Revolution and Harvey Birch, the hero of James Fenimore Cooper's enormously popular second novel, *The Spy.* Boyd was no exception, and she was ready to do just what Harvey Birch had done in a similar situation: chew up the letter and swallow it. But the colonel, eager to vent his wrath on the lieutenant, did not bother with the note. Incredibly, once again, Boyd was released and, one assumes, sent the note to Stonewall Jackson.

Just what that note contained Boyd does not specify. She had already communicated to Jackson the intelligence regarding the vulnerability of the First (Federal) Maryland, and, presumably, the note contained further information relevant to the impending battle at Front Royal. But Boyd had even more to do. On May 23, while she was reading to her cousin and grandmother, she heard the sounds of battle echoing from the hills outside of town. She went out the door and saw a chaos of blue-clad troops. As usual, Boyd found a young officer willing to talk.

"But what will you do with the stores in the large dépôt?"

"Burn them, of course," the officer replied.

"But suppose the rebels come upon you too quickly?"

"Then we will fight as long as we can . . . and . . . make good our retreat upon Winchester, burning the bridges as soon as we cross them, and finally effect a junction with General Banks's force."

Boyd tried to enlist the aid of several men, all of whom had boasted of their devotion to the South, to convey the intelligence to General Jackson, but no volunteers were forthcoming. Donning a white sunbonnet and blue dress with a white apron, she dashed into the field, through the line of fire of *both* sides. A shell burst within twenty yards of her before she approached the First (Confederate) Maryland Infantry and Hay's Louisiana Brigade. She tried to communicate with them by waving her sunbonnet in the direction of town, but the troops, uncomprehending, merely cheered her.

Boyd went down on her knees to pray and looked up to find Major Henry Kyd Douglas, Jackson's aide-de-camp, riding up to her. He had seen "the figure of a woman in white"—her dress was blue, but she wore a white sunbonnet and white apron—"glide swiftly out of town. . . . She seemed, when I saw her, to heed neither weeds nor fences, but waved a bonnet as she came on."

"Good God, Belle," Douglas gasped. "You here! What is it?"

"Oh, Harry, give me time to recover my breath." And she handed over a "little note." We can only assume that this is a different note than the one she had picked up in Winchester, since it is unlikely that she would have simply held onto it overnight and into the next day—a day in which she had the leisure to read to her cousin and grandmother. In any event, her most important intelligence was verbal, as Colonel (later Lieutenant General) Richard Taylor reported:

> Breathless with speed and agitation, some time elapsed before she found her voice. Then, with much volubility, she said we were near Front Royal, beyond the wood; that the town was filled with federals, whose camp was on the west side of the river, where they had guns in position to cover the waggon-bridge, but none bearing on the railway bridge below the former; that they believed Jackson to be west of Massanutten, near Harrisonburg; that General Banks, the federal commander, was at Winchester, twenty miles north-west of Front Royal, where he was slowly concentrating his widely scattered forces to meet Jackson's advance, which was expected some days

later. All this she told with the precision of a staff officer making a report and it was true to the letter.

It is a fact that Jackson routed the federals at Front Royal. If, instead of returning to Front Royal, Boyd had remained on the hill where she paused to wave farewell to Major Douglas with her sunbonnet, she would have seen General Taylor's men charge on the left, with Richard Ewell's command approaching on the opposite flank, and the Stonewall Brigade charging up the center. She would have seen sixteen thousand Confederate troops descend upon seven thousand federals. The panic-stricken Union soldiers failed to burn the stores lodged at Front Royal, and Jackson harvested ninety-three hundred small arms, two rifled cannon, and so much in the way of general supplies that the rebels gratefully dubbed the Union commander, Nathaniel Prentiss Banks, "Commissary Banks." The victory brought to a triumphant climax Jackson's often precarious Shenandoah Valley campaign and greatly imperiled Washington, D.C.

Given the amount of corroboration, from the recollections of Major Douglas and General Taylor, it is also clear that Belle Boyd did indeed do pretty much what she describes in *Belle Boyd in Camp and Prison*. Far less certain is just how important Boyd's information was to the victory at Front Royal. Taylor, the same man who so vividly described Boyd's staff-officer-worthy report, also recalled that "Jackson was possessed of these facts before we left New Market, and based his movements upon them." Cavalrymen like Stonewall Jackson knew the value of intelligence. Reconnaissance, after all, was a traditional cavalry mission. The general had spent at least two weeks gathering information on Yankee positions. Did Boyd's last-minute report add anything to what he already knew? Thomas Ashby, a teen-aged relative of Confederate General Turner Ashby, dismissed Belle Boyd as "just a kind of circus rider." One of the jailers who looked after Boyd at the Old Capitol, N. T. Colby, thought she was "a woman governed more by romance and love of notoriety than actual regard for the Southern cause."

Soon after her arrest and consignment to the Old Capitol, Boyd became the darling of the place. Superintendent William P. Wood ushered her into her room with a window on A Street and asked if he could get her anything. Boyd wanted a rocking chair and a fire. True, it was the end of July, but a fire would make the inhospitable place seem more like home. Wood obliged. And whatever some may have thought of Boyd's value as a spy, the Washington secessionists kept her well supplied with the finest food served to her by a "contraband" that Wood himself had assigned to be her servant.

Boyd seems to have enjoyed the attentions of numerous male inmates. She even became engaged to a Confederate prisoner, a Lieutenant McVay. He—and others—tossed notes and various tokens into her room. She often heard the sound of knives or spoons scraping the walls and ceiling of her room, as if prisoners were attempting to break through. Boyd frequently favored her fellow inmates with song, usually of a distinctly Confederate stamp. When a federal guard objected to her rendition of "Maryland, My Maryland" and, in particular, to the relish with which she delivered the line, "Huzza! she spurns the Northern scum," Boyd refused to stop singing and deliberately swept that portion of floor on which the guard had stood. Stories of a less innocent nature spread: that she behaved in prison like a slut, taunting Union soldiers with salacious remarks from her window and dressing in a manner that laid bare neck and arms. But her fellow prisoners always doffed their hats to her when she passed.

As with Rose Greenhow, Belle Boyd was never brought to trial. The opportunity to take an oath of allegiance to the Union was offered her, but, of course, she declined it in no uncertain terms. After about a month in prison, she was paroled to Richmond. Back in Dixie, she attempted a final mission that tends to bear out her Old Capitol jailer's assessment of her as a woman motivated more by an infatuation with romance and notoriety than by patriotism. It was attempted in June 1863, as the rebels advanced on Gettysburg. A friend of hers, Major Harry Gilmor, was ordered on a secret mission to enter the Union lines near Winchester. As he was about to get under way, he met Boyd, who entreated him to take her along. Gilmor decidedly did not want the flamboyant girl spy as company, but neither did he wish to offend his friend. He told her that he would have to get permission from his commander, General Micah Jenkins. Satisfied that he had put her off, Gilmor retired for the night.

When he awoke at dawn, ready, he thought, to slip out unnoticed by Boyd, he discovered that his saber and pistols were missing. Then came Boyd, skipping down the stairway, dressed in a riding habit "with a pretty little belt around her waist, from which the butts of two small pistols were peeping, cased in patent leather holsters."

There was nothing for Gilmor to do but go with her to General Jenkins, who, reading the impassioned hand signals the major made behind Boyd, refused permission.

Shortly after this episode, she sailed out of Wilmington, North Carolina, on a blockade runner bound for England. It was captured by a U.S. Navy ship, and Boyd was imprisoned at Fort Warren. She may even have been condemned to death as a traitor. Despite her earlier betrothal to the Confederate lieutenant, she exercised her charms on a handsome young mariner, Samuel Hardinge (or Harding), an officer of the ship that had captured her vessel. He helped to win her release. After further confinement in Washington's Carroll Prison, from August to December 1863, she was paroled not to the South, but to Canada. She soon left from there for England, where, in August 1864, she married Hardinge, who had been discharged from the navy. It is not clear whether his discharge was honorable or dishonorable, but he did return to the United States shortly after the wedding and died without rejoining his bride. It is possible that he was arrested and died in a Federal prison. Belle, a widow in England, staved off poverty by taking to the stage—which is where many, North and South, would have agreed that she belonged in the first place. She opened in Manchester in 1866 and then returned to America, where she made a theatrical tour of the South. It is known that she appeared in a play, *The Honeymoon*, in New York in 1868, and that she toured Ohio and Texas. She married a former British army officer, John Hammond, in 1869, and a third husband, Nathaniel High, of Toledo, Ohio, in 1885. The following year, Boyd again took to the stage or lecture circuit, offering dramatic one-woman reenactments of her career as "The Cleopatra of the Secession." Belle Boyd died in 1900.

CHAPTER FIVE

AN AGENT OF THE LINE

Very soon after he served as Rose Greenhow's courier, George Donellan realized that Confederate command needed a systematic arrangement for the continual flow of intelligence out of Washington. After all, neither he nor the likes of Betty Duvall—no matter how pretty she was—could fool all of the federals all of the time. As early as July 21, 1861, while the first Bull Run was being fought, Donellan began establishing what became known as the "Doctors' Line." On that day, he briefed a Dr. Wyvill, (or Wivill or Whyvill), a Washington physician who lived near the Navy Yard, on the operation of a line of communication that would be established "the next day." The line was a relay system of couriers and safe houses. Wyvill, for example, was to convey his dispatch to a Dr. Grymes. There was also a Dr. Kent involved and at least one other physician, whose name does not survive. Lafayette C. Baker's *History of the United States Secret Service* mentions a Dr. McC., and, certainly, there were others. Physicians, peripatetic in the mid-nineteenth century, their large black bags bulging with medicines and papers, were ideal couriers. No one would search their medical bags, and no one would question regular visits to the same house. The house in question would be located at the extreme of the territory of one doctor's rural practice. Here, the doctor-courier would deposit his dispatch, which the next physician in the relay would pick up and convey to the next safe house.

In September 1862, the Doctors' Line would be augmented by another system of couriers, the Secret Line. It was a function of the Confederate Signal Corps, which Jefferson Davis ordered Edward Porter Alexander to establish soon after the outbreak of the war. Alexander had been a lieutenant in the United States Army, who had served under Albert James Myer, an assistant surgeon with a special interest in sign language. Myer developed his system of sign language into a method of military signalling that became popularly known as "wig wag," because of the elaborate arm motions involved in sending semaphore signals with lanterns or flags. Myer became the U.S. Army's first signal officer, but his assistant, Alexander, defected to the South at the outbreak of hostilities. Alexander developed Myer's system further and put it to effective use in the Confederate army.

An efficient signal system is a great thing, but even greater is having something to transmit with those signals. Alexander found a volunteer, E. Pliny Bryan, a Maryland secessionist legislator serving as a private in the First Virginia Regiment, trained him thoroughly in the signal system, and sent him to live in Washington as a spy who was now specially equipped to transmit intelligence. Charles H. Cawood, another of Alexander's volunteers, was especially skilled in moving back and forth across the Union lines. These two men were the beginning of the Secret Line. In the spring of 1862, Porter Alexander was formally offered the position of chief signal officer of the Confederate army. He saw it as a desk job and preferred action in the field, and he declined the appointment in favor of an artillery command. William Norris—of Reistertown, just northwest of Baltimore—accepted the assignment. By early autumn of 1862, Norris was working to establish the Secret Line permanently. Confederate Secretary of War George Wythe Randolph, (who succeeded Judah P. Benjamin in that post on March 18, 1862), approved a plan for a line between Baltimore and Washington in September. A short time later, President Jefferson Davis approved an even more ambitious Secret Line running to Canada, thereby, ironically enough, making it the Confederate agent's equivalent of the antebellum abolitionist's Underground Railroad.

Later in the war, at least two other Confederate agents, Thomas N. Conrad and Benjamin Franklin Stringfellow, would develop and extend the Confederate lines of secret communication, so that by December 1862, a message out of Washington would reach Richmond in less than twenty-four hours. Indeed, by the middle of the war, the lines of communication were such that a good courier enjoyed an astonishing degree of mobility. For example, Francis Jones, blond, blue-eyed, and brooding (his young wife and child had both died), cut a romantic figure through the course of thirty-two trips across the Union lines. He traveled by sea as well as land, typically taking a blockade runner from Wilmington, North Carolina, to Bermuda, then boarding a British packet to Halifax. There he would embark by train to Montreal and Toronto, both centers of conspiratorial Confederate activity, and to Niagara Falls, where, late in the war, a Confederate "peace commission" worked to undermine the Union's resolve. He also carried dispatches from Richmond to New York and, eventually, into Maine, where rebel agents plotted an abortive uprising. Ultimately, Jones—moody and unstable—betrayed the Confederate cause, but for more than a year, from 1863 through 1864, he was a remarkably successful courier.

The system of secret communications also included a series of "safe houses," places of refuge for couriers, where they could rest, eat, hide, and pick up or leave documents. Charles T. Cockey, like William Norris from the Baltimore suburb of Reisterstown, Maryland, ran such a house and conducted other espionage activity until 1864, when he was caught in the Civil War equivalent of a "sting" operation. A Union counterintelligence agent passed himself off as a Confederate courier and was eagerly welcomed into Cockey's house.

Another Baltimorean, a dentist named Dr. Adalbert J. Volck, noted locally as a portrait painter, caricaturist, and metal-relief craftsman, was a close friend of Jefferson Davis. He ran a Baltimore safe house and also plied the Doctor's Line or Secret Line, smuggling medicine as well as would-be Confederates out of Baltimore.

By the end of the war, one safe house operator would become downright infamous. John Harrison Surratt worked for Major William Norris's Confederate Signal and Secret Service as a courier through much of the war. On December 23, 1864, Dr. Samuel A. Mudd of Charles County, Maryland, introduced Surratt to a prominent Southern actor named John Wilkes Booth. Together with a small band of conspirators, Booth and Surratt began discussing a plan to kidnap Abraham Lincoln. Surratt's father, in the early 1850s, had built a tavern and hostelry ten miles south of Washington at a crossroads known as Surrattsville. He was a rural postmaster until his death in 1862 and an ardent secessionist. He offered his tavern to the Confederate service as a safe house, and, after his death, his wife, Mary E. Surratt, and his son continued the practice. In 1864, Mrs. Surratt leased out the tavern and moved to H Street in Washington. There she ran a boardinghouse where John Wilkes Booth and his accomplices discussed strategy and at which various Confederate agents stayed. After the assassination of President Lincoln, Mary E. Surratt, who seems to have been unaware of just what Booth was planning to do, would be found guilty of conspiracy and hanged.

A regular "guest" at the Surratt tavern was Thomas Nelson Conrad, captain, Third Virginia Cavalry, chaplain for same, and spy for General J. E. B. Stuart. A native of Virginia, Conrad had graduated from Dickinson College in Carlisle, Pennsylvania, where he roomed with another Virginia youth, Mountjoy Cloud, who became a member of Conrad's espionage "ring." (Numerous Dickinson alumni joined the Confederacy, but showed their loyalty to the school by directing artillery away from campus when the Confederate army shelled Carlisle.) In 1860, on the eve of war, Conrad left Dickinson with a master's degree and took a position as headmaster of a boys' school in Georgetown. It was reported that Conrad had his pupils passing messages out the school's windows and across the Potomac. He recruited his older students for service in the Confederate army. As for himself, he was already nosing about Washington, gathering intelligence.

Not that Headmaster Conrad was overly discreet about the political sympathies he shared with his institution. Commencement orations on graduation day, June 1861, were sufficiently replete with denunciations of Lincoln, Union, and the North to arouse the ire of Washington officials, but the line was irretrievably crossed when the band struck up "Dixie" at the conclusion of the ceremonies. Conrad was arrested that evening and committed to Old Capitol Prison. Colonel William E. Doster, William P. Wood's predecessor as prison commandant, informed Conrad that he had been charged with communicating with the enemy and sending the South recruits.

No question that Conrad was very guilty on both counts, yet, as was more often than not the custom in prosecuting and punishing those accused of treason during the early part of the war, Conrad was paroled after a few days. The only condition of his parole was that he report to authorities each week, and that left plenty time for spying.

But spying wasn't enough. Conrad put together a quixotic scheme with a number of other sympathizers to assassinate Old Fuss and Feathers himself, Winfield Scott, general in chief of the Union army. Conrad procured an ancient musket and was about to proceed when one of the conspirators suggested that so momentous an act should not be undertaken without the advice and consent of the Confederate government. Assassination did not sit well with the Southern sense of honor, and Conrad was ordered to abandon his scheme. Although he and his conspiratorial band disposed of the weapon down a well near the White House, Conrad was again arrested and imprisoned in Fortress Monroe. He was soon sent to Richmond in a prisoner exchange.

Though he had yet to be ordained, Conrad became a cavalry chaplain in July 1861 and was given the rank of captain. Of course, the greater part of Conrad's time was taken up with espionage, but he was, in fact, highly thought of as a chaplain, too, and in 1863 the colonel of the Third Virginia asked that he be made official chaplain to the regiment. Even when he donned the uniform of a *federal* army chaplain, touring the Union camps, inspecting fortifications, noting troop strength and disposition, he still did his best to be a good spiritual advisor, preaching on a wide variety of edifying topics.

At first, almost no one on either side ever suspected Conrad of being anything other than a faithful man of the cloth. General Stuart informed no one of the actual nature of Conrad's duties. For a long time not even the Reverend Major Dabney Ball, the chaplain of the Cavalry Corps who had originally recommended Conrad to Stuart. Instead, Stuart let it be known that Conrad had deserted. "Well, Major," he told Ball, "your man Conrad was a fine specimen. He has deserted and there is no telling what information he has carried to Washington." If J. E. B. Stuart had had his way, Conrad would have hidden behind his Methodist broadcloth for the duration, but, remarkably successful as the chaplain was in carrying out secret missions, he found it impossible not to crow over his accomplishments. Sometimes the regiment actually cheered when he returned from a mission.

Thanks to Abraham Lincoln's loose-tongued gardener, John Watt, readers of Northern newspapers—including members of the Confederate government and military command—knew the details of the capture of two Confederate commissioners, John Slidell and James M. Mason, as they were returning from England and France following secret meetings with potential allies of the Southern cause. As a result of their mission, France and England sent their own commissioners to Richmond to negotiate a three-million-dollar loan to the Confederacy. With the Union naval blockade of Southern ports gradually becoming more effective, it was foolhardy for the diplomats to attempt to sail directly into Richmond. Instead, they would land at Washington—a perfectly reasonable destination for foreign diplomats—and make their way, secretly, of course, to the Confederate capital. Conrad's reputation had reached the rebel capital, and Secretary of War Judah P. Benjamin sent for him. His mission, the secretary explained, was to meet the French and English ministers in Washington and bring them safely to Richmond.

Betraying his relish for the cloak and dagger, Conrad prepared for his mission by dictating his own Confederate War Department pass:

> War Department, Richmond, Va.
>
> The bearer, who may be known by a gash in his tongue and a scar upon the index finger of his left hand, has the confidence of this department.

Such a document was handy for getting one through one's own lines and would certainly identify Conrad to the foreign commissioners, but, like the contract William Alvin Lloyd faithfully carried with him, it was a sure means of incrimination if it fell into the wrong hands.

Conrad, however, did not intend to get caught. He recut his beard, he procured Northern-style shoes. (Pinkerton instructed his operatives always to examine a man's shoes. At this period, most urban Northerners wore so-called "crooked shoes," with a ready-made shoe for the left foot and a mate for the right, while Southerners still wore shoes made to fit either foot, the left and right shape actually molded by repeated wearing.) Also, Conrad was careful to chew short-cut tobacco rather than the Southerner's plug. He crossed the Potomac in a boat at a point maintained by Major Norris's Signal and Secret Service and resisted the temptation to call at his parents' Maryland house for fear that Northern agents were watching it. Stopping at Surratt's tavern, he got a horse, disguised himself as a Maryland farmer, and rode into Washington.

Apparently, and despite all of his preparation, Conrad had not been told where the diplomats were staying, but Washington was a very small city, and it was an easy enough matter to inspect the registers of all the prominent hotels. The negotiators had checked into the most elegant of them, Willard's Conrad called on them, showed them his pass, gash, and scar, and, on his instructions, they surrendered to him their shoes. These Conrad took, together with the diplomats' most sensitive papers, to a cobbler of known Confederate sympathies. He hollowed out the heels, secreted the papers therein, and nailed the heels back in place.

Conrad purchased a carriage and horses, bundled his charges into it, and drove off for Maryland, where a Poolesville farmer provided a safe house. The only real difficulty the group encountered was at a culvert crossing the C & O Canal. Conrad had taken pains to find a route that avoided all the obvious and frequently used bridges, but he had not thought to make sure that his carriage top would clear this lonely culvert. Undaunted, the spy searched out a Confederate sympathizer he knew of and borrowed a saw from him. After much travail, Conrad and his distinguished passengers removed the top of their vehicle and drove through. Later, it occurred to the secret agent that he could far more simply have taken the wheels off the carriage, dragged it through the culvert, and reattached them on the other side. In any case, Conrad did convey his charges safely to Richmond. Unfortunately, there is no record of the outcome of their negotiations.

His next assignment, which came in the spring of 1862, was to ascertain the strength of the army McClellan was fielding up the Virginia peninsula in his advance against Richmond. Calling upon his "assets" in the U.S. War Department, he was able to obtain the information quickly, and, within two days, the report was in Richmond. Despite the often very effective counterintelligence work of Pinkerton, McClellan's Peninsular campaign was plagued by similar security leaks. Doubtless many of them were the work of Thomas N. Conrad. The facts are these: McClellan had wildly inaccurate information on troop strength in and around Richmond. Generals Johnston and Lee, on the other hand, had precise information. In the battles of the Seven Days, the Confederates turned McClellan back as far as the James River. It must have been a particularly chilling moment for the Union commander when a certain "Colonel Washington" (apparently Lieutenant J. Barroll Washington, aide-de-camp to General Johnston) was captured. He carried with him precise order-of-battle reports for the federal forces on the peninsula and an accurate map of current Union positions. Early in the war, the depth of Confederate intelligence was truly profound.

Indeed, Conrad had established an intelligence headquarters in the very heart of Washington, in a house known as the Van Ness mansion, owned during the war by a Confederate sympathizer named Thomas Green. From here Conrad closely directed his agents inside the U.S. War Department, including, most astoundingly, what today would be called a "mole" in the organization charged specifically with chasing down the likes of Conrad. Lafayette C. Baker's band of thirty counterintelligence operatives—the group he would later grandiosely dub the National Detective Police—had been penetrated by a double agent, Edward Norton, who warned Conrad whenever Baker was on the verge of picking up his trail.

For a Confederate spy, Washington was an exciting place to be in the wake of the Union debacle at the second Battle of Bull Run on August 29–31, 1862. With the army of General John Pope taking a beating, McClellan rushed to reinforce him. The nation's capital was now exposed as it had not been since the first battle at Bull Run. And Captain Conrad was in a position to see it all. If he could only get the word to J. E. B. Stuart to press the attack—*now*—on Washington.

The problem was that, with so many Union troops on the move, all Conrad's usual routes of egress had either been rendered unsafe for travel or were literally jammed. He decided on a circuitous course through Fredericksburg and into the Blue Ridge mountains, where he hoped either to encounter Stuart or, at least, reach a friendly telegraph station. But the going was slow, and Conrad ran out of time. Using his Secret Line relays, he sent a report to Richmond in hopes that the Signal and Secret Service there would relay it to Stuart in the field. Conrad knew it was a long shot, and, indeed, it proved much too long. Washington, for the time being, was saved, and what might have been the greatest intelligence coup of the war, what might even have brought victory to the South in 1862, failed in the delivery. Nevertheless, Conrad and his agents supplied Confederate forces with a wealth of information prior to and during the Battle of Fredericksburg on December 13, 1863.

As if determined never again to endure delay in the transmission of hot intelligence, Conrad, two days after the Confederate victory at Fredericksburg, set about extending the already well-established Doctor's Line *directly* to Richmond from a post that Lieutenant Charles Cawood, of the Signal and Secret Service, had built on the lower Potomac. Conrad erected a shack—which he dubbed Eagle's Nest—on a high cliff near a place called Boyd's Hole on the south bank of the river, taking care to mine the adjacent creeks and coves against the encroachment of Yankee gunboats. Messages could now be transferred from Cawood's post to Eagle's Nest and thence on to Richmond, reaching the Confederate capital in less than twenty-four hours.

It was well past the war's midpoint before Lafayette C. Baker began to close in on Thomas Conrad. Norton, Conrad's mole in the Baker organization, reported that the heat was on, and Conrad promptly retired from Washington—though not before telling Norton to make, of all things, a *complete* report to Baker, revealing Thomas N. Conrad as indisputably a rebel spy. It was a bold stroke, but a perfectly good tactical maneuver. After all, with Baker closing in, Conrad's usefulness in Washington was at an end. This way, at least, Norton would emerge a hero, his loyalty to the Union confirmed, and he could still contact Conrad by pretending to spy on him.

North or South, Civil War espionage operated on a shoestring, and, at this particular juncture, Conrad had to borrow $150 from a local lady with Southern sympathies in order to book passage on a river schooner bound out of Washington. He had escaped the Van Ness mansion just in time. Baker's men raided the place within an hour after Conrad's departure. When a federal officer boarded the schooner at Alexandria, Conrad lucked out again by quickly disguising himself as the ship's cook. Later, he was arrested. Feigning smallpox symptoms, he was sent to a contagious hospital. The risk of infection was frighteningly real, not only to Conrad, but to his guards. He was easily able to make his escape.

It was not until June 1863 that Captain Conrad dared to enter Washington again. What he discovered was a flashback to the period of Fredericksburg. Once again, the capital lay exposed, its troops on the march toward Gettysburg. This time, Conrad was able to ride out of Washington himself, and he meant to intercept Stuart's cavalry. Missing them by a few hours, however, Conrad, for a second time, lost a chance to bring about the rebel invasion of Washington. He returned to the city early in the spring of 1864 and, in the uniform of a federal chaplain, was preaching to Burnside's troops shortly before the Battle of the Wilderness on May 5–6, 1864.

That fall, Conrad conceived what he hoped would be his boldest stroke: the kidnapping of Abraham Lincoln. The plan was to ambush the president enroute to the Soldiers' Home, spirit him to Maryland, and, finally, to John Singleton Mosby in Virginia. In one of his postwar memoirs, Conrad claimed that James A. Seddon— who had replaced Randolph as the Confederate secretary of war on November 15, 1862—approved of the plan and sent him a letter dated September 15, 1864, ordering Mosby to give Conrad complete cooperation. In another memoir, however, he denied that either Seddon or Jefferson Davis had any knowledge of the kidnap scheme. Whatever official authorization it may or may not have had, the scheme was abandoned when Conrad learned that a cavalry unit now escorted Lincoln on his regular trips to the Soldiers' Home.

Of course, John Wilkes Booth, John Surratt, and others had also planned to kidnap Lincoln. The abortive attempt came in mid-

March 1865, less than a month before the assassination, along the very same road near Campbell Hospital just two miles from the Soldiers' Home. The nearly identical abduction schemes may or may not have been coincidence. Surratt, after all, was an associate of both Conrad and Booth, and very likely discussed the Confederate agent's scheme with the actor.

Conrad and Booth had more in common than abortive attempts to kidnap the president. For when federal officials arrested Conrad for the third time in his career, it was April 16, 1865, and the charge was not espionage, but the murder of Abraham Lincoln. At last, the spy's talent for disguise had served him ill. His present haircut and mustache configuration were precisely those of John Wilkes Booth as he had appeared on the fatal night of April 14. Sailors from the USS *Jacob Bell*, which was plying the Potomac, encountered Conrad asleep in a farmhouse. The spy was taken to Old Capitol Prison, where the case of mistaken identity was discovered, and prison superintendent William P. Wood released him, though not before introducing him to his nemesis, Lafayette C. Baker, who not only greeted him as a worthy opponent, but gave him a pass to Virginia. There he was promptly arrested again, though the charge was a vague one. Apparently tired of the federal bureaucracy, Conrad availed himself of the expedient of escape. In custody, aboard a train headed back North, he pretended to fall asleep, waited for his guards to look away, sprung for the door, and jumped off the train. He hid for a time in Virginia's Luray Caverns until he judged it safe to emerge.

After the war, Conrad married a young lady named—remarkably enough—Minnie Ball (minié balls were the conical, hollow-based bullets invented by a Frenchman, Claude Etienne Minié, and widely used by the Union army), wrote two wartime memoirs, and served as president of two colleges.

CHAPTER SIX

A FAREWELL TO ROMANCE

Mark Twain observed in his *Life on the Mississippi* that the great curse of the South, the very thing that had propelled the region into civil war, was an addiction to the romantic novels of Sir Walter Scott. Whether or not nurtured by the likes of Scott, it is clear that a powerfully romantic self-image animated Rose Greenhow and Belle Boyd and that, for the most part, it was shared by their Confederate compatriots and worked potent magic on any number of Northern government officials and military officers who compromised their loyalties to the blandishments of Southern womanhood. The Union had its female spies as well, but the two best-known—and, at that, they are fairly obscure— approached espionage in anything but a romantic spirit.

S. Emma Edmonds immigrated to the United States from New Brunswick, Canada, in 1856. She lived for a time in the West, but when war was declared she traveled to Washington, D.C., and volunteered her services as a field nurse. She was present at the first Battle of Bull Run and accompanied McClellan's army during the ill-fated Peninsular campaign. Her dedication as a nurse was heroic, as she took upon herself the hazardous duty of foraging for the fresh food her patients needed. On one occasion, a Confederate woman—crazed with grief, having lost her husband, father, and two brothers in the fighting near Yorktown—shot at Edmonds, and narrowly missed.

Edmonds would soon know what such loss meant. She was returning from foraging when she was told that a young man she had known in New Brunswick, a man with whom she was in love, had just been killed by Confederate pickets. She came back into camp just as the burial party was returning from his grave. Then and there she decided to be more than a nurse. Emma Edmonds volunteered for duty as a spy.

Her chance came when a Confederate prisoner of war, captured by scouts of the Thirty-seventh New York Regiment, revealed that a federal spy had been taken in Richmond and was to be hanged. Through an army chaplain, Edmonds made known her willingness to "fill the vacancy." Her name was sent up to headquarters, and she was summoned for an interview. An officer closely questioned her as to her views on the rebellion and her reasons for volunteering for such perilous work. She was next quizzed on her knowledge of firearms. After two years' experience on the field, even as a nurse, she acquitted herself "in a manner worthy of a veteran."

Edmonds was given a mere three days to prepare herself, as she put it, "for my debut into rebeldom." In the Thirty-seventh New York at Fortress Monroe, on the tip of the peninsula formed by the York and James rivers, there was no equivalent of James Bond's "Q," who could supply whatever paraphernalia a spy needed. Edmonds herself had to create her disguise, and it most certainly would not be the neat riding habit of a Belle Boyd, cinched with a Confederate soldier's belt just snugly enough to show her fine figure to advantage. In fact, Edmonds would not spy as a woman at all. Her disguise meant changing sex. And race.

She bought a "suit of contraband [slave] clothing, real plantation style," then went to the barber, who sheared her hair close to the head. Next, she obtained a vial of silver nitrate solution, which she used to dye her skin "black as any African." The last item was more difficult to obtain: "a wig of real Negro wool." Of course, nothing like that was to be had at Fortress Monroe. She would have to send to Washington. The Washington-bound mailboat was about to shove off when Edmonds, shorn and dyed, climbed aboard. She saw a postmaster she knew—but, obviously, he did not recognize her. As Edmonds recounts in her bibliography.

"Well, Massa Cuff," he asked, "what will you have?"

Edmonds responded in character: "Massa send me to you wid dis yere money for you to fotch him a darkie wig from Washington."

"What the ____ does he want of a darkie wig?"

"No matter, dat's my orders; guess it's for some 'noiterin' business."

"Oh, for reconnoitering you mean; all right old fellow, I will bring it, tell him."

When the postmaster returned from the capital, wig in hand, Edmonds set off for Richmond, with nothing but a few hard crackers in her pocket and a loaded revolver. By 9:30 P.M., she was past the Union's outer pickets. By midnight, she was behind rebel lines, undetected by sentries. Once she judged herself a safe distance from the picket lines, she lay down to wait out the remainder of the cold, damp night.

In the morning, she encountered a party of slaves carrying hot coffee and provisions to the rebel pickets. They gave Edmonds some of the brew and a piece of corn bread, and when they returned from the picket line, she accompanied them to Yorktown.

The slaves reported to the overseer and set about working on the fortifications. It occurred to Edmonds that, having arrived in rebeldom, she didn't know quite what to do. It was then that an officer approached her:

"Who do you belong to, and why are you not at work?"

"I dusn't belong to nobody, Massa, I'se free and allers was; I'se gwyne to Richmond to work."

That hardly satisfied the officer. "Take that black rascal and set him to work," he shouted to a civilian who was apparently in charge of the "colored department," "and if he don't work well tie him up and give him twenty lashes, just to impress upon his mind that there's no free niggers here while there's a d____d Yankee left in Virginia."

Whereas Belle Boyd gallivanted on horseback and heroically disported herself—we must assume—in bed, all in the service of espionage, Emma Edmonds was set to work with a pickax, shovel, and a "monstrous wheelbarrow." She was helping to build a parapet, breaking up gravel, shoveling it into the wheelbarrow, then pushing it up a steep plank to the brow of an eight-foot-high wall.

Her fellow slaves saved her many times when, near collapse, she was about to tumble off the parapet.

At the end of the day, Edmonds partook of the slaves' rations, which, unlike the whites', included neither coffee nor meat, and took careful note of the fortifications. She drew a rough sketch of the outer works and inventoried the ordnance with the thoroughness of a veteran: fifteen three-inch rifled cannon, eighteen four-and-a-half-inch rifled cannon, twenty-nine thirty-two pounders, twenty-one forty-two pounders, twenty-three eight-inch Columbiads, eleven nine-inch Dahlgrens, thirteen ten-inch Columbiads, fourteen ten-inch mortars, and seven eight-inch siege howitzers. She hid the drawing and the inventory under the inner sole of her "contraband shoe," the footgear worn by slaves.

Her hands blistered from wrists to fingertips, Edmonds did not think she would be able to shovel the next morning. She found a slave whose job it was to carry water to the troops, and she traded chores with him. He told her that he could get somebody else to change jobs with her the following day as well. The grateful Edmonds offered him five dollars in federal greenbacks (even as early as 1862, few people placed much faith in Confederate notes), but the slave refused, declaring that he could not take so much money. Edmonds's second day in the Confederate service was much easier than the first. She had enough leisure time to listen to the soldiers' talk and to hear about the numbers of reinforcements expected. She even saw Robert E. Lee, who had come to inspect the Yankee position and who declared that the rebels could not hold Yorktown against McClellan's siege guns. When General J. E. Johnston arrived for a council of war, Edmonds heard reports that he advised evacuation.

Having gathered this earful, Edmonds decided to take a breather by visiting with her "sable friends," as she called the slaves. She brought them some water.

"Jim," one of the men remarked to another, "I'll be darned if that feller ain't turnin' white; if he ain't I'm no nigger."

Edmonds was seized by fear, but she managed to toss off carelessly, "Well, gem'in I'se allers 'spected to come white some time; my mudder's a white woman."

The others laughed at their new companion's simple mindedness.

But, as soon as she could, Edmonds examined her complexion in a small pocket mirror she carried for the purpose of just such a self-inspection. The slave had been right. She *was* turning white. "I was only a dark mulatto color now, whereas two days previous I was black as Cloe." Edmonds applied more silver nitrate, a vial of which she carried in anticipation of inevitable fading.

After her touch-up, Edmonds returned to her post with a fresh supply of water. A group of soldiers was gathered around a man who was "haranguing them in real Southern style." Quietly, Edmonds set her water cans down and began, with great deliberation, filling the soldiers' canteens. She thought the voice of the speaker sounded familiar, and at last she recognized the man as a peddler who went to the federal camp—especially headquarters—once each week purveying newspapers and stationery. He did precisely what Edmonds was doing: just hung around and listened. Like the peripatetic physicians, itinerant peddlers made very good spies.

Now the man narrated in detail a full description of McClellan's camp and army. He exhibited a map of the Young Napoleon's entire works. Then he went on to boast: "They lost a splendid officer through my means since I have been gone this time. It was a pity though to kill such a man if he was a d____d Yankee." He told of how, at Yankee headquarters, he had heard a Lieutenant V. say that he was going to visit the picket line at such and such a time. The peddler hurried off to tell the rebel sharpshooters that a headquarters officer would be near their position and that they might capture him and obtain valuable information. Instead, the sharpshooters did what they do best. They shot Lieutenant V. as soon as they saw him. As Edmonds later recounted:

> I thanked God for that information. I would willingly have wrought with those Negroes on that parapet for two months, and have worn the skin off my hands half a dozen times, to have gained that single item. He was a fated man from that moment; his life was not worth three cents in Confederate scrip. But fortunately he did not know the feelings that agitated the heart of that little black urchin who sat there so quietly filling those canteens, and it was well that he did not.

On the evening of Edmonds's third night in the Confederate camp, she was sent with other slaves to carry supper to the outer picket posts on the right wing. Some of the pickets were white, she observed, and some black. "I had a great partiality for those of my own color, so calling out several darkies I spread before them some corn cake, and gave them a little whiskey for desert." Yankee minie balls were whistling about their heads as they ate and drank; for the outer picket lines of rebel and Yankee were less than a half-mile from one another. The other members of the supply party called to Edmonds to return with them to camp, but she replied that she would stay a while.

By and by, an officer came riding along the lines and demanded to know what Edmonds was doing there. One of the black pickets replied that "he" had helped carry out supper and was now waiting for a break in the Yankee fire before returning to camp.

"You come along with me," the officer ordered.

Edmonds was taken a few rods down the line. The officer turned to a subordinate: "Put this fellow on the post where that man was shot until I return." Edmonds was given a rifle and told to shoot at anything or anybody that approached from the enemy. "Now," said the subordinate, "you black rascal, if you sleep on your post, I'll shoot you like a dog."

"Oh no, Massa, I'se too feerd to sleep."

It was a cloudy, moonless night. It began to rain, and the pickets on either side of her had taken shelter under trees. Noiselessly, grasping the Confederate rifle as a trophy, Edmonds walked through the woods toward the Union lines. She knew that the federal pickets would fire on anybody moving toward them, so she bedded down for the remainder of the night within hailing distance of the Union picket line. At dawn, she "hoisted the well-known signal"—presumably the Stars and Stripes—and was brought back into the Union camp.

Edmonds reported to the general who had been among the officers quizzing her prior to her mission. He did not recognize her, but ordered this "darkie" to tell Emma Edmonds to report to him in one hour. She returned to her tent, chalked her face, and dressed in her own clothes. She made a full report, accepted the general's congratulations, and had the rifle sent to Washington as a memento of the war.

Like the federals, the Confederates recruited their spies from every stratum of Southern society, and physicians or peddlers or loyal slaves all made excellent couriers. Yet it is the flamboyant and seductive women who are the best-remembered among the spies of the Confederacy. It is true that Old Capitol Prison held at least one woman, accused of spying for the South, who had disguised herself as a man. Mrs. L. A. McCarty, a resident of Philadelphia, was originally arrested under the name of John Barton. Washington, D.C., was no stranger to transvestites during the war. A "certain class of women" regularly disguised themselves as soldier boys and mingled with the troops until a provost guard or a policeman was made suspicious by a soft complexion, too-shapely figure, or a high voice. Those detected were issued skirts and routinely run out of town. But when authorities searched Mrs. McCarty's trunk, they found opium, morphine, and quinine—all medicinal commodities badly needed by the Confederacy and often smuggled from North to South—as well as a revolver, military spurs, a Confederate uniform, and a new-fangled kind of iron projectile, which Mrs. McCarty's husband had invented and which she intended to offer (or sell) to the Confederate army in Richmond. It is well to remember that Mrs. McCarty of Philadelphia, transvestite in the cause of espionage, was a Southern sympathizer (or war profiteer) but not a Southern-born lady. In any event, what she did fell far short of what Emma Edmonds had done, and it is absolutely unthinkable that a Southern woman, no matter how noble the cause and how effectively the disguise might serve it, would ever pass herself off as a black, of either sex.

African-Americans, occupying the lowest caste of Southern society, were nevertheless ubiquitous throughout Dixie and, for that very reason, virtually invisible. Many Southerners feared a slave rebellion, yet few had trepidation about individual blacks. They were, in effect, fixtures, appliances to be used, at most "faithful retainers" incapable of independent action and, therefore, of little concern. Improbable as it was, and potentially disastrous as it might have been, Emma Edmonds had chosen the perfect disguise for a Union spy in the South. Allan Pinkerton similarly exploited the blindness of nineteenth-century Southern prejudice by enlisting John Scobell into the ranks of his operatives. The detective regularly examined "contrabands," escaped slaves or even freed blacks, who sought asylum in the North. They were a fertile source of behind-the-lines intelligence. In the case of Scobell, Pinkerton found an intelligent, literate man, who had worked in Mississippi and Virginia. His master had freed him a few weeks earlier, and Scobell was now eager to serve on Pinkerton's force. Not the least of Scobell's assets, as the Scots-born detective saw it, was his repertoire of Scottish ballads, learned from his master and rendered in a perfect accent. Scobell, posing as a slave, worked undercover in Maryland and Virginia with Timothy Webster and Hattie Lawton, one of Pinkerton's female operatives.

If race could be an excellent cover for espionage against the South, so could a certain combination of age and eccentricity that Southerners had long been accustomed to dismiss as harmless, especially when manifested in that species of Dixie womanhood known as the spinster lady. Miss Elizabeth Van Lew was a diminutive, birdlike Richmond spinster who cut a figure so eccentric that her neighbors dubbed her Mad Lizzie or Crazy Bet. Colonel George H. Sharpe, appointed in 1863 by the Union army's Provost Marshal General Marsena R. Patrick to head the newly created Bureau of Military Information, declared after the war that, "for a long, long time [Van Lew] represented all that was left of the power of the United States government in Richmond." He attributed to her work the bulk of intelligence gathered during 1864–65.

Her family was prominent in Richmond, and she occupied a fine mansion across the street from the church in which Patrick Henry had delivered his "liberty or death" speech. Although her mother, Elizabeth Louise Baker, had come from Philadelphia (she was the daughter of the city's mayor) and her father, John Van Lew, from Jamaica, Long Island, Elizabeth, born in Richmond in 1818, thought proudly of herself as a Virginian. But she had been sent to her mother's hometown for her education and always drew a line between herself and her neighbors when it came to the question of owning slaves. "Slave power degrades labor," she wrote in her journal. "Slave power is arrogant, is jealous and intrusive, is cruel, is despotic, not only over the slave, but over the community, the state." When she was little more than a girl, her father died. Van Lew promptly freed the family's nine slaves. If she got word that the children or relatives of her family's former slaves were being sold, she purchased them and set them free. Perhaps it was such views that isolated Van Lew and—though she was said to have been pretty as a young woman, "a pleasing pale blond" with bright blue eyes—discouraged potential suitors. She lived with her mother in the mansion on Church Hill.

Despite their unpopular and provocative views, Richmond was content to ignore Van Lew and her mother until they began visiting the Yankee officer prisoners of war who jammed Richmond's notorious Libby Prison, supplying them with food, clothing, bedding, and medicine. A local newspaper decried "these two women . . . spending their opulent means in aiding and giving comfort to the miscreants who have invaded our sacred soil, bent on rapine and murder." After the war, numerous prisoners recalled the Van Lews with gratitude, some even crediting the women with having saved their lives.

In fact, the ladies were doing much more. Van Lew was at the center of what some scholars have dubbed the Richmond Ring, a modest but effective network of spies and saboteurs that included the superintendent of the vitally important Richmond, Fredericksburg & Potomac Railroad and Mary Elizabeth Bowser, a former slave, freed by Van Lew, who sent her North to be educated. At the outbreak of the war, Crazy Bet asked Bowser to return to Richmond and secured for her a position as servant to the Davis family in the Confederate White House. During her visits to Libby Prison, Van Lew and her mother received important military information from the prisoners to whom they ministered. Union agents gave Van Lew questions, which she smuggled into prison inside the food baskets she carried. She brought out the answers in the same way and even "debriefed" newly arrived prisoners in an effort to get fresh battle information and firsthand estimates of rebel strength.

At last, the Confederate jailers grew sufficiently suspicious of Van Lew that they forbade her to converse with the prisoners. Nothing daunted, she began supplying them with books that contained tiny pin pricks spelling out questions. Prisoners pricked out answers and returned the volumes to her on her next visit. Van Lew also smuggled messages in a double-bottomed dish designed to carry hot water. On one occasion, a guard demanded to inspect the vessel. Van Lew handed it over, the guard grabbed it, and screamed in pain. She had definitely filled the bottom part of the dish with scalding hot water.

The more difficult the authorities made it for her to conduct her business at Libby Prison, the more Van Lew played on her reputation as an eccentric. She let her hair go, so that it became unkempt and matted. She wore old, threadbare clothing. She made sure she was heard talking to herself. Nevertheless, authorities revoked her permit to visit military prisons. Fortunately, Richmond's provost marshal, General John H. Winder, was an old family friend. *He* did not see the harm in humoring a crazy old lady who liked to visit prisoners of war. Winder issued a new pass.

Not all of Van Lew's activities took place in Libby Prison. Her home was a safe house for federal couriers, whose papers were hidden in the hollow tops of andirons in Elizabeth's bedroom. Some townspeople believed that she actually hid escaped Union prisoners in her house. She also coordinated the underground operations of her brother, John Newton Van Lew; Mary Elizabeth Bowser, the African-American servant who worked in Jefferson Davis's house; Walter S. Rowley, a farmer whose place was used as a safe house; Frederick W. E. Lohmann, a restaurant owner and dealer on the black market; Charles Palmer, a merchant and spy; and Martin M. Lipscomb. Like Van Lew, Lipscomb was regarded by locals as an "eccentric"; he was a victualer to the Confederate army and had a government contract to collect and bury unclaimed Yankee battlefield casualties. He was also an unsuccessful candidate for mayor of Richmond, who conducted his campaign in 1864 while he was spying for the Union. Like her Confederate counterpart, Rose Greenhow, Elizabeth Van Lew could also claim informants in the departments of War and Navy—though, clearly, she must have found methods of persuasion substantially different from those employed by the Rebel Rose.

Rose O'Neal Greenhow had been struck, it seems, from the archetypal mold that produced the Old Testament's Delilah or, if one's sympathies lie with the South, Judith of the same book. Given her personality and the Southern susceptibility of the period to self-romance, the Wild Rose just *had* to be a spy. But Elizabeth Van Lew and her so-called Richmond Ring were people either too "eccentric" or too ordinary to be spies. And, for these very reasons, they were most effective at the job. Take Samuel Ruth, identified as one of Miss Van Lew's Ring. He was a perfectly ordinary man. Born in Pennsylvania, he moved to Richmond late in the 1830s, where he mastered the growing business of railroading. By 1853, he had worked his way up to the position of superintendent of transportation for the Richmond, Fredericksburg & Potomac Railroad. The Civil War amputated the Northern portion of his railroad, and he became, in effect, superintendent of the fifty-five miles of track between Richmond and Hamilton's Crossing. But he had another job during the war. Samuel Ruth was also a Union spy and, even more important, a railroad saboteur as subtle as he was effective.

The South in the Civil War is justly celebrated for its great guerrilla-style cavalry commanders, paramountly John Singleton Mosby and John Hunt Morgan. Equally well known, but more reviled than celebrated, are the western guerrilla raiders William Quantrill and "Bloody Bill" Anderson. In their way, they, too, were brilliant and daring, though their exploits smack more of terrorism and criminality than partisan activity intended to achieve genuine military objectives. It is no coincidence that the Missourians Frank James and Jim, Bob, John, and Cole Younger served with Quantrill, while Jesse James was an alumnus of Bloody Bill's command. Although Mosby, Morgan, Quantrill, and Anderson engaged in reconnaissance well behind enemy lines and often carried out sabotage, they usually did so in uniform, and their principal *modus operandi* was the lightning raid. They are properly classed as guerrillas rather than spies, except when John Hunt Morgan and one of his best officers, Thomas Henry Hines, attempted to collaborate with Northern Copperheads in genuine fifth-column work.

Reconnaissance, which is separated by a thin line from espionage, was traditionally a function of cavalry units, and the South exploited cavalry as well as its reconnaissance role more thoroughly and effectively than did the North. To be sure, the Union had some cavalry raiders who, like their Southern counterparts, worked behind enemy lines, such as Brigadier General Judson Kilpatrick and Colonel Ulric Dahlgren. But, as the North rarely fielded spies bred so obviously to the cloak and dagger, not to mention the bedroom, as Rose Greenhow, so its operations deep within enemy territory lacked the military dash of the cavalry raid or the air of grand conspiracy that marked the Confederacy's attempts to enlist into the cause a secret army of Northern Copperheads. No, men like Samuel Ruth worked much more quietly, much more ordinarily. In fact, had Samuel Ruth not petitioned the U.S. government after the war to be compensated for his services as an informer and saboteur, we would not know he had ever been a spy.

Following the Confederate victory at Fredericksburg, General Robert E. Lee anxiously watched for signs of a mounting counter-attack from Union commander Ambrose Burnside. With Virginia reduced to a quagmire by the ceaseless rains of late January 1863, roads were impassable, leaving as Lee's only avenue of supply and reinforcement the Richmond, Fredericksburg & Potomac Railroad. And that unavoidable fact, as he awaited Burnside's next move, did not make Lee happy.

Shortly before Fredericksburg, on December 8, 1862, Lee had written to Jefferson Davis: "unless the Richmond and Fredericksburg Railroad is more energetically operated, it will be impossible to supply this army with provisions." On January 23, 1863, Lee again wrote to Davis, underscoring his desperate need for supplies and pointing out that "Great delay in the running of freight trains has been reported to me, which could be avoided by zeal and energy on the part of the agents." The general continued by suggesting that Captain Thomas R. Sharp, a Confederate officer with extensive railroad experience, be allowed to replace the R.F.& P.'s civilian superintendent, Samuel Ruth. Unfortunately for Lee and his army, Davis took no steps to relieve Ruth.

The R.F.& P. was a crucial link in the supply chain along the Confederate coast, and although Lee first commented on its apparent inefficiency before and after Fredericksburg, the fact is that Superintendent Ruth had been contributing to its sluggish operation since 1862 and would continue to do so until the end of the war. In March 1862, for example, with Ambrose Burnside menacing the important railroad junction of Goldsboro, North Carolina, Jefferson Davis personally ordered the emergency transportation of two brigades and two artillery companies to reinforce the town. A portion of the troops had to use the R.F.& P. for part of the journey. By studying regular R.F.& P. schedules between Richmond and Fredericksburg, Meriwether Stuart, writing in 1964 for *The Virginia Magazine of History and Biography*, was able to gauge the relative efficiency—or inefficiency—with which Ruth moved the troops. Mail trains customarily made the sixty-mile run in three hours, while the slower "accommodation train" took three hours, forty-eight minutes. Carrying urgently needed troops, Ruth managed to stretch this run to approximately seven hours!

Not only did he see to it that trains moved as slowly as possible, he also insured that battle damage done to the railroad's right-of-way, especially its bridges, took as long as possible to repair. A case in point is a bridge over the South Anna River, which troops under George B. McClellan put to the torch on May 29, 1862. The bridge was of strategic importance, because it linked Richmond to the Shenandoah Valley and, therefore, linked the Confederate capital to the forces of Stonewall Jackson. The R.F.& P's bridge was beyond repair, but, early in June, Henry D. Whitcomb, superintendent of the Virginia Central Railroad, whose own bridge across the South Anna had also been destroyed, proposed a quick expedient for spanning the river. He suggested that the two railroads cooperate in constructing a footbridge, which would serve two purposes: it would allow passengers to disembark on one side of the river, walk across, and continue their journey on another train; and it would allow for the passage, to and fro, of a Confederate guard sufficient to protect construction crews as they worked on rebuilding the principal bridge. Superintendent Ruth enthusiastically endorsed what seemed on the face of it, a sound plan.

But Robert E. Lee, having been trained as an engineer himself, vetoed the scheme. "I think it better," he wrote to Secretary of War Seddon, "that the R R bridge be rebuilt if practicable & at small expense." Putting up a footbridge would take time better spent working directly on the railroad bridge. No one, including Lee, suggested that the proposal was a deliberate attempt at creating delay, and, of course, the idea had not originated with Samuel Ruth. But the R.F.& P. superintendent did have a genius for capitalizing on each opportunity for delay offered him, and it is a tantalizing fact that Whitcomb, who had proposed the plan, was, like Ruth, a Northerner by birth.

That the footbridge plan had been turned down did not compel Ruth to start work on the South Anna railroad bridge. He saw to it that, for the time being, neither a footbridge nor a railroad bridge was built. By July 18, the Virginia Central had rebuilt its railroad bridge—construction had taken a mere three weeks—but the R.F.& P. would continue without any bridge at all until October, when a *footbridge* was completed. Its effect on the reconstruction of the railroad bridge, which had just gotten under way, was probably worse than anything even Lee had feared. The constant pedestrian traffic of passengers, lugging their hand baggage from one train to the other, actually hindered construction work.

Ruth's success in delaying the reconstruction of the South Anna railroad bridge seems a small enough triumph—a victory not of positive action, but of mere inaction. Yet of such "inaction" are success and failure made. The absence of the R.F.& P.'s bridge not only crippled that railroad, it overburdened and thereby impeded operations on the Virginia Central as well. It also created the conditions that could turn a single, otherwise minor railway accident into a major delay. For example, on November 18, 1862, the Richmond *Enquirer* reported:

> On yesterday morning, the upward freight train on the Virginia Central railroad becoming short of water at Sutton's, fifteen miles above Richmond, stopped for supply, and the mail train coming up a short time afterwards, was compelled to stop. Soon after this the material train, which had followed the mail from Richmond, came along, and before the engineer was aware of the danger, he was unable to prevent his train from running into the rear of the other. Three of the passenger coaches were considerably smashed by the accident, and thrown from the track. Only one person was injured—a soldier, one of whose hands was severely crushed.
>
> The down mail on the Central, was detained last evening by an accident to the freight train from Fredericksburg, about fifteen miles from Richmond.

A few days after this accident, on November 24, the South Anna bridge was at last completed. The very next day, Ruth published an advertisement in the Richmond *Enquirer:*

IMPORTANT RAILWAY NOTICE

The Bridge over Sou[t]h Anna River having been completed the trains over th[i]s Road will be run as follows:

The mail train will leave Richmond daily, at 6 o'clock a.m., and arrive at Fredericksburg at 10 a.m. Returning will leave Fredericksburg at 1 p.m., and arrive at Richmond at 5 p.m.

The accommodation train for Ashland will leave Richmond daily, [(]Sundays excepted) at 3:15 p.m. Returning will ar[r]ive at Richmond at 9 a.m.

The Freight train will leave Richmond daily, (Sundays excepted) at 7 a.m. Returning will arrive at Richmond at 1 p.m.

Freight for this road will be received and delivered at the depot of this company, on and after this day.

S. Ruth, Supt.

After seemingly interminable delay, the South Anna bridge had been completed, so Superintendent Ruth published a perfectly routine advertisement. Nothing of the cloak and dagger here; just a railroad man doing his job.

In fact, the advertisement was not *quite* routine. Ordinarily, a simple announcement would have been made, and passengers would have been advised to call at the RF& P offices for a timetable. Instead, Ruth published a detailed schedule of operations over a critical—and vulnerable—section of railroad. The advertisement would have been as informative to the Union army as it was to the Southern patrons of Samuel Ruth's railroad. Yet, on the basis of this advertisement, no one could actually accuse Ruth of aiding the enemy. Nor, on another occasion, could he have been charged with sabotage when he failed to ship out urgently needed provisions *in the absence of the required C.S.A. requisitions.* The secretary of war himself, James A. Seddon, wrote to Peter V. Daniel, president of the R.F. & P., on January 24, 1863: "You are fully aware of the importance of prompt and regular communication with the Army near Fredericksburg. . . ." Doubtless, President Daniel and his superintendent *were* aware, but, then again, Ruth was simply following correct railroad and military procedure when he held up the shipments. The proper forms, after all, had not been filed. War or no war, Ruth was being a good bureaucrat—never mind that a good *Confederate* would have shipped the provisions with or without the requisitions or, at least, would have made a positive effort to obtain the requisitions.

For three years, then, Samuel Ruth conducted his railroad in like manner. He may or may not have had a hand in various wrecks that occurred during his tenure. That is impossible to determine. But it is a fact that he took advantage of whatever circumstances presented themselves in order to create delay and inefficiency and to communicate to the enemy information relevant to available transport. Nothing dashing or daring here, but effective nonetheless.

Just because Ruth's methods avoided the usual trappings of espionage did not mean that his work was without danger. At 4:00 P.M. on Monday, January 23, 1865, Samuel Ruth was arrested in his office at Eighth and Broad streets, Richmond. The charge was treason.

In addition to supplying federal commanders with information and subtly sabotaging railroad operations, Ruth helped convey across Union lines various individuals who wanted to abandon the Confederacy. One or more of these persons, once they were safe in the North, must have freely discussed the role Ruth and others, including a J. H. Timberlake and one Isaac Silver, had played in their escapes. Some of this loose talk drifted back to Richmond, and Ruth was confined to the military prison known as Castle Thunder. The Richmond *Whig* and the *Sentinel* published accounts of the arrest, the *Sentinel* observing that "Mr. Ruth has been long and favorably known in this city as a most efficient [!] railroad officer, and a respectable, prudent and cautious man. His friends are slow to believe him guilty."

And so was the Court. On February 2, 1865, the *Sentinel* and *Whig* both reported that Samuel Ruth had been "honorably discharged, there not appearing against him the first particle of evidence." That's how good a spy Ruth was.

By the last year of the war, Elizabeth Van Lew and the Bureau of Military Information had established a courier and safe house system that was at least as elaborate as the Doctors' Line and Secret Line of the Confederacy. Five safe houses or relay points were established between Richmond and Union army headquarters. Van Lew or a black servant would carry a dispatch to a family-owned farm house south of the Confederate capital. Another courier would transport it to the next safe house—perhaps in a hollow egg or stitched into clothing—and so on up the line to General Grant's camp. Some messages were ciphered. Others were written in invisible ink between the mundane lines of family letters. By the time Grant was closing in on Richmond, Miss Van Lew was sending to him, by her couriers—and in time for the general's breakfast— fresh flowers from her garden together with intelligence concerning the movements and strength of rebel forces in and about Richmond.

The flowers were a nice touch. Even nicer was Van Lew's offer to a certain Captain Gibbs, the new commandant of Libby Prison. With housing in short supply in Richmond, Van Lew graciously offered room in her spacious home to Gibbs and his wife. Not only did this serve to remove suspicion from her, but it also brought to an end impromptu searches by rebel agents, who kept the Van Lew house under continual surveillance.

The only real, physical threat to Van Lew's safety came on April 2, 1865, when, in the face of Grant's approach, the Confederate government evacuated Richmond. Following that event, Crazy Bet unfurled a huge American flag and flew it from atop her roof. It was the first Stars and Stripes raised in Richmond for four years. A mob gathered, threatening not only to pull down the banner, but to burn down the house as well. Now Van Lew gave her neighbors a chance to test just how "crazy" she was. She pointed to the faces in the crowd that she knew, and she declared that, if anything happened to her, the Union army would avenge her. The threat was enough to disperse the crowd. Indeed, General Grant ordered an advance guard into Richmond especially to protect Elizabeth Van Lew.

It was apparently an easier matter for Samuel Ruth to gain acquittal from a Richmond court on charges of treason than it was, after the war, for him and Elizabeth Van Lew to make good their claims to compensation for services rendered the United States government. Like William Alvin Lloyd, Ruth, Van Lew, and others of the Richmond Ring endured lengthy and frustrating battles of petitions and rejections. Unlike Lloyd, who had only a martyred president as mute testament to his services, Ruth was able to obtain endorsements from George H. Sharpe, head of the Bureau of Military Information, and Ulysses S. Grant, among others. Although Secretary of War Stanton rejected Ruth's petition—together with those of F. W. E. Lohmann and Charles M. Carter (a Richmond Ring courier)—Ruth persisted and, ultimately, received a cash reward as well as an appointment from President Ulyses Simpson Grant to a post in the Internal Revenue Service.

Soon after his arrival in Richmond, General Grant called on Miss Van Lew and took tea with her on her veranda. After his election to the presidency, he rewarded Van Lew with the office of postmistress of Richmond, and he asked Congress to appropriate for her the lordly sum of fifteen thousand dollars. Parsimonious to a fault after a long and expensive war, Congress declined to vote the funds. More the pity for Elizabeth Van Lew, who had spent much of her wealth caring for prisoners and maintaining her network of spies. Nevertheless, she was hardly destitute when she died in 1900. Friends and families of the prisoners she had fed, comforted, and doctored raised funds sufficient to supply her with a steady income for the balance of the nineteenth century.

CHAPTER SEVEN

LICENSE TO DIE

South and North, there were plenty of men and women who persisted in taking a romantic view of espionage, and for such individuals, the most romantic thing a spy could do is die. For the first two years of the war, it was easy enough to entertain such heroical-tragical fantasies, since neither side made it a regular practice to execute spies. This was especially true in the case of women, whose actions military officials were loath to take seriously and upon whom levying a harsh sentence was almost unthinkable. So flagrant and arrogant a spy as Rose Greenhow suffered, like most others, nothing more than arrest, confinement, and eventual "parole" to the South. Historian John Bakeless quotes a comment in one Confederate regimental history, that the ladies of Winchester, Virginia, "did a little spying in which they were almost always perfectly safe."

As the war ground on, individual lives became cheaper and romantic sentiment cheaper still. Federal officers sentenced to death Jane Ferguson, a young Tennessee woman who disguised herself as a Union soldier and infiltrated Union lines. The sentence, however, was reversed. Pauline Cushman, a beautiful actress, was expelled by federal officials from Nashville as a dangerous secessionist, whereupon she was eagerly embraced by Confederates totally unaware that she was actually a double agent whose expulsion was meant to ingratiate her with the rebels. For the

Union, she procured important military maps and drawings of fortifications until, in the last year of the war, soldiers of Braxton Bragg's command found her out and arrested her. She was sentenced to be hanged—and was saved from that misfortune only by the timely arrival of federal troops.

It was far easier for military authorities to pass the sentence of death upon men. Even a hardened realist could not deny the heroism evident in the death of Confederate courier Private Sam Davis. At the time of his execution in 1863, he was lauded in the Confederate press as a latter-day Nathan Hale. Charged with spying in the vicinity of Pulaski, Tennessee, Davis was offered his life in exchange for revealing his sources.

He refused. He was hanged.

Nor did military authorities suffer qualms over the execution of boys. David O. Dodd, a seventeen-year-old Arkansas lad, was apprehended with coded documents and maps of federal fortifications. He was offered his life if he would reveal his sources. Like Sam Davis, he refused. It was a heroic act, yet the closer we look at a boy under sentence of death, the harder it is to see any romance or glory in this often inevitable consummation of the spy's vocation. Dodd was arrested on Christmas Eve, 1863, by federal troops occupying Little Rock. The night before, he had taken Mary Swindle Brantly to a dance. Little more than two weeks later, on January 8, 1864, she watched him hang.

Mary Brantly described Dodd as "rather small for his age," an "extremely modest, little fellow," but "unusually handsome and manly." The townspeople of Little Rock petitioned the occupying forces to spare their David. As for the courier himself, his only request was that he be shot rather than hanged. Both the petition and the request were denied. The boy wrote a letter:

> Military Prison, Little Rock
> January 8, 10 o'clock A.M., 1864

My Dear Parents and Sisters:

   I was arrested as a spy and tried and was sentenced to be hung today at 3 o'clock. The time is fast approaching, but, thank God! I am prepared to die. I expect to meet you all in Heaven. I will soon be out of this world of sorrow and trouble. I would like to see you all before

I die, but let God's will be done, not ours. I pray to God to give you strength to bear your troubles while in this world. I hope God will receive you in Heaven; there I will meet you.

Mother, I know it will be hard for you to give up your only son, but you must remember it is God's will. Goodbye! God will give you strength to bear your troubles. I pray that we may meet in Heaven. Goodbye! God will bless you all.

> Your son and brother,
> David O. Dodd

He was hanged from a tree on the campus of St. John's College, his alma mater. A regiment of federal troops bore witness to the execution. One soldier fainted in the ranks. Another afterward tearfully confided to Mary Brantly's father that "he would have refused to be present had he known that a mere boy and not a man was to be hanged."

The boy was buried in the presence of his family and a Methodist minister. "No prayers or funeral services of any kind were permitted," Mary Brantly noted.

The Union also had its martyred spies. Spencer Kellogg Brown entertained no romantic notions about espionage. For him, it was hard work, quite literally: menial and back breaking.

Brown had been raised in Kansas Territory, battleground for proslavery and antislavery, or "free state," factions, which fought so brutally in the years preceding as well as during the Civil War that the rest of the nation dubbed the territory "Bleeding Kansas." At age fourteen, Brown, an abolitionist, was already fighting. A force of three hundred proslavery men attacked and overran his hometown, Osawatomie, burning his family's house and taking him prisoner. (The fanatical abolitionist leader John Brown subsequently defeated the proslavery attackers with only forty men.) Spencer Brown was put in the home of a proslavery physician, who announced his intention to convert the boy to his views. Brown ran away and went to live in upstate New York with relatives.

He did not return to Kansas until 1860, and when he did return, he was hardly made to feel welcome. With the election of Abraham Lincoln, he was warned to quit the territory, especially on account of his name, notwithstanding the fact that he was no kin to John

Brown. Spencer Brown went to St. Louis, enlisted in the U.S. Army, and fought in Missouri. He left the army when his term of enlistment expired and, in 1861, joined the navy, which assigned him to the *Essex,* a Mississippi River snag boat that had been crudely converted into an ironclad. It was part of a small fleet of similarly modified or hastily constructed vessels deployed on missions to support ground troops in western Kentucky by helping to reduce Fort Henry on the Tennessee River and Fort Donelson on the Cumberland. It was vital to the operation to gather information on the strength and disposition of Confederate river batteries in the vicinity of Rebel-held Columbus, Kentucky. Twenty-year-old Brown volunteered for the hazardous mission.

On the afternoon of January 30, 1862, Brown and a comrade named Trussel had a dinner of fried oysters and passed the afternoon ashore playing billiards. They returned to the *Essex* at nightfall and left word that they were to be awakened at 2:30 in the morning. It was a terribly cold 3:00 A.M. when the two men rowed away from the ironclad in a skiff. Brown and Trussel planned to pass themselves off as deserters from the Union army, and to this end Brown allowed himself to be handcuffed. The cold was so intense, however, that he removed the iron cuffs until they had rowed within sight of Columbus. They had also brought with them two fine saws and files. But, deciding that these objects would be incriminating if they were discovered during a search, they threw them overboard.

The pair suffered in the cold until dawn, when they were taken on board the steamer *Charm,* or, rather, "effected a landing" on the vessel. Their repeated attempts at hailing anyone on the steamer had been unsuccessful, and they were actually on deck before anyone noticed them. Explaining that they were deserters from the North, they were taken to a "floating battery" commanded by a Captain Guthrie. The captain removed Brown's irons, but remained suspicious enough to pay a call on Major General Polk in his headquarters at Columbus. After he returned from this consultation, Guthrie interrogated the pair, who said that they wished to join the Confederate army, and lodged them aboard the floating battery for three days. Finally, on February 4, they were transferred to a gunboat, named *General Polk* after the area commander, and placed under guard. They were, however, treated more like guests than men being held under suspicion. Their guards shared grog with them, gave them a fine dinner, and allowed them a tour of the gunboat that included a close examination of her four rifled Parrott guns, which were mounted on a carriage and slide peculiar to the Confederate navy and superior to anything in the North.

At this point, it finally occurred to the Confederate commanders that they had better examine the men separately. During their initial interrogation, when they had both been present, they answered Guthrie's questions, Brown later recalled, "in a way that seemed remarkably like prevarication to each other." This experience prompted them to settle on a common cover story, so that, by the time they were individually questioned, they did not fatally contradict one another.

They continued aboard the gunboat, taking careful note of batteries and fortifications along the river. The plan was to be put ashore, ostensibly to enlist in the army, but the officers and crew of the *General Polk* wanted them to sign aboard their vessel. Unless they could get ashore, Brown and his comrade would have no way of returning to their own lines. At last, Brown succeeded in convincing the men of the *General Polk* that, eager as they were to serve, to remain aboard the gunboat was to risk hanging if they were captured by federal forces. Their only chance was on land, in the army. On February 6, then, they were deposited at Island Ten and enlisted into the company of Captain Gray, an engineer.

Their first assignment was hard labor, building a house. Next, they were given the opportunity of cleaning a sixty-eight-pounder cannon, and afterward put to "all sorts of job-work." At last, Brown had had enough and tried to convince Trussel to make a break for the Union lines. But, no, Trussel wanted to gather more information concerning fortifications, guns, and torpedoes—and, finally, to confirm a rumor that the rebels were about to evacuate Columbus. They were assigned to an engineer named Pattison, who put them to work as surveyors, an ideal situation for spies. It even occurred to Brown to sabotage the survey by reporting false distances, but, fearing discovery, he reconsidered. It was a good thing. All the land that he and two black assistants "chained,"—i.e., measured with surveyor's chains—was rechained as a check on what Brown had done.

Brown and Trussel decided that, once Union forces took Madrid, the spies would make their break. Their plan was delayed, however, when Trussel contracted dysentery. Trussel begged Brown to leave without him, but the faithful spy would not. On a Monday morning, as Brown was about to prepare some tea for Trussel, he was arrested by an Irish lieutenant of sappers, who took him to the commanding general.

"This young man, General, was standing on the bank yesterday all day long, and we suspect him of being a spy, and about to give information to the enemy."

Spencer Brown was remanded to the custody of a Colonel Scott, Twelfth Louisiana Volunteers, who soon marched off with him to Tiptonville. Brown relieved one of the soldiers of part of his load during the long march and was thereby able to get the loan of a pair of blankets, which were his only comfort during the cold, muddy nights. Nor was Brown fed—and *that* he refused to take like a good, obedient prisoner. He haled an officer and "gave him a good blowing up." The officer sent the colonel to him. "I asked him if he had orders to starve me, and he, repenting, took me upstairs and gave me a good breakfast," which bucked up Brown sufficiently to start him spying again, "taking a good and comprehensive view of the fort [Fort Pillow, midway between Cairo and Memphis on the Mississippi River], breastworks, caliber of the guns, etc."

During his two-week "imprisonment" at Fort Pillow at the end of March and beginning of April, Brown played whist and ball with his guards and, more remarkably, taught "the officers sword practice and the men bayonet exercise. . . . The weather was fine, and I enjoyed myself famously, without any apprehensions for the future." At length, Brown persuaded an officer—by promising that he would join his company—to speak to General Villipique to gain his release. The general briefly interrogated Brown, who pledged to go to Corinth and enlist. On his word alone, Brown was given a pass, transportation, and five days' provisions. He lingered three days, however, to take in the rest of Fort Pillow.

Brown started off for Corinth, Mississippi, through Memphis, where he tarried a few hours, studying its defenses. He was seated beside General Trudeau and his aide on the train to Corinth and "obtained much valuable information" in the course of the ride. Brown spent the night at Grand Junction, where he allowed himself to be recruited by a "man belonging to the First Louisiana Cavalry Volunteers." They reached Corinth together, then journeyed on to Iuka, where the man's regiment was headquartered. Brown declined to be sworn in until he received the bounty money payable to all volunteers.

It was the morning of April 6, 1862, and Brown began to hear the sounds of the fight at place called Pittsburgh Landing, just across the Tennessee line from Corinth. The North named the action after a nearby church, Shiloh Chapel, and it would prove to be one of the bloodiest, most chaotic battles in a war that was already a mounting litany of chaotic, bloody battles. Brown saw his chance to return to his lines. At eleven in the morning, his company was ordered to fall in. Brown, never officially sworn in, managed to get his name on the muster roll, secured a superannuated double-barrel shotgun, ten rounds of ammo, and "an ambitious but extremely emaciated horse." Iuka was eight very rugged miles from Shiloh Chapel, and as with every step the noise of battle increased in volume, Brown's mind raced with the thought that he might be "brought into a fight against my friends."

Progress was painfully slow, due to the rugged terrain. After a brief retreat, the march was continued all day and night: "I, whose every nerve seemed pounded to a jelly, and whose eyelids seemed glued fast, was only kept awake by the hope of escape." At last, after midnight, they made camp. In the morning, Brown talked to some farm boys and learned that the Tennessee River was only a mile and a half away. It was now that Brown, mounting his thin old horse, made his break. He reached the river, at the best gallop his mount could manage, in a quarter of an hour. Exhausted, Brown nonetheless cast off his shoes, trousers, and overshirt, and plunged into the Tennessee. The cold was so intense that he had to turn back. He stripped completely naked now save for the rebel cap he had acquired at Fort Pillow, and he steeled himself for another try. This time he made it to an island in the middle of the river, where, after a long search, he found an old, split dugout. It carried him, hip-deep in water, to the opposite shore about a mile downstream from the island.

Spencer Brown ran for two miles until he saw a plowman. The farmer, terrified by the naked apparition before him—a wild man torn and bleeding from brambles and the flinty terrain—misdirected Brown. After another five miles, however, Brown managed to find a man who was willing to part with "some wretched clothes and a piece of bread and bacon." His feet still bare, Brown walked another three miles until he found a "Union man," who put him on the back of a mule and took him another thirteen miles to the Union camp at Savannah, Tennessee. The federals were as suspicious of Brown as the Confederates had been and placed him under guard until, at length and after a two-hour wait in the rain, he was taken before General Grant, to whom he made his report.

Astoundingly, all we know of this mission comes from a letter Brown wrote to his grandfather in Utica, New York. He was lucky that his letter, detailing acts of espionage, never fell into the wrong hands. But Spencer Kellogg Brown's luck ran out early in August 1862, when he volunteered to destroy a ferryboat the Confederates used to bring supplies across the Mississippi to Port Hudson. The young man carried out his mission successfully. He was near a Union vessel carrying forty men, so he must have felt safe enough to row ashore in a small boat with four other soldiers. Two civilians, claiming to be Union men, drew Brown away from the others and started a conversation. Perhaps the young man proved as loquacious with them as he had in his letter to his grandfather. In any case, as they talked, a group of Confederate guerrillas leaped out of their hiding place and captured Brown and his four companions.

The spy was sent to Richmond, where he was tried for the crime of espionage. He was sentenced to be hanged on September 25, 1863. On that day, at eleven in the morning, he was taken from his cell in Castle Thunder and brought to the gallows. The *Richmond Whig* reported the execution:

> A short but impressive prayer was offered; at the conclusion of which the condemned man, unaccompanied, mounted the scaffold. In a few moments Detective Capehart followed and commenced to adjust the

rope over the neck, . . . in which [Brown] assisted, all the while talking with the officer. Taking off his hat, to admit the noose over his head, he threw it to one side, and, falling off the scaffold, it struck a gentleman beneath, when the prisoner turned quickly, and, bowing, said, "Excuse me, sir." After getting the rope on his neck arranged . . . Detective Capehart commenced to pinion the arms of the condemned, to which he submitted composedly, simply remarking, "Isn't this hard, captain?" His ankles were then tied together and his hat given to him. Capehart then shook hands and left him. A Negro came on the scaffold with a ladder and proceeded to fasten the rope to the upper beam, the prisoner meanwhile regarding him with the greatest composure. The rope being fastened, the Negro was in the act of coming down, when the prisoner looked up at the rope and remarked, "This won't break my neck. 'Tisn't more than a foot fall. Doctor, I wish you would come up and arrange this thing. I don't want to have a botched job of it." The rope was then re-arranged to his satisfaction, and the cap [hood] placed over his head. The condemned man then bowed his head and engaged a few seconds in prayer, at the conclusion of which he raised himself, and, standing perfectly erect, pronounced in clear voice, "All ready!"

Elizabeth Van Lew, who was among the citizens of Richmond witnessing the execution, recorded another of Brown's remarks. As he was marched to the scaffold, he turned to the crowd and asked, "Did you ever pass through a tunnel under a mountain? My passage, my death is dark, but beyond all is light and bright."

Of all Civil War spies, the most professional and least encumbered by fantasies of romantic adventure was Timothy Webster. We first encountered this most trusted of Allan J. Pinkerton's operatives as a "mole" burrowing into the Maryland conspiracies against the life of President-elect Abraham Lincoln. Pinkerton hired Webster away from the New York City Police Department in 1853 and quickly discovered that the man was fearless. "No danger was too great for him," observed his employer, "no trust too responsible." Furthermore, Webster combined great physical prowess with a chameleonlike ability to adapt to whatever circumstances and company in which he found himself. This talent might have gotten him into trouble on at least one occasion. After completing his infiltration of the Maryland conspiracy, in which he was fully accepted as a radical secessionist and potential assassin, Webster traveled to Cincinnati by way of Pittsburgh to meet with Pinkerton and their new client, Major General George McClellan. Perhaps a conspiratorial air, so painstakingly feigned in Maryland, clung to Webster yet as he walked into the barroom of his Pittsburgh hotel.

Two men were discussing what action the federal government should take in response to the riotous reception Baltimore had given the Sixth Massachusetts Regiment as it marched to the relief of Washington on April 19, 1861. One of the individuals cursed the president and General Winfield Scott for having failed to burn Baltimore and teach the rebels a good lesson. Webster, in an effort to avert all possibility of confrontation, started to leave the saloon, when the loudmouthed man challenged him, demanding to hear his opinion on the matter.

"I think," said Webster, "that the President and General Scott understand their duties much better than I can inform them, and I suppose they do not wish to destroy the property of many who are true to the government."

"This is all nonsense. There is not a single Union man in the whole city."

"I think you are mistaken," Webster replied with his customary coolness. "I am sure there are thousands of them there."

"Are you a Southern man?" the barroom dictator angrily asked.

"No, sir, I was born in New York."

"What is your name?"

"You will find my name upon the register of the hotel, if you desire it, and as I do not wish to have any further controversy with you, I bid you good morning."

A crowd had gathered around Webster and the other man. One of them now demanded to know the contents of a telegram Webster had just received. Another man piped in: "I believe he is a d____d spy; let us see what he has got!"

Webster broke free of those nearest him and backed to the door. In a calm but determined voice he declared: "Gentlemen, I am no spy, and if any of you attempt to trouble me further, some of you will assuredly get hurt!"

"Hang him! Hang the spy!" came the cry from the mob.

Webster at last drew his revolver.

"Gentlemen, we have had enough of this nonsense. You can talk about hanging me, and perhaps there are enough of you to do it, but, by God, the first one that attempts to put his hands upon me is a dead man!"

"Come on," said one of his assailants, "he is only one against twenty, and we will take him dead, or alive!"

It was at this moment that Allan Pinkerton arrived. Facing two revolvers, the mob backed down.

Pinkerton and Webster left Pittsburgh for Cincinnati and the headquarters of General McClellan. On May 13, 1861, scarcely six hours after the general's request for "observations made within rebel lines," Pinkerton sent Webster to Louisville and, through Bowling Green and Clarksville, to Memphis. "He made friends of all he met," Pinkerton observed, "and cleverly ingratiated himself into the good graces of those whom he believed might be of service to him."

He partook of soldiers' fare in the rebel camp, shook hands warmly with raw recruits, joked and laughed with petty officers, became familiar with colonels and captains, and talked profoundly with brigadier-generals. He was apparently an enthusiastic and determined rebel, and in a few cunningly-worded sentences he would rouse the stagnant blood of his hearers till it fairly boiled with virtuous indignation against Yankees in general, and "Abe Linkin" in particular.

Webster's talent in sustaining a *role* of this kind amounted to positive genius, and it was this that forced me to admire the man as sincerely as I prized his services. . . . he was naturally as inscrutable as the Sphinx. Many of his associates were of the opinion that he was cold and unfeeling, but *I* knew there could be no greater mistake than this; *I* knew that a manlier, nobler heart never existed than that which beat within the broad breast of Timothy Webster.

When necessary, the Sphinxlike operative could become the chatty, entertaining boon companion, the hero of the card-table, the storyteller of the bar-room, or the lion of the social gathering, as the exigencies of the case might require. He could go into a strange place and in one day surround himself with warm friends, who would end by telling him all he desired to know. In a life-time of varied detective experience, I have never met one who could more readily and agreeably adapt himself to circumstances.

During his Southern sojourn, Webster represented himself as a Baltimorean, and, indeed, he could give intimate, graphic accounts of the troubles there. He could give vent to his outrage over the oppression visited by Northern troops and "Lincoln hirelings" upon "friends of the cause."

In Memphis, Webster discovered that a "safety committee" was avidly tracking newcomers and arresting them on the slightest pretext. On the train, Webster had been watching a dark, "sharp-visaged, long-haired individual," who wore a broad-brimmed hat. As Webster was checking into his hotel, the dark stranger walked into the lobby, looked about, approached another man, took him by the arm, and escorted him out. Webster overheard "two citizens" remark:

"What does that mean?"

"It means that the stranger is under arrest."

"Under arrest? And who is the man who arrested him?"

"Oh, he is a member of the safety committee."

"But what crime has the stranger committed, that he should thus be taken into custody?"

"Nothing, perhaps; but the fact that he is a stranger from the North is sufficient to mark him as an object of suspicion."

"Isn't that a little severe?"

"Severe? It's a necessity in these times. For my part, I am in for hanging every Northern man who comes here, unless he can give the most satisfactory proof that he is not a spy."

Now Webster took note of men shadowing *him*. Accordingly, the agent adopted an air of conspicuous leisure, lounging in the barroom of the Worsham Hotel, reading and smoking. He saw three Confederate officers conversing at the bar.

"Yes, gentlemen, that is a true principle," remarked the one the others called Doctor, a flabby-faced, bulbous-eyed man wearing a uniform overladen with gold lace. "It will not do to let a man set foot on Kentucky soil until the Northern troops disregard the neutrality of that State."

"I beg pardon, sir," Webster put in. "Will you permit me to ask one question?"

The three officers turned to the stranger with some surprise.

"Certainly, sir; certainly," invited the doctor.

"Do you suppose that Kentucky will allow the Northern army to march through the State without showing fight?"

"Not by a jug-full. The moment the Northern army crosses the Ohio river, Kentucky will rise in arms and take sides with the South."

"If she doesn't," said Webster passionately, "she will prove herself unworthy of the respect of any true Southern men!"

That did it. The doctor's face shone, and he laid his hand on Webster's shoulder.

"May I ask where you are from?"

"I was born in Kentucky and reared in Maryland, and I am now direct from Baltimore."

"Baltimore!" cried all three men. A round of vigorous handshaking followed.

"Baltimore!" repeated the doctor, red-faced with excitement and the effort of so enthusiastically shaking Webster's hand. "My friend, we are always glad to meet a Baltimorean, for we know there is many a true man in that city who would help us if he could. May I ask your name, sir?"

"Webster—Timothy Webster."

"A devilish good name. Mine is Burton. My friends call me Doctor Burton. Allow me to introduce you to Colonel Dalgetty and to Captain [later Pinkerton says Lieutenant] Stanley of the Arkansas Rifles."

The four men drank a health to Kentucky and became instant friends, all eager to talk to Webster—who was no less eager to hear all they had to say.

"Webster, we've got to do some hard fighting in these parts, and that before we are many days older," said Doctor Burton.

"I think you are right," Webster replied. "We must fight it out. From what you have told me, however, I am sure the Lincoln troops will find you fully prepared to give them a warm reception here."

"That they will, sir; that they will! We have one full regiment and four or five companies besides, at Camp Rector, and General Pillow has thirty-seven hundred men at the camp in the rear of Fort Harris, which is a little above us on this side of the river. We expect to move with him, and if there is an attack made upon us every man in the town will instantly become a soldier."

127

"Have you arms enough for all of them?"

"Arms? Let the Yankees count on our not having arms, and they will meet with a surprise party. In two hours' notice we can have from eight to ten thousand men ready to march."

"No doubt of it, Doctor; but how do you expect to get two hours' notice?"

"Lord bless you, Webster, we have men watching the movements of the Yankees at Cairo, and the minute they make a move we are notified. Then our signal gun is fired, and every man is mustered."

After a few more drinks, one of the men, Lieutenant Stanley, removed his uniform hat and put it on Webster's head. "Excuse me, Mr. Webster, I merely wish to see how you look in one of our hats." He stepped back to admire. "By the gods, nothing could be more becoming! My dear fellow, you must have one by all means, if you stay among us." And the party proceeded to a hat shop, where Dr. Burton bespoke a "secession chapeau" for Webster.

"Now, my dear fellow," the doctor declared, "you can consider yourself at home!"

"Perfectly at home," said Colonel Dalgetty.

"Henceforward you are one of us," added the lieutenant.

Hat firmly planted on his head, Webster left the barroom with the others. There, watching him, was the dark stranger who had arrested the man in the hotel lobby. He was watching Webster now, but the detective pretended not to notice. His new friends harbored no suspicions, as they introduced him to a large number of soldiers and citizens.

Webster spent the balance of the evening inspecting the fortifications along the river. The next day, his friends invited him to visit Camp Rector, near Mound City, about eight miles from Memphis. After their tour of the encampment, the party retired to a Mound City hotel for drinks. There, in a doorway, was the dark stranger in the broad-brimmed hat.

"That fellow is one of the safety committee," said Dr. Burton as he filled his glass.

"He appears to be looking for some one," remarked Lieutenant Stanley.

"Reckon he is," put in the doctor. "He's always looking for some one. And, by-the-bye, those chaps are doing a heap of good for the cause just now. A Northern man stands no show for his life in these parts if the safety committee spots him. They hang 'em on suspicion."

"That's right," said Webster. "I believe in hanging every Northern man that comes prowling around. They don't deserve a trial, for they have no right here anyway."

Even as he said this, Webster thought of the man in the broad-brimmed hat. He reasoned that he had not yet been arrested because the safety committee was waiting to see if he would attempt to return North. There would be no way to escape with the information he had gathered so far unless he could give the broad-brimmed gentleman the slip. He returned to Memphis—though not before a Colonel Gaines, an artillery commander, took Webster by the hand. "Webster," he declared, "you'd make a good soldier. Hang me if I wouldn't like to have you on my force."

The next morning, the detective looked for the agent of the safety committee. Not finding him, he boarded a train for Chattanooga, always taking time for conversation with rebel officers, who were all too eager to share information. At Grand Junction, he changed to a northbound train and headed for Jackson, Mississippi. It was then that the man of the broad-brimmed hat reappeared, this time in company with another agent, "an ill-looking man of herculean proportions."

At Jackson, Webster stepped off the train and spoke to a conductor, making certain that his shadows would hear him.

"How soon will there be a train for Humboldt?"

"In twenty minutes."

"Do you know anything about the hotels there?" The conductor named a hotel, and Webster boarded a train for Humboldt. The two "safety" men took seats in the same car.

As the train rolled out, a woman approached Webster.

"Pardon me, sir; may I occupy a portion of this seat?"

"Certainly, madam, certainly."

She sat beside him and whispered: "You are going to Humboldt?"

"I am."

"You are a Northern man?"

"Madam!"

"Believe me, I am not an enemy. I have been sitting in the rear part of this car. I heard two men talking, and have reason to believe they were speaking about you. They said they would stop at the same hotel with you in Humboldt, and keep a close watch over you, and if you attempt to go northward they will arrest you, take you back to Memphis, and deal with you as they would with any Northern spy. I advise you to be very careful, sir, for your life depends upon it."

With that, the lady rose and left before Webster could so much as acknowledge the information or thank her.

At Humboldt, Webster managed to exit the car without being seen by his shadows. He hid behind a pile of baggage and watched them. They seemed unconcerned at having temporarily lost sight of their prey and walked toward a saloon. After all, they knew that they would see him at the hotel. Webster quickly boarded a northbound train headed for Louisville. Once across the Kentucky line, he removed his "secsesh" hat and put on the one he had worn from the North. Soon, Webster was in Cincinnati and had filed a complete report with Allan Pinkerton.

That hat would come in handy again. Under orders from McClellan, Pinkerton sent Webster and another operative, John Scully, to Baltimore, which, since the April 19 uprising against the Sixth Massachusetts Regiment, had been governed by a series of three military commanders but was still a hotbed of conspiracy. Webster was set up as a "gentleman of means and leisure" living at Miller's Hotel. He and Scully had their pictures taken at a local gallery, holding a large Confederate flag between them, Dr. Burton's gift hat perched securely on Webster's head.

Webster, as Pinkerton had observed, was a consummate actor, whose cover was accepted without question. But even an agent as talented as he was imperiled by the two great flaws in Pinkerton's operation. The Chicago detective made no attempt to separate espionage from counterespionage. Webster was overexposed. He worked as a spy in Tennessee, as a counterespionage agent in Washington, and, now, as a double agent in Baltimore, infiltrating rings of Confederate conspiracy while pretending to bring them intelligence from Washington. Secondly, Pinkerton never established lines of secure communication for his operatives. *They* gathered the intelligence, and then *they* had to figure out a way to bring the information back to Washington. Something was bound to go wrong.

Webster was holding court at a Baltimore saloon, a meeting place for Confederate sympathizers. Bill Zigler, known as a "ruffian and bully," one of the ringleaders of the mob that had attacked the First Massachusetts, walked into the saloon.

"Hello, Webster! You're *here,* are you? By G___d, I've been looking for you!"

"Did you speak to me, sir?" Webster asked in his customary measured tone.

"Yes, I spoke to you, sir!" Bill mimicked. "I say I've been lookin' for you, and when I've spoke my piece I reckon this town will be too hot to hold you many hours longer."

"I don't understand you."

Zigler laughed. "You've been playin' it fine on the boys here for the last three weeks, but d___n you, I'll spoil your little game!"

"What do you mean? You speak in riddles."

"I'll tell you what I mean! Gentlemen, that man is leagued with the Yankees, and comes among you as a spy."

Dead silence in the barroom. Then, from one of the men:

"Oh, nonsense, Zigler. You must be drunk to make such an assertion as that. There is not a better Southern man in Baltimore than Mr. Webster."

"I am as sober as the soberest man here, and I reckon I know what I am talking about. I saw that fellow in Washington yesterday."

"I can well believe that you saw me in Washington yesterday, for I certainly was there. I have been telling these gentlemen what I saw and heard while there."

"Maybe you have, but I'll bet ten dollars you didn't tell 'em that you had a conversation with the *chief of the detective force* while you were there!"

What was Webster to do? He displaced the panic he must have felt with feigned rage.

"You are a liar and a scoundrel!" he cried—or, at least, those are the words Pinkerton attributes to him.

"I am, eh?" Zigler hissed between clenched teeth as he lunged toward Webster.

The ex-New York cop let fly a right to Zigler's head. The man fell between two tables, shook himself, and, "with a roar like that of a baffled beast," rushed Webster with a knife. By that time, however, the detective had produced a revolver.

"Coward!" exclaimed Webster with righteous indignation. "If I served you right I would shoot you down like a dog; and I am afraid I can't resist the temptation to do so anyway, if you don't immediately leave the room. Go! and in future be careful who you accuse of being in league with the accursed Yankees."

Zigler put his knife away and slipped out of the barroom with a backward glance.

"I'll fix you yet, d____n you!" he swore.

"I cannot conceive," Webster said to his companions, "what that fellow has against me, that he should try to defame my character by such an accusation."

Laughter was general.

"I'd as soon suspect Jeff Davis of being a Yankee spy," said one of the men.

If anything, the encounter with Zigler raised Webster in the estimation of the rebel enthusiasts. Webster announced that he was traveling south and that he was willing to carry letters and messages to friends and relatives. On September 26, 1861, he and John Scully took passage on the steamboat *Mary Washington* and sailed down the Chesapeake to Fair Haven, Maryland. From here they proceeded southwest to Leonardtown, where they rendezvoused with another of Pinkerton's operatives, William H. Scott. Using the letters and messages the Baltimore secessionists entrusted to Webster, the three men ingratiated themselves with rebel sympathizers throughout southern Maryland and obtained intelligence on the secessionist movement in the state.

The detective returned to Washington, made his report to Pinkerton, and then reappeared in Baltimore, where his secessionist friends were so impressed, they decided to induct him into a secret society called the Knights of Liberty. At midnight, Webster was led, blindfolded, to a Baltimore alleyway. Sam Sloan, who was leading him, rapped on a door.

"Are you white?" called a voice from inside.

"Down with blacks!"

And the door swung open. At the head of a flight of stairs, another password was demanded:

"Halt! Who comes there?"

"Long live Jeff Davis," replied Sloan.

Sloan presented Webster to a man he addressed as "Most Noble Chief."

"Mr. Webster," the chief inquired, "is it your desire to become a member of this knightly band?"

"It is."

Next, Webster submitted to an oath and a ceremony very similar to what he had experienced earlier, in Perrymansville, when he infiltrated the conspirators against Lincoln. He was, in effect, knighted.

"I, Timothy Webster, citizen of Baltimore, having been informed of the objects of this association, and being in full accord with the cause which it seeks to advance, do solemnly declare and affirm, upon my sacred honor, that I will keep forever secret all that I may see or hear, in consequence of being a member of this league; that I will implicitly obey all orders, and faithfully discharge all duties assigned to me, no matter of what nature or character they may be; and that life or death will be held subordinate to the success and advancement of the cause of the Confederacy and the defeat of the bloody tyrants who are striving to rule by oppression and terrorism. Should I fail in the proper performance of any task imposed upon me, or should I prove unfaithful to the obligations I have here assumed, may I suffer the severest penalty for treason and coward-ice, as well as the odium and contempt of my brother knights."

Absurd as the fraternal-lodge trappings of this secret society were, it seemed to Webster that these men were part of a deadly serious plot to invade Washington. Not only were they in constant communication with the Confederate military command, but, they claimed, they were at the head of an army of ten thousand Baltimoreans, ready to rise and join the rebel army. Furthermore, the Knights of Liberty had access to a vast cache of arms, and they commanded a network of satellite organizations throughout the state of Maryland. When Webster reported all of this to Pinkerton, the decision was made to put an end to the Knights of Liberty—without, however, compromising Webster's cover. Using Webster's contacts, Pinkerton was able to install two more of his operatives in the organization. Webster and the pair arranged with the deputy provost-marshal of Baltimore to raid a midnight meeting of the Knights when the two new operatives would be on guard duty and Webster would be addressing the meeting. The guards would admit the federal troops to an outer hall, and, at a prearranged moment in Webster's speech, they would enter the hall itself.

"The dissolution of the Union is one of the inevitable necessities of Lincoln's election," Webster addressed the Knights, "and it will be our mission to strike directly at the heart of the abolition party, and bury its foul carcass beneath the smoking ruins of Washington city!"

That was the signal. The federals rushed in, and Deputy Provost Marshal McPhail announced, "Gentlemen, you are our prisoners. I advise you to give in gracefully. We are too many for you."

There were no trials. The ringleaders were sent for a time to Fort McHenry, and the rest, with the anticlimax customary in the Federal prosecution of sedition and conspiracy, were released after taking an oath of allegiance. Yet, according to Pinkerton's frankly biased view, the Knights of Liberty had been decisively defeated, and all *organized* conspiracy had been brought to an end in Baltimore and throughout Maryland.

On October 14, 1861, Timothy Webster left Baltimore for Richmond, traveling down the Eastern Shore of Virginia until he reached Eastville, Northampton County, on October 22. There he found a Mr. Marshall, who made his living smuggling goods, mail, and passengers through the Union lines in the shadow of federal gun emplacements. Marshall's business would become a common one as the war ground on and the Union naval blockade tightened. It was also risky. Marshall had owned a fine sloop, which the federals captured. Now his operating vessel was a mere dugout, thirty-one feet long, five feet wide, and running under three sails—main, fore, and jib. From Eastville, Marshall would transport Webster, together with eight other men, mostly Baltimoreans, all pledged to enlist in the Confederate army, to Gloucester Point, York County.

The passage was made in the dark of night, in rough water, and with a strong gale. Webster himself played lookout. A Union gunboat was sighted, but the dugout slipped by, sailing a total of thirty miles in three-and-a-half hours.

"Who comes there?" hailed a sentry as they neared Gloucester Point.

"Marshall—mail boat!"

"Stand, Marshall, and give the countersign!"

"No countersign."

"Sergeant of the Guard, Post No. 1!" the sentry called out.

"Who's there?" came the reply.

"Marshall, with mail boat and passengers."

"Sentinel, let them pass."

A few minutes later, the passengers were in the midst of a rebel camp. After pausing to survey the strength and disposition of troops at Gloucester Point, Webster obtained from a Colonel Crump a pass to Richmond, where he registered at the Spotswood Hotel and began a reconnaissance of the city's defenses. After a time, he returned to Baltimore, where he was warmly greeted by the paroled members of the Knights of Liberty. In Baltimore, Webster managed to pick up valuable information concerning a scheme to smuggle Confederate-bound supplies out of the city. The operative sent a message to Pinkerton, who saw to it that the merchants involved in the scheme were shadowed. After their goods were packed and carefully labeled for a foreign port, federal authorities seized the cargo at the dock. Ironically, the only trouble Webster had in Baltimore was from another Pinkerton agent, who arrested him as a rebel spy. This was quickly cleared up and turned to Webster's advantage, for it heightened his credibility among the city's Southern sympathizers. Stories were placed in the *Baltimore American* and the *Baltimore Gazette* of November 22, 1861, detailing his "escape" from federal custody.

Once again, Pinkerton dispatched Webster to Richmond, this time in company with John Scobell, the Scottish-ballad-singing "contraband" who had volunteered for service with the detective. They were to proceed together as far as Leonardtown, whence Scobell would continue on through Dumfries and Centreville, and Webster would make his way to Richmond. At a hotel in Leonardtown, Webster encountered a tall, dark-whiskered man, who struck the operative as nervous. Webster remarked this to the innkeeper, who replied that the gentleman had good reason to be jumpy. He was a deserter from the Union army.

"Was he an officer?"

"He says he was a surgeon, and had served in the regular army on the Pacific coast for a number of years. His family are Southerners, and he says he concluded to throw up his commission and join our side."

Webster learned that he, too, was on his way to Richmond, that his name was Dr. Gurley—and that he was carrying messages to Judah Benjamin, at the time Confederate secretary of war. The detective quietly strolled to the black section of Leonardtown in search of Scobell. Finding him, he told Scobell that he would point out to him the errant surgeon. Webster next returned to the hotel, where he had arranged with the innkeeper an introduction to Dr. Gurley. Introductions made, the two men had a drink and resolved, come morning, to continue their journey to Richmond together. With that, Gurley left the barroom.

"There is going to be a shower," observed Webster, "and the Doctor will have to walk fast to escape it."

Within the hour, Dr. Gurley reappeared at the barroom. He was hatless, his clothing torn and soiled, his face pale, and his lips trembling. To Webster's "astonished" inquiry, Gurley responded that he had been attacked and robbed, knocked unconscious. Worst of all, the dispatches to Secretary of War Benjamin had been taken.

"Never mind," said Webster consolingly. "The loss of the papers won't amount to much; when we arrive in Richmond you can communicate verbally the nature of the papers you have lost."

"That's the devil of it," said Dr. Gurley. "I don't know their contents; they were intrusted to me by men who are working in the interest of the South, and as they were sealed, I have no more idea than you have what they contained."

Of course, it was Webster who had dispatched Scobell to waylay Dr. Gurley. Now he was not only in possession of important Confederate communications, but had succeeded in preventing them from reaching the secretary of war himself. As to sending the information northward, Scobell had arranged it through an underground network composed of Southern blacks who called themselves the Loyal League.

Webster returned to Washington and by Christmas 1861 was preparing yet another foray into rebeldom. Each expedition yielded not only intelligence based on observation, but a wealth of Confederate communication. For Southerners entrusted northbound mail and dispatches to Webster, and Southern sympathizers in Washington gave him letters and messages to carry to Richmond. All, of course, he and Pinkerton intercepted and read.

As usual, the operative made his way to Leonardtown, Maryland, and the inn of John Moore, a Southern sympathizer who customarily arranged boat passage across the wide Potomac. It was a bitter winter night when Webster, sharing a jug of punch with John Moore, asked the innkeeper what the prospect was for crossing the river that night.

"We can't cross here at all any more, Webster. The damned Yankees are too sharp for us."

Webster asked if there was no other way to cross.

"There's a way for some people, and I guess you are included in the number."

The innkeeper directed Webster to Cob Neck, about fourteen miles from Leonardtown, where a wide inlet could accommodate a boat and the swampy, overgrown pine forest was suited to concealing activity. Moore asked only one favor—that Webster escort into Virginia two ladies, wives of rebel officers, and their three children, who had been living in the North and were eager to join their husbands. The operative agreed.

With the wind against the little boat, the vessel had to make many tacks to cross the river. It was a slow passage in rough water. At last, a storm blew up, bringing high winds and an icy rain. A gust ran the vessel aground about a hundred feet from shore. Webster ordered the boatman to lower sail and jumped into the shallow water, carrying two children in his arms. After depositing them safely on shore, he helped carry the ladies and the remaining child across. They had a mile to walk through a pelting, icy rain to reach the nearest shelter. After seeing to the ladies and children, Webster, still in his wet clothes, lay down on the floor to sleep. By the light of the fire, he saw a package, which he examined and discovered was addressed to Judah Benjamin. Webster pocketed the package and fell asleep.

In the morning, he awoke in an agony of swollen joints. However, he packed the women, children, and himself into an ox cart and set off for Hop Yard Wharf on the Rappahannock. There they boarded a steamboat bound for Fredericksburg, where Webster had to remain for two days because the exposure he had suffered in the icy river and storm had triggered a severe attack of rheumatism. The ladies, whose children and whose own lives Webster had saved, were anxious to reach Richmond and so left him in Fredericksburg, as Pinkerton wrote, in the care of "absolute strangers." However, Webster used their absence as an opportunity to examine the contents of the package they had left behind. He found maps of the country surrounding Washington, marked with the disposition and strength of Federal troops and other information.

After two days at Fredericksburg, Webster, still aching, boarded a train for Richmond. He called on Judah Benjamin, delivering to him various letters Southern sympathizers had given him in Washington. Benjamin, in turn, furnished Webster with passes enabling him to travel freely. He was joined in Richmond by Mrs. Hattie Lawton, another Pinkerton operative, who passed herself off as Webster's wife or sister (reports vary on this point). Webster also made contact with one more Pinkerton man, a Mr. Stanton, who was scheduled to return to Washington. Webster gave him the package that the ladies had intended to deliver to Benjamin. When Pinkerton examined the documents he recognized the handwriting as that of James Howard, a clerk in the Washington, D.C., provost marshal's office. Howard was arrested and confined to the Old Capitol Prison. Webster lost a week, confined to bed with his rheumatism. He then joined a war contractor named Campbell on a journey to Nashville, through Knoxville and Chattanooga, then on to Bowling Green, Kentucky, and back to Richmond through Manassas and Centreville, gathering intelligence at each point. After collecting northern-bound dispatches from Secretary Benjamin, Webster set out for Washington.

By January 1862, apparently having completely recovered from his rheumatism and armed with southern-bound correspondence, Webster was ready for another trip south. At Leonardtown, Hattie

Lawton had made the acquaintance of Washington Gough, a wealthy Southern sympathizer who aided blockade runners in crossing from Maryland to Virginia. Webster also became a favorite of Gough and, indeed, ingratiated himself with secessionist sympathizers throughout Maryland. Webster was equally well respected by Virginia Confederates. When a Leonardtown man named Camilear crossed the river into Virginia and was arrested by rebel authorities, his friends and relatives turned to Webster for help. (He did, in fact, secure the man's release.) Webster and Lawton left Leonardtown together for Richmond. Unfortunately for the detective, the weather again turned bitterly cold and damp, aggravating his rheumatic condition. After a night's sleep in a Richmond hotel, Webster awoke in great pain, unable to move.

Incapacitated, Webster could not communicate with Pinkerton for several weeks. Presumably, Hattie Lawton was too involved in caring for her invalid partner and too fearful of compromising them both to attempt any communication herself. Pinkerton worried about both his operatives, as did General McClellan. Finally, early in February, McClellan advised Pinkerton to send one or two agents to Richmond to try to locate Webster. The detective chose Price Lewis and John Scully, both of whom had worked with Webster in Baltimore. For once, Pinkerton even exercised some caution in the matter of using the same men both for espionage and counterespionage. Not that Lewis and Scully had *never* worked in a counterespionage capacity; they had participated in searches of the Washington residences of several prominent Southern families, including those of the Phillipses and the Mortons. Pinkerton had reason to believe that Mrs. Phillips, having been paroled from "Fort Greenhow," and Mrs. Morton might be living in Richmond, so, before sending Scully and Lewis on their way, he ran down a number of sources in order to determine the present whereabouts of these two families. The Phillips family, he learned, had returned to South Carolina, while the Mortons had gone back to Florida. It seemed safe enough, then, to send the two operatives to Richmond.

The pair reached Richmond without difficulty and checked into the Exchange Hotel. The next morning, they set out in search of Webster, stopping first at the offices of the *Richmond Enquirer*, on behalf of which Webster had carried letters and purchased Northern goods. The two agents were directed to the Monumental Hotel, where they found Webster, helpless, attended by Mrs. Lawton. A Mr. Pierce, who had befriended Webster, was also in the room, so Scully and Lewis were careful not to betray their mission. On their second visit, the pair found Webster in company with a Captain McCubbin, an officer of the provost marshal's office with whom Webster had also become friendly. Half jokingly, McCubbin asked Scully and Lewis if they had registered as required with Provost Marshal Winder. Webster was disturbed by an undercurrent of suspicion in McCubbin's levity, but, in his invalid state, there was nothing he could do about it.

Scully and Lewis reported to General Winder's office, and informed the provost marshal that they were natives of England and Ireland, come to the South to set up a smuggling operation. Winder received them so cordially that, after the interview, the pair left, congratulating themselves on having allayed all suspicions. They called again on Webster, but a few minutes after their arrival in his hotel room a detective from the provost marshal's office knocked on the door. General Winder, he said, wanted just one more piece of information from them: what *parts* of England and Ireland did they come from?

When the detective left, Webster implored Scully and Lewis to get out of Richmond immediately.

"We certainly cannot be suspected," Scully said, "and I am confident that you are alarming yourself unnecessarily."

But Webster insisted. "I tell you that man never would have come here with that question unless there was something wrong."

At that moment, there was another knock on the door. George Cluckner, a provost marshal's detective, entered the room with Chase Morton, son of ex-Florida Governor Morton, whose Washington, D.C., house Scully and Lewis had searched.

If Pinkerton is to be believed, that search had been conducted with such gentility and consideration that Mrs. Morton, her daughter, and her two sons thanked Scully and Lewis, telling them that if anyone involved in the search were ever taken prisoner and brought to Richmond, they would do their best to secure kind treatment for them. Now, however, Scully panicked. Without a word, he walked out the door. Lewis bumbled through the introductions and followed Scully, who was waiting for him at the top of the stairs. They were about to descend when the door to Webster's room opened, and Cluckner called out: "Are your names Lewis and Scully?"

"Yes, sir," answered Lewis.

"Then I have orders to convey you to General Winder's office."

While the two Pinkerton men waited in an anteroom of the general's office, Chase Morton, accompanied by an officer, entered.

"Don't you remember me?"

No, Lewis answered, he did not.

"Don't you remember coming to my mother's house, in Washington, as an agent of the secret service of the Federal government, and making a thorough search of our premises and its contents?"

"You are mistaken, sir. I know nothing of what you are alluding to."

"I am not mistaken, and you are the man!"

Scully attempted to bluff it out. "Perhaps this gentleman will say that he recollects me, next," he said.

"Yes sir," said Morton, "I recollect you also . . . . "

General Winder now entered.

"How do you do, Mr. Lewis, and how is Mr. Seward?"

After further questioning and lame denials, the two operatives were sent to Henrico Jail. Four days later, Winder summoned Scully to his office. Lewis, in the meantime, formulated an escape plan with other prisoners. They were held in cells separated from the main part of the prison and, using an improvised saw made by filing teeth in a knife, they managed after several days to saw through the bolts on the cell doors. During exercise period in the prison yard, one of them, Charles Stanton, volunteered to be buried in an ash heap piled against the yard wall so that he could go to work on the outside door when the other men had been called back to their cells. Stanton, a sailor, had been captured while he was on an undercover mission purely of his own invention and execution. He had come south with the intention of obtaining command of a Confederate gunboat, which he would then run through the Union lines. While some of the prisoners distracted the aged jailer, the others quickly dug a "grave" in the ash heap, Stanton lay down, and the ashes were heaped over him, save for his face, which was covered with straw. The other prisoners returned to their cells, and one of them placed in Stanton's bed a straw dummy they had fashioned. After the old jailer made his nighttime cell check, the prisoners waited for Stanton to start on the door, which would be the signal to leave their cells. Stanton, however, had a problem. The jailer passed by the ash heap and took note of the small pile of straw atop it. For reasons known only to himself, the jailer struck a match and was about to ignite the straw when a gust of wind blew it out. He patted his pockets for another match, but, failing to find one, walked on. Stanton emerged from the ash heap and began to work on the lock. The operation required more force than had been anticipated. A group of black prisoners, captured in an attempt to escape to the North, began to sing as loudly as they could, covering the noise of the others as they worked on the door.

At eight in the evening of March 18, the prisoners emerged from Henrico Jail. Their problem now was Richmond's strict nine o'clock martial law curfew. They had to make for the countryside as quickly as possible. Through many a bitter winter campaign, Union soldiers learned to scoff at clichés about the "sunny South." As they huddled near the Chickahominy, waist deep in icy mud, the fugitives shivered and suffered. They pushed on, rarely daring to build a fire. And the second fire they did build drew a detachment of Confederate soldiers. Price Lewis and his fellow escapees were prisoners once again. Returned to Henrico Jail, each was clapped in double irons.

Perhaps to forestall another escape attempt, authorities quickly convened the court martial of Price Lewis. A short time before, John Scully had been court martialed and, largely on the strength of the Morton family's testimony, was found guilty of espionage. Lewis was quickly convicted as well, and both men were sentenced to be hanged a week hence.

Throughout the ordeal, the pair had been separated and were now confined in separate cells of a prison called Castle Godwin. A day after they were brought to Castle Godwin, Lewis was given a message that John Scully, seriously ill, had requested to see him. In fact, Scully had feigned illness, so that the authorities would permit the visit. They discussed their situation and concluded that nothing was to be done. Scully, a Roman Catholic, announced that he wanted a priest to hear his confession.

"You will not tell him what you know of Webster, and his connection with this matter, will you?" asked Lewis.

"I don't know what I will tell him. I have not decided what to say, nor do I know what I will be commanded to relate."

Lewis argued at length with Scully. It is impossible to determine whether this exchange, which Pinkerton recorded in his memoir, is a figment of the anti-Catholic prejudice characteristic of the period, a conviction that "popery" was, by definition, conspiratorial, or a real and unforeseen hazard of espionage. Whatever Scully may or may not have revealed to his confessor, he did, upon promise of a pardon, betray Timothy Webster. When Lewis learned of this, he, too, "opened his mouth."

After some sessions of questioning in Webster's hotel room, a provost marshal officer, whom Pinkerton identifies as Cashmeyer, was dispatched to arrest Webster and transport him to Castle Godwin. Mrs. Lawton protested that Webster was too ill to be moved, but Cashmeyer pointed out that his orders were to convey Webster to Castle Godwin—dead or alive. Hattie Lawton was also arrested. Pinkerton recorded that, when Webster was brought into General Winder's office, another prisoner exclaimed, "My God! They will send the dead here next."

The "Cashmeyer" to whom Pinkerton referred was undoubtedly Philip Cashmeyer, a German immigrant and prewar Baltimorean who was employed by Provost Marshal Winder as a special detective. Ironically, in the spring of 1864, Elizabeth Van Lew would successfully recruit him for service in her Richmond Ring. After the war, federal officials called on Cashmeyer to identify various Richmond loyalists entitled to compensation for supplying intelligence to Union forces.

Webster's trial was swift, and he was sentenced to be hanged on April 29, 1862. Allan Pinkerton read of the trial, conviction, and sentence in one of the Richmond newspapers that regularly reached his office. He, General McClellan, and Secretary of War Stanton appealed the sentence through diplomatic means, but to no avail. As to Webster, his only request was that he be shot rather than hanged. This General Winder denied.

Pinkerton's most effective agent was taken from his cell at five in the morning and brought to the Richmond fair grounds, which had been transformed into Camp Lee. Hattie Lawton bade him farewell at the cell door, and he announced, "I am ready!" At ten minutes past eleven, Webster was brought to the scaffold. Stiff and agonized by his rheumatism, he slowly ascended the stairs. The noose and hood were placed over his head, the signal given, and the trap sprung.

Webster fell to the ground beneath the gibbet; the noose had slipped.

"I suffer a double death," Webster was heard to mutter.

The noose was refitted, so tightly that the condemned man remarked, "You will choke me to death this time."

Alone, in miserable agony, Timothy Webster died the death of a common criminal. Hattie Lawton, Price Lewis, and John Scully were all paroled to the North after brief prison terms. There is no way to gauge the sufferings that may have been wrought upon Lewis and Scully by a troubled conscience.

CHAPTER EIGHT

Stringfellow

At ninety-four pounds, blond, gray-blue-eyed Benjamin Franklin Stringfellow had just the right last name. He was, in fact, so slight—so much a string fellow—that, like every other Confederate military officer he approached, Captain John F. Lay, commander of the Powhatan Troop (later Company E, Fourth Virginia Cavalry), refused to enroll him for service. He refused, that is, until Stringfellow made a point. He left the captain, captured three of his sentries, then marched them back to the reluctant officer at the point of a gun and again asked to enlist. Captain Lay needed no further convincing.

In May 1861, during the days immediately following Virginia's decision to secede, Captain Lay's company was posted near the Potomac. Federal troops had occupied Arlington, and now General P. G. T. Beauregard needed to know what was going on in Alexandria. Were Union troops there, and, if they were, what was their strength and what were they doing? Most likely, Captain Lay sent Private Stringfellow into Alexandria. If so, this hazardous mission was his first espionage assignment. In any case, it was shortly after this that Stringfellow was attached to the reconnaissance group of the Confederate Cavalry Corps, which included John Singleton Mosby, soon to win fame as the Gray Ghost guerrilla raider, and Redmond Burke. Large-framed as Stringfellow was slight, Burke apparently served as Stringfellow's principal mentor in the art of scouting, if not espionage proper. Redmond Burke was killed on November 25, 1862, attempting to evade capture at Shepherdstown, West Virginia.

The reconnaissance unit of the cavalry corps boasted at least three Burkes. In addition to Redmond, there was Captain John Burke, whose specialty was espionage rather than scouting, and who was a master of disguise. He had at some point in his career lost one eye and so could appear with or without a glass substitute. Civil War spies frequently used disguises: Thomas N. Conrad became adept at radically altering his beard and mustache, Stringfellow made a rather attractive girl, but John Burke is the only Civil War agent who could appear at will with one eye or two. A third Burke, whose first name is not recorded, was a double agent in the service of the Union. He made a convincing Confederate, however, his commander once remarking that, "If I had a thousand such men I could whip a brigade of Yankees."

Some time during the war, after a series of exploits that strain credibility, Frank Stringfellow was commissioned a lieutenant and attached to Major William Norris's Signal and Secret Service. It is not known precisely when this occurred, but his name must have been familiar to Norris early in the existence of the service he commanded. For, toward the end of 1861, Stringfellow was ordered to meet E. Pliny Bryan, who would be among the first to serve with Norris when the Signal Corps was officially established on July 31, 1862. The two men got together in Manassas, at the Stone House Hotel. Bryan's secret mission at the time sounds almost ludicrous. He collected newspapers. But, as we have seen, the Northern press was prodigal in broadcasting the details of troop strength, deployment, and command. This seems an espionage windfall, but even this intelligence came at a price. Often, Confederate agents and sympathizers in various Northern cities simply bundled the papers together and figured out a way to smuggle them south. But this quickly brought the agent or sympathizer under suspicion, and the bundles were not easy to carry in secret. Bryan's scheme was to set up Stringfellow in Alexandria, where he would have access to Washington newspapers. Stringfellow would daily glean the papers for military information, which he would summarize in brief, easily concealed documents, and then transmit the documents to couriers working the Doctors' Line.

One of Bryan's assets in Alexandria was a dentist Stringfellow identified in a memoir as Richard M. Sykes. (John Bakeless, in his 1970 *Spies of the Confederacy*, points out that no dentist named Sykes appears in the Alexandria city directories of the period. As Stringfellow made it a habit to protect those who worked with him, the absence of the name does not necessarily render his story suspect.) Posing as a dental apprentice, Stringfellow was to live with Sykes, using his office to communicate with couriers. Bryan was careful to work up a cover story of some depth. Stringfellow would call himself Edward Delcher, who was a real person—a Baltimore dental assistant now serving the Confederacy in the western theater of the war, far from Baltimore or Alexandria. Bryan had acquired from Delcher's family the young man's baptismal certificate, and he counterfeited a medical certificate stating that Delcher was unfit for military service. A glance at this certificate and one look at the ninety-four-pound Stringfellow would convince any prying federal agents that "Edward Delcher" was legitimately a civilian. Bryan also borrowed from the Delcher family one of Edward's suits, which bore the label of a Baltimore tailor. Good federal agents, especially Pinkerton's detectives, were especially fond of examining clothing in minute detail. Finally, Bryan furnished Stringfellow with detailed information on Delcher's background, should he have to answer any questions.

Thus armed with his new identity, Stringfellow collected newspapers, digested them, sealed the gleanings in an envelope, and deposited the newspapers themselves in a dry well under the floor of the dental office, since a federal detective might find the sight of so many discarded newspapers suspicious. Bryan had told Stringfellow to leave his envelopes in a special place beneath the eaves of the dentist's house. This he did at night. Each morning, the envelope was gone. Interestingly, on August 23, 1861, Rose Greenhow reported in a dispatch to Richmond that "a line of daily communication is now open through Alexandria." Perhaps one of the couriers with whom she worked, and whom either she or Thomas Jordan had recruited, was responsible for carrying Stringfellow's digests.

On at least one occasion, Stringfellow had direct contact with a rebel courier. In February 1862, an emergency patient, groaning in agony, his face swathed in a towel, appeared in Dr. Sykes's office. Stringfellow ushered him in ahead of a Union army major who was in the waiting room. The major, hearing more moans coming from the treatment room, never suspected that the emergency "patient" was a courier bearing the secret information that Lincoln had personally ordered General McClellan to advance on Manassas by February 22. This either confirmed or anticipated similar decisive information Rose Greenhow supplied Beauregard during the days immediately before the first Battle of Bull Run. After delivering the message, the "patient"—still swathed—walked through the waiting room, passed the federal major, and out the door.

Later, Stringfellow's cover was nearly blown by a circumstance one might think the spy would have taken steps to avoid. In Alexandria lived Emma Green, Stringfellow's "intended." Instead of carefully approaching her—perhaps through Bryan or some courier—to explain his mission and the need for absolute secrecy, Stringfellow merely avoided her and hoped that no awkward situation would arise. It is understandable, perhaps, that Stringfellow would not want to alert anyone, even his sweetheart, to his presence. But Alexandria was a small town, and the two were bound to meet.

It happened in the worst possible place: Dr. Sykes's office. Emma Green, who had brought her grandfather to the dentist, saw Stringfellow in the waiting room and greeted him with all the delighted surprise a well-bred young woman of the period might allow herself. Another patient, whom Stringfellow suspected of being a Pinkerton operative, was in the waiting room, so there was nothing for Stringfellow to do but tell the young lady that she was mistaken: he didn't know her, and he had never seen her before.

Fortunately for the spy, Green caught on and quickly apologized for her "mistake."

Still, Stringfellow could hardly relax. The most terrible truism of the Civil War was that the battle lines divided not only governments, but families. While Dr. Sykes was a solid Confederate sympathizer, his wife, daughter of a Union officer, was not. Of course, Sykes did not tell her who his young apprentice really was, but both Stringfellow and Bryan feared she might someday become suspicious and alert federal authorities. What neither Bryan nor Stringfellow had anti-cipated was that Mrs. Sykes, apparently feeling that she and the doctor were growing apart, would attempt to use the dental apprentice to make Sykes jealous and, therefore, more attentive. Repeatedly, she flirted with Stringfellow in front of the dentist—and that, at last, was enough to breach his loyalty to the South.

It was Mrs. Sykes who warned Stringfellow that her husband was about to go to the authorities. That night, the spy fled—not by the front door (for a detachment Union cavalry, perhaps members of the provost guard, was on the march) but through a back window. He made for the home of Sam Whiteside (as with Sykes, no Whiteside appears in Alexandria city directories), a safe house, where he had secreted his Confederate uniform. From a distance, he saw Union cavalry search the Whiteside home. Waiting until they had left, Stringfellow entered, secured his uniform, and left.

Union war records list numerous arrests of civilians for possess-ing a Confederate uniform, usually hidden in a trunk. Mrs. L. A. McCarty, for example, who was lodged with Rose Greenhow in Old Capitol Prison, had been found with a uniform, as well as various items of contraband and the prototype of a new artillery projec-tile. In most cases, these uniforms were not kept for sentimental reasons or as souvenirs. They were, in fact, for clothing spies who, like Stringfellow, were in imminent danger of capture. A Confeder-ate soldier found behind the lines in civilian clothing could be hanged as a spy. In uniform, however, he could be held only as a prisoner of war. Frank Stringfellow was able to escape Alexandria and make his way to Yorktown, where he rejoined J. E. B. Stuart's cavalry in the spring of 1862. For the balance of the spring and summer, Stringfellow was sent on scouting missions behind Union lines during McClellan's Peninsular campaign and the beginning of General John Pope's campaign against Lee. Such reconnaissance missions, while highly dangerous, were conducted in uniform, so cannot properly be called espionage.

Stringfellow's next assignment as a spy came toward the end of August, a few days before the second Battle of Bull Run, when Stuart sent him to Warrenton, Virginia, to reconnoiter river pas-sages and to identify the extreme right flank of Pope's army. Stringfellow wore the blouse of a Union officer, though he hedged his bet by wearing a Confederate shirt and trousers. He was operating at night, when he hoped the hybrid nature of the uniform would not be noticed and when, if he were captured, he could discard the blouse and reasonably claim to be in legitimate Confederate uniform. Stringfellow was able to learn the location of General Pope's headquarters—at Catlett's Station—which he reported to Stuart, who staged a quick raid, capturing horses, taking three hundred prisoners, and obtaining a wealth of Pope's papers. "Gaining the knowledge of the enemy's location, his force, the position of his reinforcements, and his *notions* of where *we* were, and what we were trying to do, was of great value to us [in fighting second Bull Run—a rebel victory]," Stringfellow himself recalled.

After serving as a uniformed courier during the second Bull Run battle, Stringfellow's next major mission came early the next year, when he was assigned to establish a line of communications out of Washington. This seems to have been separate from the Doctors' Line and the Secret Line, and it is not clear whether the assignment came solely from J. E. B. Stuart or through Major William Norris. It does seem clear that Stringfellow had very little knowledge of the other regular lines of communication coming out of the capital. This may suggest that the operation was conducted independently of Norris's Signal and Secret Service Bureau or, if Norris had a hand in it, that he was employing the sound espionage practice of telling his agents only what they absolutely had to know and nothing more.

Stringfellow performed his work with the aid of a cavalry detachment under Captain John Farrow. Two other men, Charles Arundel and the other unidentified, accompanied him through Fairfax County. The home of Arundel's family, at some distance outside Alexandria, served as a safe house. Not far from the house, Stringfellow waylaid a Union sutler and his wagon, appropriating needed supplies, some money, and, most important of all, the sutler's pass signed by the provost marshal. Afterward, he set off for Alexandria, from where he would cross to Washington. In Alexandria he would recruit agents for the line and pay a call on his "intended," Emma Green, whom he had not seen since the brief and highly unsatisfactory encounter in Dr. Sykes's office.

Pausing to see his sweetheart was not Stringfellow's only rash action on the mission. Fifteen miles outside of Alexandria, and while he was still wearing a Confederate uniform, the agent called at the house of a woman who was known to be a Union sympathizer. Night was coming on, and he needed a place to sleep. Stringfellow explained to the woman that he was on his way to visit his fiancée, whom he had not seen for two years. That was enough to convince the lady, despite her political leanings, to afford him shelter. But the apparently guileless youth got even more. Obviously, he could not enter Alexandria in the uniform of the Confederacy. Stringfellow persuaded the woman to keep his grays for him—as we have seen, a dangerous thing for a civilian to do—and to lend him some of her son's clothes.

Now just one problem remained. What if the lady's son saw Stringfellow ambling by in his clothes? The spy needed an especially inconspicuous way of entering Alexandria. He knew of a woodcutter in the vicinity, Olander Devers, a staunch Confederate, who regularly drove his wagon into the city. At this point in Stringfellow's narrative there occurs one of those passages that strain credibility. The spy did not enter the Devers house by means of the door, but through a hole in the base of the chimney. Two logs had been loosened there and a blanket hung inside the cabin to stop drafts. Stringfellow does not say how he knew about the loose logs. Perhaps, as John Bakeless speculates in his *Spies of the Confederacy,* it was "a specially devised entrance for secret service use." In any case, the spy made his sudden appearance, narrowly avoided decapitation at the keen edge of the startled woodsman's ax, procured his wagon, and, showing the stolen sutler's pass, drove into Alexandria. Devers, who followed some distance behind his wagon, picked it up in Alexandria.

Obviously, Stringfellow could not set up again as Dr. Sykes's assistant. Indeed, he was always in grave danger of being discovered by Sykes. Instead, he called on an unidentified storekeeper, a solid Confederate sympathizer, and posed as R. M. Franklin, "store-helper." His next order of business was to see Emma Green, whom the storekeeper fetched for him. Stringfellow reports that he spent "many happy days in the city," presumably in Green's company—though he was also busy recruiting men for the line and, using his sutler's pass, at least twice venturing into Washington. There he was able to recruit agents who either worked at, or managed to penetrate, the headquarters of Major General Henry ("Old Brains") Halleck, at the time general-in-chief of the Union Army.

While Stringfellow was in Alexandria, he was fortunate enough not to encounter Dr. Sykes. Turning a Washington corner, however, he nearly collided with a Union army captain, whom he had helped capture in the raid on Catlett's Station the year before. Stringfellow never forgot a face, and neither did the federal captain. The spy ran, and the officer ran after him. Stringfellow ducked into the open door of a house belonging to a friend of his mother's. In postwar popular lectures, Stringfellow recalled that, when he entered, his mother's friend was mending a tablecloth. She rose from her work, comprehended the situation instantly, and called out, "Here, Frank." With this, she lifted her fashionably commodious hoop skirt, and the slightly built Stringfellow crawled under it just as federal soldiers dashed through the door. They asked: Had anyone come into the house? Why, yes, the woman answered. A man had run in and then right out again, through the back door. Satisfied, the soldiers left to continue their pursuit.

Like so much in Stringfellow's career, this incident calls for a willing suspension of our disbelief. That, after the war, Stringfellow was, like Thomas N. Conrad, a respected Christian minister does not necessarily mean he was incapable of spinning quite a yarn. However, John Bakeless points out that "a girl in Fauquier County, Virginia, is known to have hidden her fiancé in exactly the same way." To be sure, stranger things than this happened in the course of the War Between the States, and the farcical nature of this episode is quite in keeping with the tone of much that is known to be true of Civil War espionage.

But the news that greeted Stringfellow when he left Washington and Alexandria and returned to the Arundel house was hardly funny. Charles Arundel and Stringfellow's other, unnamed companion had been killed. Remarkably, the sutler he had waylaid was spending the night at the Arundel house. With Stringfellow's newly trimmed hair, clean-shaven face, and city clothes, the sutler did not recognize him. They even shared a bedroom.

Stringfellow rejoined Captain Farrow and the cavalry. They raided a federal outpost, capturing twenty-five Yankees and thirty-five horses, but Stringfellow was wounded in the process and

Farrow killed. The spy's next misfortune was his capture shortly before the Battle of Gettysburg. He must have been taken in uniform, however, for he was quickly handed over in a prisoner exchange. Hard upon his release, he was part of a raid designed to capture a Union general to exchange for General William H. F. "Rooney" Lee, who, having been wounded in the leg, was taken by federal raiders at the Battle of Brandy Station on June 9, 1863. Stringfellow's mission failed to turn up a general.

At around this time, Stringfellow was notified that his mother had become a casualty of war. She had been hit by a shot fired during an engagement in the vicinity of her house at Raccoon Ford, near Verdiersville, Virginia. J. E. B. Stuart dispatched Stringfellow on a reconnaissance mission that would allow him to visit his mother. Carrying with him a brand-new biography of Stonewall Jackson, intended as a gift for the invalid, he paused on his way to the house to poke around in a Union encampment and, in particular, inspect the unguarded tent of General Samuel P. Carter. Not only did he capture the general's papers—which included the divisional payroll, detailing strength, personnel, and organization— he obtained a Union captain's uniform. He thought about taking the general's, but it didn't fit. After a skirmish, during which he dropped the Jackson biography, Stringfellow got away. Federal troops, finding the biography, assumed that they had killed Stringfellow.

When he reached his family's house, the spy saw that it was occupied by Union soldiers. He went up to a window and scratched on it, hoping to draw the attention of one of his family's slaves. It worked only too well. The slave, having been told that Stringfellow was killed escaping from General Carter's tent, looked out the window, thought she was seeing a ghost, dropped the oil lamp she was carrying, and started a minor blaze. Stringfellow, meanwhile, disappeared into the night.

Later, the spy managed to alert another slave—Uncle George— who dressed him in women's clothing and sneaked him into Mrs. Stringfellow's room. Suddenly, there was a knock at the door. Stringfellow hid himself in a closet as the Union army surgeon entered. Although the family slaves had been informed of young Frank's death, it was thought best to withhold the information from his frail, wounded mother. Now, presenting her with the Jackson biography, it was the doctor's sad duty to break the news.

All the while, the dead man waited in the closet, jotting down various items of military information the surgeon let slip.

Difficult to believe? John Bakeless had the story, in part, from Stringfellow Barr, the spy's grandson. Bakeless goes on to state that Frank Stringfellow's notes remained on the closet walls undisturbed for years until someone whitewashed over them, "happily so lightly that traces can still be seen." These Bakeless confirmed by "personal examination."

For the balance of 1863 and into early 1864, Stringfellow was once again engaged in cavalry reconnaissance duties rather than espionage. Toward the end of this period, a party of Stuart's men captured a federal captain. Among the papers he was carrying was a federal pass made out for Sallie Marsten, who lived near Culpeper Courthouse. Stringfellow questioned the captain, who explained that he had secured the pass in exchange for Miss Marsten's company at a regimental dance. The captain asked Stringfellow to deliver a letter to Sallie Marsten, presumably explaining why he had been compelled to stand her up.

Stringfellow delivered the letter, and he did more. For he knew the Marsten family well. Sallie Marsten had met the captain when she crossed federal lines in search of her brother, a Confederate soldier missing in action. Now Stringfellow would put the pass to better use. He called on the Marstens, who dressed him in Sallie's best ball gown and sent him off to the dance, pass in hand. There he heard much discussion of troop movement and the news that Ulysses S. Grant had been named to the post of general-in-chief. It was valuable information that accurately boded the North's new resolve to take the offensive.

The spy would have liked to hear more, but a lieutenant who had entertained suspicions about "Miss Marsten"—she had a pass, but she came to the dance alone—made inquiries and discovered that her would-be escort had been captured. The lieutenant quietly called "Miss Marsten" out of the dance. He took her to a secluded spot—perhaps for questioning, perhaps for something more amorous—whereupon Stringfellow produced a brace of derringers and forced the hapless lieutenant to drive him beyond the Yankee outposts.

Of all Stringfellow's apparently fantastic adventures, this is actually one of the more easily believed. We have already seen a transvestite Confederate spy in Mrs. McCarty and a transvestite, transracial spy for the Union in Emma Edmonds. Throughout the war, federal authorities exposed, as it were, numerous women masquerading as men in the ranks. It is also a fact that Lieutenant Thomas Post, of the First Georgia Regiment, attended a federal military ball disguised as a girl, and a colonel invited him to dinner afterward! Captain Frank Battle, visiting his family in Nashville, deceived occupying federal forces by passing himself off as a female.

J. E. B. Stuart was fatally wounded at the battle of Yellow Tavern on May 11, 1864. After Stuart's death, Stringfellow seems to have reported to Generals Wade Hampton, Fitzhugh Lee, and Robert E. Lee himself. Jefferson Davis sent him to Washington at the time of Lincoln's second inauguration, where he assumed the uniform and identity of a federal soldier named Robert Hawkins, who had been furloughed to convalesce from a wound. Stringfellow's mission was to deliver some documents to a foreign legation in the capital and to make contact with a Union officer who was offering to sell military secrets.

All seems to have gone reasonably well, though his meeting with the Union officer was inconclusive. Then Stringfellow committed the same kind of apparently rash act that had served him well before. On his arrival in Washington, he had checked into Willard's Hotel. After a short stay there, he moved on to a series of boarding-houses. Finally, feeling that he was being watched, he deliberately moved into a boardinghouse that catered to federal detectives! It was a lapse into bravado, perhaps, or a stroke of cunning calculation. For the last place a Union operative would think to find a rebel spy was in the room next to his.

Or hers. It seems that a woman detective in the house did become suspicious, and Stringfellow realized it. He tried to befriend her, and even played checkers with her, since she apparently had a passion for the game. But she did not let up. At last, during dinner one night, she proposed a toast to Abraham Lincoln. Stringfellow, with a history of having disguised himself as a woman, and who had many times worn the uniform of a Union soldier, now demurred. He never drank alcoholic beverages, he said. The lady detective then suggested that he drink the toast in water.

That was when something possessed Benjamin Franklin Stringfellow. Perhaps it was the accumulated pressure of four years of deceit. Who knows? The spy raised his glass and drank to the health of *Jefferson Davis.*

He then vanished, securing other lodgings, but not for long. Early in April he learned that the Confederate government had evacuated Richmond, and he decided that the time was now ripe for his own evacuation from Washington. Before he could leave, he was interrogated by a detective, who, however, was unsure of Stringfellow's identity. The spy referred him to a traitorous Union officer—a daring move, but one that would at least buy him time. For, Stringfellow was aware, if the officer was tempted to reveal Stringfellow's identity, he would first have to ponder the consequences: that Stringfellow would, in turn, reveal him as a traitor. The spy gambled that the officer would vouch for him.

Stringfellow did not wait to find out. He made use of one or more of the Confederate lines out of the city. However, he had not gone very far when he was stopped by a federal cavalry patrol, the leader of which demanded his papers. Unsatisfied, the cavalry officer detained Stringfellow and announced that he would have to be taken to a higher authority. The spy *ate* as many as he could of the secret documents he carried on his person. Despite Stringfellow's appetite, a survey of Washington's defenses, sewn into the lining of his coat, was quickly discovered, and Stringfellow was shipped to Port Tobacco, Maryland, for further interrogation.

With the war rapidly nearing its end, spies posed little threat, and the federal officer in charge at Port Tobacco informed Stringfellow that five hundred dollars would set him free. The officer had overestimated the financial resources of the Confederate secret service, however. Stringfellow did not have the money. Nevertheless, the spy managed to escape and, after twenty-one tortuous days of running and hiding, reached Virginia. By this time, however, Abraham Lincoln had been assassinated and Secretary Seward assaulted. The nation was gripped with rumors and theories of a grand conspiracy against the president and his cabinet. Reasonably renowned as a rebel spy, Stringfellow, who had been in Washington just prior to the assassination and who, like many other Confederate agents, had lodged in Mrs. Surratt's safe house and may well have procured horses, carriage, and a driver from her, was suspected of complicity in the assassination. Learning of the accusations against him, he made use of the Secret Line to get out of Virginia and out of the United States. He found refuge in Hamilton, Ontario. After the hysteria following the Lincoln tragedy died down, Stringfellow returned to the United States, lectured on his exploits, and, yes, even married Emma Green.

CHAPTER NINE

SECRET SERVICES

T he evidence suggests that, by any standard, Timothy Webster was an extraordinary spy. Certainly, he was the most effective of Pinkerton's operatives engaged in espionage, as opposed to counterespionage activities. Unfortunately, the bulk of Pinkerton's Civil War records was lost when his office was consumed by the great Chicago Fire of 1871, and it is not possible to say precisely what information Webster or any other Pinkerton agent procured and how that information affected military strategy. Historians of the period generally agree, however, that Pinkerton was remarkably effective as a counterintelligence officer, but equally ineffective, even disastrous, as a gatherer of positive intelligence. With only eleven detectives in Washington, a city fairly bursting with men and women willing to supply information to the Confederacy, Pinkerton was instrumental in reducing the torrent of information flowing out of the capital to something more than a trickle. In March and April 1862, a Washington-based spy was able to furnish an accurate, if partial, list of the units with which McClellan embarked at Alexandria for the Virginia Peninsula. Four months later, in part due to the vigilance of Pinkerton and his men, spies who did succeed in getting in and out of Washington supplied information on General Pope's army that was so riddled with error as to be useless. From this point on, it is also apparent that the quantity and quality of Confederate intelligence greatly diminished until June 1863, when the frequency of intelligence reports reaching Confederate commanders again increased. By that time, Pinkerton was out, and Lafayette C. Baker had taken over counterintelligence operations in and around Washington.

What General McClellan most wanted from Pinkerton's intelligence assets behind rebel lines were estimates of troop strength. Early in the Peninsular campaign, Pinkerton's men were reporting Confederate General Joseph Johnston's troop strength at between one hundred thousand and one hundred twenty thousand. Six weeks later, as Lincoln was pressing McClellan to invade Richmond, Pinkerton's operatives estimated the strength of defending forces at two hundred thousand. Such figures were more than sufficient to daunt the Union's hyper-cautious Young Napoleon, who, Lincoln said, was chronically afflicted with a bad case of "the slows." Though, in reality, Johnston could have mustered no more than fifty thousand, and the troops deployed around Richmond numbered about one hundred thousand, McClellan was convinced that he was badly outnumbered and declined to take the offensive. He retreated from Richmond, suffered serious losses, and was relieved as commander of all the Union armies on November 7, 1862.

Pinkerton's agents in the South were not wholly ineffective. Mrs. E. H. Baker, another of the detective's "lady operatives," was dispatched to Richmond in November 1861 to learn what she could of the ironclad naval vessels and battering rams reportedly under construction at the Tredegar Iron Works. Mrs. Baker was friendly with a Captain Atwater and his family, of Richmond, with whom she stayed while she carried out her mission. Atwater agreed to take her on a tour of the iron works, but mentioned that he could not leave immediately because he was due to observe a test of a new "submarine battery." The submarine vessel was designed to approach surface ships undetected and to release two or three divers, who would plant an explosive charge below the waterline of the ship, and return to the submarine with a wire connected to the charge. After the submarine withdrew to a safe distance, the charge could be set off. Baker demurely invited herself along to witness the test. It was a success—the submarine sank a scow—and Baker made a quick sketch of the vessel, procured other information concerning it, and returned to Washington through Fredericksburg and Leonardtown.

She reported to Pinkerton, who conveyed the information to General McClellan and the secretary of the navy. Baker noted that a gray-green float, barely visible on the surface of the water and containing breathing apparatus (what a modern submariner would call a snorkel), betrayed the presence of the boat. Federal ships were instructed to be on the lookout for such a float, and within three weeks a Union vessel reported having caught the float and its air tubes in her drag rope, disabling the vessel and drowning all aboard.

It is likely that the vessel, which Baker, Pinkerton, and others feared would bring about the destruction of the Union naval blockade, would have proven no more reliable or effective than the far more famous *H. L. Hunley* of 1863, usually acknowledged as the world's first full-fledged submarine. Thirty feet long, five feet deep, and less than four feet wide, the *Hunley* was propeller driven, deriving her power from an eight-man crew who turned a crankshaft. When water was let into her ballast tanks, the *Hunley* submerged and could stay underwater for about two hours, that is, as long as the available air held out; there was no snorkel. Unlike the vessel Baker had seen, the *Hunley* towed at the end of a two-hundred-foot line a copper cylinder packed with ninety pounds of black powder. The submarine would pass under a surface ship, elevate a bit, and drag the towline against the target's keel. When the bow or keel made contact with the torpedo, the charge went off, blowing a hole in the hull.

Or so the theory went, and General P. G. T. Beauregard himself predicted that the *Hunley* would spell the end of the Union blockade. In practice, however, the submarine proved a grisly failure. She submerged handily enough but was not always so easy to raise. During one test, while she was on the surface with her hatches open, a steamer next to her got under way and, in her wake, pulled the *Hunley* over on her side, which flooded her. She sank with the loss of six crewmen—two men and the skipper were able to jump overboard before she went under. The vessel was refloated, the inventor himself, H. L. Hunley, was put in command, and he set out for practice dives. On October 15, 1863, she dived, air bubbles were seen, and she never resurfaced. Apparently a hatch had sprung a leak or had been closed improperly. All hands, including Hunley, drowned. Refloated a third time, the sight of the crew—"contorted into all sorts of horrible attitudes, some clutching candles . . . others lying in the bottom tightly grappled together"—so appalled Beauregard that he forbade the *Hunley*'s further use as a submarine. It was fitted with a spar torpedo—in effect, a hull-punching battering ram—and joined CSS *David* as a ram. On February 17, 1864, at 8:45 P.M., *Hunley* rammed the nine-gun federal sloop *Housatonic*. Pierced through to the powder magazine, the vessel was rocked by an explosion, heeled to port, and sank stern first. Five crew members were drowned, but the water in this part of Mobile Bay was so shallow that most of the *Housatonic*'s crew were able to save themselves by clinging to masts and rigging that remained above the surface as the ship settled to the bottom. The *Hunley* did not fare as well as its victim. Its hull cracked by the exploding magazine, it went down with the *Housatonic*. All hands perished.

Pinkerton was always on the lookout for good recruits, and, one morning, while he was with McClellan's army advancing up the peninsula, he came across a group of soldiers gathered around a man who amounted to a stand-up comic. He was about thirty years old and delivered his monologue in perfect deadpan, at which his audience roared. Furthermore, he stuttered prodigiously. Intrigued, Pinkerton asked a soldier who the fellow was. Stuttering Dave, he was told, the funniest man in the regiment.

Pinkerton asked to borrow David Graham, who, it turned out, was eager to venture behind rebel lines and "have s-s-some fun before I g-g-get home." In fact, Pinkerton discovered, the stuttering was an act, executed, however, with perfect naturalness. The detective disguised Graham as a peddler of notions—needles, pins, thread, and buttons—and turned him loose.

He walked right into a rebel camp.

"B-b-boys, I'm most d-d-darned hungry, w-w-w-what do you s-s-say to givin's me a b-b-b-bite to eat; d-d-dang my buttons, I'm willin' to p-p-pay for it in t-t-trade or cash."

Notwithstanding their amazement at his having gotten into camp, the soldiers shared their mess and swapped stories. While Stuttering Dave entertained the rebels, he took in the camp and

Hero of the War of 1812 and the Mexican War, Winfield Scott (1786–1866) was the septuagenarian general-in-chief of the Union army at the start of the Civil War. Although he was succeeded early in the conflict by the thirty-five-year-old George McClellan, Scott took two actions that were important for counterespionage and espionage; he devised the so-called Anaconda Plan—a naval blockade of Confederate shipping—and he hired Lafayette C. Baker, a former California vigilante, to spy on the Confederates in their capital. *(Library of Congress)*

Brigadier General John Winder, C.S.A., provost marshal of Richmond, was in charge of Confederate counter-espionage. Spies feared him, but the Union's first behind-the-lines agent, William Alvin Lloyd, operated successfully right under his nose, plying him with groceries, cash, and a twelve-hundred-dollar custom-tailored dress uniform (*not* the one in the photograph, however, which shows Winder before the war in the uniform of a U.S. Army captain). *(Library of Congress)*

The famed Civil War photographer Mathew Brady, or an assistant, took this photograph of Rose O'Neal Greenhow, the most celebrated of the Confederacy's many spies in Washington, D.C. Greenhow and her daughter, called Little Rose, are posed in front of the window to their room in the Old Capitol Prison. The boards crudely nailed across the window were intended to prevent the Rebel Rose from passing messages to couriers on the outside. *(Library of Congress)*

The Old Capitol in Washington, D.C., was built in 1815 to house Congress while the original Capitol, burned by the British during the War of 1812, was being repaired. During the Civil War, the building was converted into a military prison. After it was abandoned by Congress, but long before it became a prison, the Old Capitol served as a boardinghouse, which was run by Rose O'Neal Greenhow's aunt. Rose herself nursed South Carolina's John C. Calhoun through his final illness in 1850, when he lodged in the boardinghouse. Through one of the war's more bizarre coincidences, Rose and her daughter were imprisoned in the very room in which Calhoun had died. *(National Archives and Records Administration)*

Major General George B. McClellan, handsome and youthful, was dubbed the Young Napoleon by the Northern press. A fine administrator who was beloved by his men, McClellan nevertheless suffered from a flaw no commander can afford: He was afraid to lose. Overcautious and hesitant, he repeatedly declined to take the offensive. Early in the war he hired Allan J. Pinkerton to supply his army with intelligence concerning the enemy's number and disposition. The private detective and his "operatives" continually fed him grossly inflated estimates of Confederate troop strength, which served only to confirm the general in his chronic inaction. *(National Archives and Records Administration)*

Allan J. Pinkerton (smoking a pipe) is shown here with some of his "operatives" near Cumberland Landing, Virginia, on May 14, 1862. The detective and his men were quite effective at counterespionage—catching rebel spies—but sadly inept when it came to espionage—spying on the Confederates. *(National Archives and Records Administration)*

A portrait of Belle Boyd, "the Cleopatra of the Secession." A Northern correspondent who interviewed this celebrated Confederate spy for the *New York Tribune* could muster no more flattering description than "without being beautiful, she is very attractive. Is quite tall, has a superb figure, an intellectual face, and dressed with much taste." What she lacked in pulchritude, however, she made up for in spirit and a certain willingness to please—especially when it came to young federal officers. *(Library of Congress)*

On May 24, 1844, Samuel F. B. Morse, inventor of the telegraph, transmitted the world's first message over a line strung from Baltimore to Washington: "What hath God wrought!" Within a decade, 23,000 miles of telegraph lines networked across the nation, and during the Civil War, both armies (but especially the Union) ran thousands of miles more. While much military intelligence was transmitted over the lines, spies seemed to have made surprisingly little use of the telegraph, trusting to secret couriers instead. *(National Archives and Records Administration)*

Both the Union and Confederate armies used signal towers like this one, photographed in 1864 at Cobb's Hill, near New Market, Virginia, to transmit the lantern and flag semaphore signals that were critical to coordinating troop movements, relaying commands, *and* conveying intelligence. During the Civil War, intelligence, insofar as it struggled to gain official military status, was largely the stepchild of the signal corps or signal service. The Confederate Army had a department that was sometimes (but not consistently) called the Signal Bureau and Secret Service, headed by Major William Norris, whose original mission had been to establish signal stations on the Virginia Peninsula and across the James River. Soon, Norris's mission expanded from the transmission of intelligence to the gathering of intelligence as well. *(National Archives and Records Administration)*

Neither the Union nor the Confederate army gave much organized, official support to spies, but commanders on both sides did believe in reconnaissance and made extensive use of scouts and cavalry to gather information. In addition, the Union Army experimented with observation balloons and established a balloon corps. Balloons, like the *Intrepid*, shown here being inflated at the Battle of Fair Oaks, Virginia, in May 1862, remained tethered to the ground, while their landlinks included telegraph wires that allowed the aerial observers to transmit details about enemy position and movement. The Confederates, sufficiently impressed with the Union's balloons to attempt a few ascents of their own, lacked the technology to develop a regular aerial corps. *(National Archives and Records Administration)*

Alexander Gardner photographed scouts and guides serving with the Union's Army of the Potomac at Berlin, Maryland, in October 1862. Many scouts were uniformed and, therefore, were regarded as reconnaissance personnel rather than spies. However, many others were civilians, in civilian clothing, hired to undertake missions that ranged from observation to behind-the-lines infiltration. Thus the distinctions among "scouts," "guides," and "spies" were often obscured. For accounting purposes, spies were generally listed as scouts or guides on military rosters and ledger books. While most Civil War-era commanders admitted a need for *scouts* and *guides,* few were willing openly to admit that they employed *spies. (National Archives and Records Administration)*

Newspapers sent their reporters into the field to cover the war in extensive detail. Neither the North nor the South was able to regulate press coverage, and censorship was unheard of. The result was that newspaper reports, which regularly published details of troop strength and disposition as well as strategy, were often a commander's most valuable source of intelligence about the enemy. Southern military leaders, in particular, saw to it that a steady and timely supply of Northern newspapers reached them. The photograph shows a *New York Herald Tribune* field wagon with correspondents. *(National Archives and Records Administration)*

Elizabeth Van Lew, the Union's most effective spy in Richmond, freed her family's slaves, including Mary Elizabeth Bowser, whom she sent North for an education then asked back to Richmond, where Miss Van Lew got her a job as servant in Jefferson Davis's wartime home, the so-called White House of the Confederacy. Bowser faithfully reported all that she saw and heard there. *(National Archives and Records Administration)*

This ruined railroad bridge at Fredericksburg, Virginia, was photographed in April 1863 by Union Captain A. J. Russell. The figures on the far side are soldiers of Barksdale's Mississippi Brigade, which saw heavy fighting at Fredericksburg. It is said that this is the only wartime picture of Confederate soldiers taken by a Union photographer. Samuel Ruth, superintendent of transportation for the Richmond, Fredericksburg & Potomac Railroad, was a Union sympathizer who became a member of Elizabeth Van Lew's "Richmond Ring" of Union spies. Ruth used his position with great skill to sabotage Confederate rail transportation, seeing to it that repairs to this bridge and other crucial links to Richmond were delayed as long as possible. *(Library of Congress)*

Pauline Cushman, a beautiful actress of Creole descent, was "expelled" by Federal officials from Nashville as a dangerous secessionist. She was then eagerly embraced by the Confederates, who were unaware that she was actually a double agent whose expulsion was staged for the purpose of ingratiating her with the rebels. For the Union, she procured important military maps and drawings of fortifications until, in the last year of the war, soldiers of Braxton Bragg's command arrested her. Sentenced to be hanged, she was saved only by the timely arrival of Federal troops. *(Library of Congress)*

George H. Sharpe, seated left, organized the Bureau of Military Information, the closest thing the Union Army had to an official intelligence service. However, like its Confederate counterpart, the Signal Bureau and Secret Service, it failed to coordinate spotty intelligence efforts by disparate groups who answered to various lower-echelon commanders. *(Library of Congress)*

Miss Elizabeth Van Lew, known to her Richmond neighbors as "Crazy Bet" and dismissed by them as a harmless, if annoying and eccentric spinster, was, in the words of George H. Sharpe, "for a long, long time . . . all that was left of the power of the United States government in Richmond." Sharpe attributed to her work the bulk of intelligence gathered during 1864–65. *(Valentine Museum)*

James M. Mason was one of a small legion of Confederate diplomats and intriguers sent to England to persuade that nation's government to recognize the Confederacy as a sovereign state. Europe was the scene of intense covert activity during the Civil War, as North and South jockeyed for diplomatic advantages and sought to buy up foreign arms. When Mason and his fellow Confederate agent, John Slidell, were arrested on the high seas by a Union naval commander, who brazenly boarded the British steamer *Trent* on November 8, 1861, the United States and Great Britain hovered precariously close to the brink of war. *(National Archives and Records Administration)*

Georgia-born James D. Bulloch had been a sailor since age sixteen, when he joined the U.S. Navy. After fourteen years of service, Bulloch had attained nothing beyond the rank of lieutenant. He resigned his commission in 1853 to become skipper of a commercial mail steamer between New York and New Orleans. Bulloch lived near New York City, where his half-sister was married to Theodore Roosevelt, Sr., father of the future twenty-sixth president of the United States. But, when the war broke out, there was no question where Bulloch's allegiance lay. Confederate Secretary of the Navy Stephen R. Mallory sent Bulloch to England to buy or commission to be built six commerce raiders, arm them, and recruit the crews to man them. *(Collection of G. J. A. O'Toole)*

Coolly intellectual and ultra-urbane, Henry S. Sanford was officially United States minister to Belgium. In fact, Secretary of State William Seward put Sanford at the center of a network of spies and paid informants. His mission was, through means covert as well as diplomatic, to counteract Confederate efforts to enlist the political and material support of European nations in its war against the Union. Sanford's most formidable opponent was James D. Bulloch. *(Library of Congress)*

The great Italian patriot and nationalist Giuseppe Garibaldi was the focus of two bizarre, half-baked, and badly botched diplomatic schemes to enlist him into the cause of the Union. Abraham Lincoln was prepared to make him a major general, but Garibaldi wanted nothing less than supreme command of the Union army and the authority to emancipate the slaves. On these points negotiations broke down, and the "Washington of Italy" remained in his homeland. *(Library of Congress)*

On Saturday, July 11, 1863, conscription commenced in New York City. On the following Monday, a week of rioting broke out. These "Draft Riots" quickly took on racial overtones as Irish laborers, fearful that emancipated slaves would usurp their jobs, turned their wrath against the city's African Americans. On July 14, the Colored Orphan Asylum at Fifth Avenue and 46th Street was set ablaze, the rioters cheering the flames. A small band of Confederate agents attempted, with little success, to organize the New York Draft Riot—and others that broke out across the country—into full-scale rebellion. *(Library of Congress)*

Major General Judson Kilpatrick was a fearless commander—especially where the lives of his men were concerned. His subordinates dubbed him "Kilcavalry," and William Tecumseh Sherman simply called him "a hell of a damned fool." With the enthusiastic approval of Abraham Lincoln, Kilpatrick led an unsuccessful guerrilla-style raid on Richmond. Papers found on his subordinate, Colonel Ulric Dahlgren, revealed that the assassination of Jefferson Davis was part of the mission. Outraged Confederates published the papers, to the embarrassment of Northern officials, who denied any knowledge of an assassination plot. *(Library of Congress)*

Ulric Dahlgren, son of Union Rear Admiral John A. Dahlgren, joined the army and was commissioned a captain at age eighteen. (He is pictured here, standing, in the uniform of that rank.) On July 6, 1863, in the aftermath of Gettysburg, Captain Dahlgren was shot in the foot at Boonsboro. His leg was amputated above the knee three days later. During his convalescence, Dahlgren was jumped in rank to colonel—at twenty-one the youngest man to hold that rank in the Union army. Wooden leg and all, he eagerly joined Judson Kilpatrick's raid on Richmond. The operation went sour, Dahlgren was killed, and papers ordering the assassination of Jefferson Davis were found on his body. Confederates buried Dahlgren in an unmarked grave as a gesture of contempt, but Richmond's Union underground "resurrected" the young officer's body, reburied it, then saw to its safe return to Admiral Dahlgren at the end of the war. *(Library of Congress)*

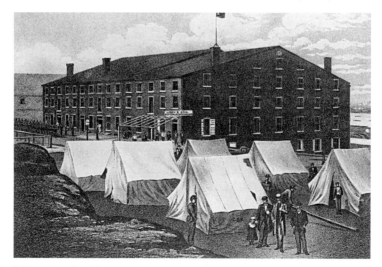

Before the Civil War, this building on the James River in Richmond was the warehouse of Libby and Sons, ship chandlers. During the war, it was converted into a prison (for officers only), which quickly acquired a reputation as a hellhole second only to the prison at Andersonville, Georgia. The liberation of Libby Prison was ostensibly the principal object of the ill-fated Kilpatrick-Dahlgren raid on the Confederate capital. *(Library of Congress)*

The Confederacy had two Virginia prisons called Castle Thunder, one in Petersburg and this one in Richmond. A converted tobacco warehouse, it was the counterpart of the Union's Old Capitol Prison, a place for political prisoners, including those charged with treason and espionage. Inmates were reportedly treated harshly here and with gratuitous cruelty. After the fall of Richmond, Union authorities used Castle Thunder to hold Confederate officers and men charged with war crimes. *(Library of Congress)*

Mary Surratt's Washington, D.C., boardinghouse sheltered any number of Confederate spies and couriers during the war. Her son John was a longtime Confederate courier. It was under Mrs. Surratt's roof that John Wilkes Booth hatched his plot to kidnap Abraham Lincoln, and when that scheme failed, the actor decided on assassination. Mrs. Surratt was hanged, along with Louis T. Powell (alias Lewis Paine), David E. Herold, and George A. Atzerodt, on July 7, 1865. *(Library of Congress)*

John H. Surratt was the only one of John Wilkes Booth's associates who had any official connection to the Confederate "secret service." He was a courier, his family's Maryland tavern served as a safe house for other couriers, and his mother's Washington boardinghouse harbored Confederate agents and sympathizers. Surratt schemed with Booth to kidnap Lincoln. After the assassination, he fled to Europe and became, of all things, a papal guard. He was extradited to the United States, stood trial for conspiracy, but was acquitted. His mother, Mary E. Surratt, was not so lucky. *(Library of Congress)*

Although many contemporary Northerners and later historians attempted to paint John Wilkes Booth as part of a grand conspiracy, he was, as he wrote in a letter to his sister, "A confederate doing duty upon his own responsibility." While the assassination of Abraham Lincoln—the most sinister covert act of the Civil War—almost certainly carried no sanction from the Confederate government, Booth, in his getaway, did make use of the South's well-developed avenues of secret communication and travel in and out of Washington, D. C. *(Library of Congress)*

The "Navy Yard Bridge," over which John Wilkes Booth and his accomplice, David Herold, escaped into Maryland on their way to Surratt's tavern after the assassination of Abraham Lincoln. *(National Archives and Records Administration)*

Sergeant Boston Corbett, the man who claimed to have shot John Wilkes Booth in a Virginia tobacco barn. *(National Archives and Records Administration)*

Early in the war, Lafayette C. Baker, a former vigilante from the California gold fields, walked into the office of Winfield Scott, the Union army's general-in-chief, and volunteered himself as a spy. Scott sent him to Richmond, where, after a brush with Jefferson Davis himself, he returned to Washington and eventually became head of an agency he christened the National Detective Police. A notorious self-promoter who was censured late in his career for having illegally spied on Andrew Johnson during the impeachment proceedings against him, Baker brought the manhunt for John Wilkes Booth to a successful conclusion. *(Library of Congress)*

made the customary estimates of troop strength. At one point, a company commander suggested that he enlist.

"C-Captain, I d-d-don't think you would want me; I t-t-tried t-to enlist s-s-s-sometime ago, b-b-b-but the d-d-doctor said, m-my f-f-fits and stuttering b-b-being so b-b-bad, he c-c-couldn't p-p-pass me."

Mere reconnaissance wasn't enough for Stuttering Dave. Seeing how the ammunition was stored in wagons, he decided to set fire to it by laying a train of powder from the wagons, running a distance, and touching it off like a fuse. He bided his time until midnight and set to work. Amid flash, flame, smoke, and thunder, Stuttering Dave ran back to the Union lines.

In fairness to the rebels, the federals could be just as credulous in their reception of spies masquerading as what enlightened people of the era called "mental defectives" and plainer folk called "simple-minded." Dr. William Passmore was an Englishman by birth but a Confederate by conviction. He got himself up as an imbecilic itinerant peddler and wheeled a produce cart all through General Ambrose Burnside's camp during several weeks preceding the Battle of Fredericksburg on December 13, 1862. Bearing a pass signed by the general himself, he sold his goods directly to Yankee soldiers and officers, who were apparently quite garrulous in his presence. After all, what harm could an addle-pated pushcart vendor do?

If Stuttering Dave Graham was a born entertainer, George Curtis, in Pinkerton's estimation, was a born detective. A New Yorker, Curtis served in an infantry regiment of that state until Pinkerton obtained his discharge for the purpose of his joining the secret service. In April 1862, the operative sailed down the Potomac in McClellan's steamer *Commodore*, landing at Old Point Comfort. From here he made his way to Richmond. Halted by pickets at the outskirts of the city, Curtis was forthright, telling them his name, asking to see their commander, General Hill, and refusing to take no for an answer. (Pinkerton's narrative does not say whether this was Ambrose Powell Hill or Daniel Harvey Hill, both of whom were serving in the defense of Richmond).

The general asked Curtis what he wanted.

"In the first place, I spoke falsely to your pickets when I told them

I was from Norfolk. My name is Curtis, and I am from Washington. As to my business, I deal in what the Yankees are pleased to term contraband goods; yet I don't see how gun-caps, ammunition of all kinds, and quinine should be considered contraband, for the simple reason that I, as a dealer, find a better market South than North for my goods. My desire is to get through to Richmond, where I hope to be able to effect contracts, with Secretary [of War Judah] Benjamin, to furnish my goods to the Confederate government."

Hill was skeptical. How did you get through the Union lines? he asked. Curtis replied with no elaborately fabricated story, but told the truth:

"I came down on the 'Commodore,' General McClellan's boat, three days ago."

Hill not only gave Curtis a pass to Richmond, but also letters to carry to the city. The detective would deliver the messages, of course, but not without reading them first. Yet the intelligence payoff was bigger than might first appear. Posing as a merchant, Curtis soon became friendly with a man named Mr. Leroy, who confessed that he was a dealer in contraband. Curtis, naturally, reciprocated the confidence, and, in the course of a long stroll through the streets of Richmond, the two formulated a plan of partnership.

Within a week, it became apparent to Curtis that the contraband merchants not only enjoyed a profitable trade supplying the Confederate forces with goods, but that they also furnished a steady supply of military intelligence. Just how this was accomplished, Mr. Leroy soon disclosed to him.

"Why," he said, "haven't you heard of the subterranean headquarters?"

No, Curtis replied, he had not.

"Then come along with me. I ought to have told you about this before, as it is intimately connected with our business."

Leroy took the detective to a large and elegantly furnished room on the third floor of a hotel. A number of men were reading or writing at tables.

"Here," Leroy said, "are the subterranean headquarters, although they are above the top of the ground instead of beneath it. I need not tell you that the name is given as much to mislead as for any other purpose."

Leroy went on to explain that the subterranean headquarters functioned as a bureau of intelligence managed in part by the government and in part by merchants in Richmond and in Baltimore. It served the related purposes of gathering intelligence and ensuring that needed contraband goods got through from Baltimore. Leroy said that the headquarters employed some fifty couriers and agents. Leroy asked Curtis to travel to Yorktown, then under siege by McClellan, and deliver some dispatches from the subterranean headquarters to General John Magruder. Curtis complied, but made a detour to the Union camp, where he delivered the dispatches to Pinkerton's field superintendent. Subsequently, Pinkerton used Curtis as a double agent, intercepting and copying the dispatches he carried from the subterranean headquarters and sending the originals on to their intended destination. ("I concluded," Pinkerton later wrote, "that if the information intended for the rebels could first be had by us, after that, they were welcome to all the benefit they might derive from them"). Pinkerton does not specify how long Curtis was active as a double agent. It could not have been long, for Pinkerton's days as an intelligence officer were by this time numbered. One would conclude that, positioned as he was, Curtis was a valuable asset. Significantly, although he operated in Richmond and was, therefore, nominally an *intelligence* operative, his actual mission, intercepting Confederate intelligence regarding Union forces, was a function of *counterintelligence*, the one job at which Pinkerton's department excelled.

From nearly the beginning of the war through 1862, Allan Pinkerton, with his small band of detectives, directly in the employ of General George B. McClellan, was the closest the United States government came to having an official department of intelligence. Beginning in August 1861, Lafayette C. Baker ran intelligence—or, more frequently, counterintelligence—operations at the behest of General Winfield Scott and Secretary of State Seward, who had organized an unofficial "Treason Bureau." After Scott's retirement, Baker reported to Secretary of War Edwin Stanton. Pinkerton's department and Baker's operated simultaneously from August 1861 to January

1863, by which time, after McClellan's fall from power, Pinkerton had left Washington. Not only was no attempt made to coordinate the two departments, on at least two occasions members of one organization were under the surveillance of or arrested by members of the other.

Early in 1863, acting on orders from the army's new general in chief, Fightin' Joe Hooker, Brigadier General Marsena R. Patrick, provost marshal general, created a Bureau of Military Information under the command of Colonel George H. Sharpe, assisted by Captain John McEntree and John C. Babcock, a civilian. Its function was to organize the loose array of spies, scouts, and couriers attached to the army. Whereas Pinkerton had no more than eleven operatives in Washington, and Baker commanded about thirty men, Sharpe administered approximately two hundred spies and scouts, whom the official payroll lumped together as "guides." The bureau by no means supplanted the prerogative of individual field commanders to hire their own spies and assign their own scouts, but it was a step toward coordinating intelligence-gathering activities and, even more important, interpreting intelligence data in a meaningful and timely manner.

The need for such interpretation should have been made apparent to both armies by dozens of incidents. The best known, however, is the so-called "Lost Order Episode," which involved what *should* have been the single most important intelligence find of the war. On September 13, 1862, two ordinary soldiers of an Indiana regiment stumbled across three cigars—a lucky day for them. Wrapped around the cigars was a piece of paper: Robert E. Lee's "Special Order No. 191," which gave in detail his plan of operations in western Maryland. Doubtless, the soldiers enjoyed the cigars, but they also had the presence of mind and sense of duty to deliver the document to their superior officer. Eventually, it did find its way on up to General McClellan. Whether through delay in interpreting the document, in getting it to McClellan, or through the Young Napoleon's customary unwillingness to take decisive action, the intelligence, significant as it was, served no tactical purpose. It simply was not exploited.

Sharpe worked to streamline the transmission of intelligence. Taking as his code name "Colonel Streight," he attempted to audit all information personally, intelligence gathered not only from spies, but from scouts, cavalry detachments (the traditional agents of forward reconnaissance), newspapers, prisoners of war, and— that most novel means of Civil War observation—balloonists. While the War Department's *War of the Rebellion: A Compilation of the Official Records of the Union and Confederate States Armies* contains a great deal of raw data gathered by men under the command of the Bureau of Military Intelligence, details of the bureau's actual operation are few and far between. That it was an effective intelligence-gathering organization is attested by Robert E. Lee's biographer, Douglas Southall Freeman, who stated, "For the first time on Virginia soil . . . the federals knew more of what was happening on the south side of the Rappahannock than Lee knew of what was taking place north of the river." A resident spy reporting to the bureau located a gap in Lee's line at the Battle of Chancellorsville on May 2–4, 1863, that made it possible for Hooker to surprise the enemy by marching to the Confederate rear. Moreover, whereas estimates of troop strength gathered under Pinkerton had been in error by 100 percent or more, Hooker, at Chancellorsville, was supplied by a Richmond-based agent with estimates accurate to within one-quarter of 1 percent. At Chancellorsville, bureau counterintelligence also performed brilliantly, preventing Lee from observing Hooker's complex maneuvering. In despair at the lack of information reaching him, the Confederate commander wrote to Jefferson Davis, "I have no means of ascertaining the truth." Provost Marshal Marsena Patrick crowed, "the rebels have not the slightest idea what we are about." Not all of the Confederates' troubles were due to the actions of the bureau. A Confederate courier did reach Richmond with some vital intelligence, but, in one of those slapstick moments that characterize so much of Civil War espionage, he had forgotten the key to the cipher.

Unfortunately, General Hooker failed to exploit the rich intelligence he had been furnished. Despite initial surprise and dearth of information, Lee was able to mount a devastating attack on Hooker's right flank. The Union commander had been alerted to Lee's movements, but he did not act in time. Chancellorsville ended in federal defeat—though at an exceptionally high cost to the Confederates.

The War Between the Spies

At Gettysburg between June 27 and July 4, 1863, General George G. Meade put to far better use intelligence gathered by bureau men from Confederate prisoners of war. Gettysburg was pivotal in every sense. It seemed to mark the Union's new resolve to win a war that had so far offered mainly defeat and heartbreak, and it also turned on Meade's critical decision to press the attack. During a lull in the campaign—for the engagement was too long to be called a battle—Meade, concerned that the Confederates were about to mount an offensive, had to decide whether or not to withdraw. Prisoner interrogation, properly interpreted, revealed that the rebel forces were far more worn down than the federals. Meade stood his ground and turned what could have been a bloody draw into a victory that eventually pushed the Confederate army back into Virginia.

The Bureau of Military Intelligence did not carry out its work unchallenged. The indefatigable Lafayette C. Baker, whose men had occasionally stumbled over Pinkerton's operatives, repeatedly attempted to usurp what Provost Marshal Patrick saw as the bureau's prerogatives. One modern historian claims that Patrick and Baker engaged in a "running feud" throughout the duration of the war, and it is a fact that Patrick issued an order stating that any civilian visiting the army and bearing a pass from Lafayette C. Baker was summarily to be sent back to Washington. And even Meade, having failed fully to capitalize on Gettysburg by declining to pursue the retreating rebel forces, turned bitter against the bureau. In the aftermath of the campaign, he used the bureau men detailed to him not as valuable intelligence officers, but as military policemen. Generals Patrick and Meade argued with one another, and Meade called the bureau "good for nothing" and inferior to the cavalry as an instrument of intelligence gathering.

When Ulysses S. Grant became general in chief of all the Union armies in March 1864, the Bureau of Military Intelligence was again put on a solid footing. There is good evidence that, by war's end, even the activities of Elizabeth Van Lew and her so-called "Richmond Ring" were under bureau direction. In the West, however, the authority of the bureau was felt far less. Most likely, this was a function of geography rather than military politics. For the war in the West was very different from that in the East. No great cities were lost or won, and no decisive strategic ends were achieved. Nevertheless, men fought, and men died—and intelligence was gathered.

In the West, Grant chiefly depended for intelligence on Grenville Mellon Dodge, the Massachusetts-born Iowa engineer who would, after the war, mastermind the construction of the Union Pacific Railroad. Dodge had worked in intelligence as early as 1861, when General John C. Frémont, ever zealous to quash rebel activity in the areas under his command, assigned Dodge to track down rumors of guerrillas and sabotage. Grant put Dodge's talents to more effective use coordinating a loose network of frontier scouts and spies. Dodge also drew on his engineering background to develop a new method of estimating troops strength by calculating the area a given body of soldiers occupied on some well-defined space, like a road. He kept minutely detailed topographical maps—the kind he would later use to build the transcontinental railroad—and was so meticulous in his record keeping that, three years after the war, when a War Department official demanded from Dodge an itemized accounting of his expenditures for secret service activities, he referred the official to a document that had costs for 1863–65 figured literally to the penny: $17,099.95. Such precision is the more amazing given the nature of the intelligence assets Dodge exploited—mostly locals, including escaped slaves. After organizing the First Tennessee Cavalry, made up of citizens loyal to the Union, he pressed the men to recruit their relatives as spies. Dodge commanded about one hundred agents, jealously guarding their identities by replacing their names with code numbers. Even among headquarters staff members, agents were referred to by number rather than name. Despite these precautions and Dodge's injunction to avoid unnecessary heroics, at least half of his agents were captured or executed.

(One of them saved his own life by joining the Confederate army. He served so well that he was promoted to first sergeant, but, as soon as he could, he slipped back over the Union lines and, still attired in his rebel uniform, reported to Dodge.)

Typical of the local talent Dodge recruited was Philip Henson, a thirty-five-year-old Mississippian. Although all his family members were confirmed Confederates, Henson was a Union man, who, however, had the sense to keep his sentiments to himself until he could do something about them. When the Union army penetrated northern Mississippi, Henson volunteered for undercover work. Given his background and the fact that he seemed slow—even stupid—no one would suspect him of espionage. He simply rode into the Confederate camp, strolled in his shuffling manner up to General Sterling Price's headquarters, and struck up a drawling conversation with the sentries there. He asked them what was up, and they, obligingly enough, told him. Then the spy waved goodbye, ambled slowly to his horse, rode off, and made a complete report at Union headquarters. Later, when Dodge needed intelligence from Vicksburg, because the federals were closing in on the important Mississippi River town at the beginning of 1863, he again called on Henson. Instead of skulking about, Henson asked his family's neighbor if he wanted to visit his sons who were serving with the Confederate army at the Vicksburg fortress. Henson even had a horse to lend, and the neighbor was more than happy to go. When pickets challenged them, all the pair had to say is that they were visiting "our boys" at Vicksburg. Henson was still faced with the problem of how to circulate through the ranks in order to get a thorough firsthand view of the town, its fortification, and the strength and disposition of the troops. He located General John C. Pemberton and started telling him how badly the federals were treating Southerners in occupied territory. This gave Pemberton an idea. He asked Henson to make a circuit of the town's fortified perimeter and tell this story to the troops. It would let them know what they were fighting for—to protect their families, women, and children. And it gave Henson just the license he needed to gather all the information Grant would need as he laid siege to the town.

The nearest thing to a rebel counterpart of the Bureau of Military Information was, of course, the Confederate Signal Service, headed by Major William Norris. An 1840 graduate of Yale, Maryland-born Norris practiced law in New Orleans until 1849, when the lure of gold took him to California. Once there, however, instead of prospecting, he accepted an appointment as judge advocate to the U.S. Pacific Squadron, which gave him experience with military police activities. He sailed to Valparaiso, Chile, in 1851, where he married the daughter of a former U.S. consul and returned to the United States, settling at the family estate, Brookland, northwest of Baltimore. In 1858, this lawyer and administrator of military justice became president of an enterprise called the Baltimore Mechanical Bakery, a state-of-the-art facility in which Norris apparently took much pride.

His business career was not destined to last long. On April 27, 1861, a pro-Confederate organization called the Maryland Chasseurs held a drill and demonstration in Baltimore. One of their members received an announcement of the event that bore a handwritten note: "Can you not bring Mr. Norris with you?" Within a few weeks, Norris transported himself, his wife, and five children to Richmond. On July 18, 1861, General John Magruder authorized Norris to establish a system of signals on the Virginia Peninsula and across the James River. By May of 1862, Captain Norris was officially made Magruder's signal officer, and on July 31 he was appointed chief of the newly created Confederate States Army Signal Corps.

Originally, the Signal Corps was a very small force consisting of ten officers and ten sergeants, later increased to one major, Norris (who was promoted from captain), ten first and second lieutenants, and a total of thirty sergeants. In addition, privates were detailed to the service as required. When the signal corpsmen were not engaged in signal duty, they were often detailed to observe the enemy or to act as scouts and couriers. In this way, the mission of the Signal Corps—variously called the Signal Bureau, Signal Service, and Signal and Secret Service Bureau—came to include espionage. From his Richmond office, first located on Belvin's Block on Fourteenth Street between Main and Franklin, then moved to the south side of Bank Street, between Ninth and Tenth, Norris commanded an agency responsible for, as he himself summarized it:

(1) management of the entire signal corps and cipher system of the Confederate States Army—therein is included also
  (a) manufacture and collection of all signal apparatus and stores;
  (b) manufacture, collection and distribution of all cipher apparatus

(2) management and supplying of secret lines of communication on the Potomac
(3) translation of cipher messages received or sent by the War Department, heads of bureaus, or officers of the army
(4) provide transportation across the Potomac for agents, scouts and others passing from and to Baltimore and Washington
(5) observing and reporting all movements of the enemy on the Potomac
(6) procuring files of the latest Northern newspaper for the Executive Department
(7) obtaining books, "small packages," etc. for heads of bureaus
(8) forwarding letters from the War or State Department to agents, commissioners, etc. in foreign countries.

By January 1863, the service was fully operational. Not that it was to be immune from the kind of administrative rivalry that also afflicted the various federal secret service operations. In 1863, an Independent Signal Corps was established, with headquarters at Petersburg, Virginia. It was commanded by James F. Milligan, a Confederate army captain with a naval background. He had served in the U.S. Navy during the Mexican War, resigned in 1850 to join the revenue service, then, when Virginia seceded, accepted a commission as lieutenant in the Virginia State Navy. When he was skipper of CSS *Empire,* plying the waters near Norfolk, Milligan set up a system of land signals in the Norfolk area and soon transferred to the army, where he was commissioned a captain and made signal officer of the Department of Norfolk. Although Milligan's service cooperated with Norris's, a rivalry—one historian calls it a feud—developed between the two men and lasted for the war's duration. On May 31, 1863, Lieutenant R. A. Forbes, Second Company, Independent Signal Corps, accused Norris of drunkenness while aboard a flag-of-truce boat and of revealing the Confederate Signal Corps cipher alphabet. A court of inquiry, held on July 29 to August 15, fully exonerated Norris, calling the charges "loosely made without due care and investigation."

Despite intramural squabbles, the Signal and Secret Service brilliantly administered the Secret Line, the trans-Potomac intelligence courier system that was superior to anything the federals had at least until very late in the war. Beyond the courier system, the activities of the service are so obscure that, well into the twentieth century, numerous historians have denied that the Confederates ever had any "secret service." However, it is apparent that Signal and Secret Service activities extended to sabotage. It was a lieutenant attached to Norris's command, J. L. Doggett, who arranged a guide for a raiding party, led by Confederate naval lieutenant John Taylor, which burned and sank the USS *Alleghanian* in Chesapeake Bay, off the mouth of the Rappahannock on October 28, 1862. Captain E. Pliny Bryan, one of the first men to volunteer for secret service with the Signal Corps, became a pioneer in the development of torpedoes and mines. And at least one Signal and Secret Service officer, Lieutenant James Carey, a Baltimorean, was captured—in civilian clothes—as a spy.

Norris's administration of the Secret Line brought his service into contact with at least two agents of the British government, Colonel Arthur James Lyon Fremantle, of Her Majesty's Coldstream Guards, and Fitzgerald Ross, as well as with some of the Confederacy's best-known spies and saboteurs, who may or may not have been officially attached to the service. These included Thomas N. Conrad and Captain Thomas H. Hines, architect of the ill-fated Northwest Conspiracy. The irrepressible Frank Stringfellow was also officially commissioned a lieutenant in the Signal Corps. Norris's command even extended to a name made infamous in the aftermath of the Lincoln assassination. John H. Surratt, whose mother was hanged as a conspirator in the president's death, served under the major as a courier.

In the fall and winter of 1864–65, the Confederate Congress debated at least two bills providing for the establishment of a "Bureau of Special and Secret Service," "special service" being one of the many contemporary euphemisms for espionage. Given the prevailing amateurishness of most Civil War intelligence work, the bill was quite extraordinary, projecting the bureau as an agency not only to recruit and manage spies, but to engage in many aspects of unconventional warfare, including the development of new weaponry. While the rebels' Congress was considering matters of intelligence, it seems that the executive branch of the Confederate government was taking its own steps to centralize current secret service activities. Evidence suggests that, during the winter of

1864–65, the State Department took over the Secret Line and may also have assumed control of other secret service activities. At war's end it was Judah P. Benjamin, then secretary of state, who personally destroyed the department's secret service records.

As for Norris, he was captured in the fall of Richmond and held for a time on suspicion of having stolen money belonging to Union prisoners. He was soon cleared of the charges and, on June 30, 1865, took an oath of allegiance to the United States. After a trip to New York, he settled with his family at Brookland. He wrote to a former comrade-at-arms that "I am less & less satisfied & more loathe the Yankees," and he contemplated moving to Chile in order to introduce the Confederate signal system to the Chilean army; he had been promised the rank of colonel. It is doubtful that he ever went. Certainly, he was still in Maryland at the end of 1866, when he wrote a letter to the lawyer defending John H. Surratt, who had been accused of complicity in the conspiracy to assassinate President Lincoln. In the letter, Norris stated that Surratt had served him as a courier, but that he had no role in any Confederate secret service conspiracy against Abraham Lincoln. In 1870 and again in 1875, Norris entertained the possibility of becoming a signal officer in the Egyptian army, but the job fell through. In the 1870s and 1880s, we know Norris lectured on the battle of the *Monitor* and *Merrimack,* publishing an eyewitness account of the fight in 1874. He also lectured during the same period on the Confederate secret service. In 1890, Brookland was destroyed by fire, and, six years later, while he was watching workmen rebuilding his house, the seventy-six-year-old former head of the Confederate Signal and Secret Service suffered a fatal stroke.

CHAPTER TEN

CHIEF OF THE NATIONAL DETECTIVE POLICE

A s the star of Allan J. Pinkerton had risen with the fortunes of George B. McClellan, so it fell with his. On November 7, 1862, the Young Napoleon, having failed to beat Lee to Richmond after the costly Antietam campaign and, thereby, having lost his chance to take that city, received a telegram from Major General Henry Wager Halleck:

Major General McClellan, *Commanding, &c.:*

General: On receipt of the order of the President, sent herewith, you will immediately turn over your command to Major General Burnside, and repair to Trenton, N.J., reporting, on your arrival at that place, by telegraph, for further orders.

Very respectfully, your obedient servant.

Pinkerton left Washington, too, and the business of espionage proper. He continued to serve the Union, however, by ferreting out fraud and corruption—a rich field for police work during the war.

Pinkerton's appointment as a government detective had never been made official at a very high level. He had been hired by his friend and associate, George McClellan, and it was Pinkerton himself who dubbed his operation the "secret service." Lafayette C. Baker, putting together a parallel, sometimes rival, never cooperative organization about a year later, also called his organization the

175

"secret service," though he later rechristened it the National Detective Police. Like Pinkerton's appointment, Baker's was not a function of any official agency. As McClellan had hired Pinkerton, General Winfield Scott hired Baker. There was one significant difference: when Pinkerton was hired, he was a nationally famous private detective; Baker just walked into General Scott's office and asked for a job.

Baker had been born in Stafford, New York, on October 13, 1826. His great-grandfather was Remember Baker, one of Ethan Allen's Green Mountain Boys and a tough backwoodsman, who endured numerous Indian depredations, including the amputation of his toes. When Lafayette Baker was thirteen, his family moved to the vicinity of Lansing, Michigan, and during the years 1848 to 1860, he wandered through New York, Philadelphia, and, finally, California, where he set up, during the Gold Rush days of San Francisco, as a jack of all trades—among which, it was rumored, was the profession of claim jumping. By the mid 1850s, Mormon leader and entrepreneur Sam Brannon joined other prominent San Franciscans, including future governor Leland Stanford, in organizing a Committee of Vigilance to do the job that the city's inept and corrupt police force consistently failed to do. By 1856, there had come into being an army of some two thousand vigilantes, each known by an assigned number. Baker was number 208.

That was the extent of his experience as a "detective" when, in April 1861, he wandered into Willard's Hotel, Washington, D.C., and engaged General Hiram Walbridge of New York and William D. Kelley of Philadelphia in a conversation about the perilous state of the nation.

As the always self-promoting Baker recalled it, General Walbridge announced, "you are the man of all others to go into this secret service; you have the ability and courage." Shortly thereafter, Congressman Kelley and George W. Wright, congressman from California, escorted Baker to Scott's office. Since Baker's father had fought under the general during the War of 1812, Baker was introduced as the son of "an old friend, with discretion, ability, and courage to do what was necessary." Scott and Baker spoke privately, and the general arranged another interview for the following day. On that occasion, a little more than three months before the first

Battle of Bull Run, Scott confided that he had been unable to obtain definite intelligence concerning rebel forces at Manassas. It had not been for lack of trying; of five men who had been sent to Richmond, two were confirmed dead, and the rest were presumed captured. "Young man," Old Fuss and Feathers concluded, "if you have judgment and discretion, you can be of great service to the country."

Baker did not set off for Richmond at once. He traveled first to New York "to arrange unsettled affairs" and returned to Washington at the end of June. When Baker finally agreed to make the hazardous trek into Dixie, General Scott took from his vest pocket "ten double eagles of coin" and wished him the best of luck.

On July 11, just ten days before first Bull Run, while Rose Greenhow was already actively acquiring intelligence for General Beauregard, Baker took off, his mission to assess the disposition and strength of Confederate forces in and around Richmond as well as along the way. Given the sievelike condition of Union security, Scott decided that no one in the Federal lines should be informed of Baker's mission. Scott's decision meant that the spy's first task was to penetrate *friendly* forces. Baker needed a plausible cover. He went to a "daguerrean establishment" and bought at the bargain price of four dollars an old box that had once contained a camera. He slung it across his back and, thus "disguised" as one of numerous itinerant photographers then making a living capturing early scenes of the war, set across the river to Alexandria, Virginia.

Just four miles outside of Washington he came upon the Second Maine Regiment and called on the colonel, who asked him to "take a view of the camp, including his tent and the principal officers standing in the foreground." Baker said he would oblige, had a good dinner compliments of the colonel, and headed for the hills, box in hand. He told the officer that he would first take to the high country to get an overall view of the camp and then return to photograph headquarters.

Of course, he did not return, but went forth "toward the heart of rebeldom." Baker believed that he had crossed the federal lines, but was shocked to hear a shouted, "Who goes there?" The sentinel took him to the headquarters of Union commander Samuel P. Heintzelman, who, "with his usual nasal twang," cursed Baker: "Oh! you villain, you, you. Trying to get through my lines, are you?

I've a good notion to cut your head off! But I'll fix you, you rascal; I'll send you to General Scott." With that, Baker was escorted back to Washington and the office of Winfield Scott. "With an expression that indicated both amusement at the *ruse,* and its failure, and confidence in me, the old veteran said: 'Well, try again!'"

Baker employed a simpler maneuver the second time. He sneaked into the ranks of a column of Union soldiers advancing over the Long Bridge into Virginia. But a sharp-eyed lieutenant saw him, seized him by the collar, put him under guard, and shipped him back to the capital.

Finally, Baker decided to attempt entry through Maryland. He went on foot to Port Tobacco, found a black man with a boat, gave him one of Scott's gold pieces, and was rowed across the river into the Confederacy, landing just below Dumfries, Virginia. It was the very route the rebels would develop into one of several regularly used secret lines of communication. It was, in fact, largely the route by which John Wilkes Booth, four years later, would leave Washington after his final, fatal performance at Ford's Theatre.

Now that Baker was in the Southland, it occurred to him that he had neglected to formulate any real plan of action. He wandered in the woods four miles from the Potomac. Two soldiers suddenly appeared and took him prisoner, intending to take him back to camp, eight miles away. Soon thirsty from the march, the three men stopped at a roadside beer shop. The soldiers invited their prisoner to drink, and while Baker—as he more than once pointed out in his self-serving *History of the United States Secret Service*—"never indulge[d] in stimulants," he accepted the offer and, in return, began to treat his captors. They soon drifted into sleep, and Baker quietly resumed his way, this time heading for Manassas Junction.

He did not get far. "I am a peaceful citizen, unarmed, and on my way to Richmond," he protested to the four cavalrymen who ordered him to halt. They searched Baker and found some letters he had apparently *wanted* to be found, including two from Reverend Shuck, a missionary who had returned from China by way of California, where he met Baker; at this time, Shuck was a popular Confederate army chaplain. True, the illiterate cavalrymen were unable to read the letters for themselves, but Baker obliged with a rendition of the choice parts. Despite the implied endorsement from

Reverend Shuck, the soldiers arrested Baker and took him to the Brentsville headquarters of General M. L. Bonham.

When the splendidly uniformed Bonham came into the room, Baker deliberately remained seated with his hat on—clearly telegraphing the message that he was totally ignorant of things military, including "the deference due to the commanding officer." This behavior is early evidence of the quick thinking, cunning, and attention to detail that, for better and for worse, would mark his subsequent career as chief of the National Detective Police. Later, for example, when Baker was engaged in ferreting out deserters, he learned to look for the "clue to a deserter's character . . . in his bronzed face, [even though] his dress and positive declarations indicated the life of a quiet citizen." Or he observed a hand that might reveal a callous where the gunlock had pressed in the march. Or he caught sight of the red line sewn into government-issued socks. There was one deserter from the Twelfth New York Battery who covered his traces so well that nothing about him aroused Baker's suspicion. But the detective detained the man nonetheless, waited until he dozed off in his office, then shouted: "Fall in, men!" The unfortunate individual sprang to his feet, looked around, and prepared to march.

"Where did you come from, and where are you going?" Bonham shot as he confronted Baker.

"I came from Washington, and am on my way to Richmond."

"Take off your hat, sir," Bonham thundered. "How dare you come inside of my lines?"

"I am a loyal and peaceful citizen of the United States, engaged in an honorable and legitimate pursuit. I have business in Richmond, and desire to go there."

"Well, I will see that you *do* go there. I believe you are a Yankee spy, and I'll send you to General Beauregard at once."

Baker, in irons, was transported to Manassas Junction and was deposited at Beauregard's headquarters where, exhausted, he fell asleep until nine the next morning, when Beauregard began his interrogation.

"So you are going to Richmond, are you?"

"Yes, if I can get there; but am willing to return [to Washington] if you will permit me to do so."

"No; I prefer that you should go to Richmond. Where do you reside?"

"I have lived in California the last ten years; but formerly lived in the South."

"What part of the South?"

"Knoxville, Tennessee."

"How long since you were in Knoxville?"

"Ten or twelve years."

"What is your name?"

"Samuel Munson."

"Yes, I see from your letters that is your name; but what was your name before you turned spy?"

"I am no spy."

"I believe you are; and, if I was satisfied of it, I would hang you on that tree. Orderly, take this man out and put him in the guard-house."

Samuel Munson was the name of a Knoxville man Baker had met in California. Having learned something of his family—Munson's father was a prominent judge—Baker decided his identity was as ripe for appropriation as any. The detective does not, however, explain how he obtained letters addressed to Munson, nor does he specify whether or not the letters from Reverend Shuck were addressed to Baker or Munson. It is possible, of course, that Baker simply faked all the letters in his possession, addressing them all to Munson.

If Baker was scared, his appetite was unaffected by his emotions. "I am very hungry; can you give me breakfast?"

"You will find breakfast in the guard-house."

To the officer in charge of the stockade, Baker asked, "Sir, I am very hungry—can you give me something to eat?" When Baker took from his pocket one of General Scott's double eagles, the smiling rebel inquired, "What will you have?"

Baker ate the breakfast that was sent him, giving to the officer the bottle of "sour wine" that accompanied it. That and the gold piece had put him on good terms with his jailer, who asked what he was in for. Baker replied that he didn't know, but would be obliged if he were allowed—under guard, of course—to walk around outside. Saying this, he produced another coin.

The accused spy and a guard went to the local hotel, where Baker treated his man to a drink, and then took "a general survey of all the troops in the immediate vicinity of Manassas Junction."

> My accommodating guard then took me to all the camps, pointed out the different intrenchments in course of erection, the names of the several regiments and brigades, who commanded them, their strength, &c. When I had obtained this information, my guard met drunken friends, and left me to go where I pleased. Fearing I should be missed, I immediately returned to the guard-house.

It was there that Baker was met with an example of Confederate counterespionage. Two fellow "prisoners" began asking him a battery of questions, meanwhile complaining bitterly of ill treatment. One asked Baker to carry a letter to his wife in Washington. The detective consented, then reported to the guard-house. "You have a spy in the stockade," he told the lieutenant, and handed over the letter. Later, Baker saw the lieutenant and the "spy" in conversation.

Even passing this "test" did not prevent Baker's removal to Richmond. There he was held not in Castle Thunder, the prison specially reserved for suspected spies, but in a railroad engine house. After four or five days, he was taken to Spottswood House, which served at the time as Jefferson Davis's residence. In the heat of the season, the president wore a light linen coat, without vest, collar, or cravat.

"You have been sent here from Manassas as a spy! What have you to say?"

Baker protested his innocence, and Davis asked substantially the same questions as Beauregard. Afterward, Baker was returned to the engine house. Three days later, he was brought back to the executive mansion, but was sent back to the engine house without another interview, as the president was otherwise engaged. After another week, he was again brought before Davis.

This time, the president was more interested in espionage than counterespionage. "How many troops do you suppose there are in Washington and its vicinity?" he asked.

"I have no means of knowing; probably 75,000 or 100,000, with more daily arriving."

"Who commands the Yankee troops?"

"I suppose, General Scott."

"Where are his headquarters?"

"In Washington."

And so on. Baker strained his ingenuity to make replies that consisted of nothing more than common knowledge or that were so general as to be useless. He was returned to the engine house, only to be recalled again later. This time, Jefferson Davis meant business.

"What is your name, sir?"

"Samuel Munson."

"Where were you born?"

"In Knoxville, Tennessee."

"What is your business here?"

"The settlement of certain land-claims in California for a man whose agent I am."

"Who is the man?"

"Rev. Mr. S____, of Barnwell Court-House; now I believe a chaplain in the army." (Baker may have been a skillful spy, but he—or his ghostwriter—was not a careful editor. Just a few pages earlier in his account from *The History of the United States Secret Service,* he had spelled out the name of Reverend Shuck.) Although Baker had on his person the letters and documents relating to Shuck, Davis was still unconvinced. He asked more questions about the defenses in and around Washington, to which Baker made noncommittal answers. Finally:

"Do you consider yourself a Southern man?"

"Yes, sir, I do."

"Do you sympathize with the Southern people?"

"I do."

"Are you willing to fight with them?"

"Yes, sir."

"Will you enlist?"

"No, sir."

"Why not?"

"Because I am here on business which I ought first to accomplish."

Baker was again returned to the engine house. After three more days, he was brought back to Davis. The president sat at his desk, writing. Reclining upon a lounge half asleep, and looking much like a man who had imbibed strong drink too freely, was Robert Toombs, at that time, Confederate secretary of state. He roused himself somewhat when Baker entered the room.

"Have you any other way of proving that your name is Munson," Davis asked, "excepting the letters found in your pocket?"

"I am not acquainted here, sir, and do not know any one."

The president launched into a series of more detailed questions relating to railroads and troop disposition, then he returned to counterespionage.

"You say you are originally from Knoxville. Can you give me the name of any persons you know there."

"It has been a good many years since I lived in Knoxville, but I remember some persons who were there when I left." Baker gave the names of several people he knew to be residents of Knoxville.

"Would they know you?"

"I think so, though a residence of eight years in California has, no doubt, changed me very much. If I should see them, I think I could make them remember me."

Davis rang a bell, a messenger appeared and was given a name.

The reason for the delay, for the days of detention in the engine house, became terrifyingly clear to Baker. Davis had needed the time to locate someone from Knoxville. Baker's thoughts desperately turned to escape. But how? Davis kept writing. Toombs, recumbent, closed his eyes.

The president's messenger had left the door ajar, and Baker quietly drew his chair toward the door, such that he could look out into the hall. On a small table he saw blank cards on which waiting visitors were instructed to write their names. The card was then sent in to the president before he granted an audience. Baker saw the messenger reenter the hall with a stranger, who wrote his name on a card, which he then handed to an orderly, who brought it in to Davis. With the president engrossed in writing and Toombs in slumber, Baker, seated by the door, obligingly extended his hand for the card. The orderly offered it, Baker read the name it bore, and motioned to the orderly to lay it on the president's table. Davis looked at the card and directed the orderly to admit the caller.

The Knoxville visitor entered, Baker sprang from his seat, grasped the stranger's hand, and burst out with, "Why, how do you do, Brock?"

The somnolent Toombs raised himself up. As for Brock, he was clearly taken by surprise, but, not wishing to appear ignorant in front of the president and his secretary of state, replied: "Yes, I know him, but I can't call his name now."

"My name is Munson, of Knoxville. Don't you remember Judge Munson's son who went to California?"

"What, Sam Munson?"

"That's my name."

"Oh yes," said Brock, turning to Davis, "now I remember him. Yes, I know him very well."

"Do you know his people there?" asked Davis.

"I know his father, Judge Munson, very well."

Secretary Toombs at last stood up. "That will do, sir," he told Brock, "that will do."

After seeing Brock out the door, Toombs held a whispered conversation with his president. A guard was summoned and escorted Baker back to the engine house.

Next morning, Brock appeared at the engine house. This would be difficult, thought Baker. Fortunately, however, Brock did most of the talking. You know so-and-so? he would ask. Oh, Yes, Baker replied. Then would come an allusion to some humorous anecdote about so-and-so, at which Baker burst into laughter.

Brock reported favorably to Jefferson Davis. Two days later, an officer brought Baker a parole paper. The spy pledged not to leave Richmond without orders from the provost marshal, and he was free—free to make all the observations he wished to make. Of course, the delay in getting across the Potomac in the first place, and his later detention rendered his intelligence regarding the situation at Manassas useless. The Union had already fought and lost the first Battle of Bull Run.

There was yet one more close call in Richmond, when a man came up to the spy, slapped him on the shoulder, and proclaimed, "Hallo, Baker! What are you doing here?" Which touched off a battery of queries and denials, terminating in the stranger's remark: "Well . . . I never saw two men look so much alike in my life!"

The next task was to get back to Washington. Two miles outside of Richmond, Baker was stopped by a Confederate officer, who demanded a pass. The spy had one, but the soldier was not satisfied and ordered Baker to accompany him to Fredericksburg. At this point, Baker faked a limp and prevailed upon the officer to take the pass to the commanding general and leave him with a soldier. Baker proposed to his guard that they stretch out in the shade. They did so, the guard fell asleep, and Baker—though it "was no pleasure to me to subject him to punishment or even censure on my account"— took the trooper's revolver and rode off on his horse. Bye and bye, he encountered some rebel soldiers of "Dutch"—that is, German— extraction, who were fishing the Potomac. He bought a meal from them and then declared, "I want to buy that boat. What will you take for it?"

"I no sells dat poat."

"I'll give you twenty dollars for it, in gold."

"It's worth more as that to us. The Yankees ish breaking up all poats on the Potomac."

That night, Baker stole the boat and was pushing off when he heard one "Dutchman" shouting to the other: "Meyer! Meyer! the poat ish gone! the poat ish gone!"

One of the men leveled his musket at Baker. "I did not want to kill 'mine host,'" Baker recalled, "but the law of self-defense again demanded a sacrifice." He fired his purloined pistol and felled the "Dutchman." The second soldier fired a shotgun at Baker, but missed; the spy returned fire, and the soldier ran.

At last, Baker worked his way back to Washington and the office of General Scott. He had been gone three weeks. While the Manassas intelligence was too late to serve any purpose, Baker did have information regarding fortifications around Fredericksburg and Richmond, as well as "resources and plans of the rebel chiefs, and the blockade running of the Potomac." Scott was pleased with what Baker had done, but decided to employ him principally as a counterespionage agent. It was in this capacity that Baker, amateur spy, earned the confidence of Secretary of State William Seward, who was determined to discover even the merest hint of disloyalty throughout the North and stamp it out.

The program of Seward's informally organized "Treason Bureau" suited the former vigilante well. Although northern security was

185

laughable, as Rose Greenhow and others proved, it wasn't for want of paranoia and wholesale arrests. During the first few months of the war, more than a thousand political prisoners—persons suspected of aiding the rebellion—were arrested and detained for months, usually without a hearing, let alone a trial. John P. Potter, representative from Wisconsin, headed up a House Committee to Investigate Government Employees, which made ruthless use of a network of informers. While Baker's zeal as an investigator and arresting officer endeared him to Seward, he rapidly earned a reputation as scoundrel, who would stop at nothing—short of outright physical torture—to extract a confession. He would hold a suspect in the basement of the Old Capitol Prison, interrogating him continuously and for days. He employed such "brainwashing" methods as sleep deprivation, and he was not above using phony witnesses to scare a confession out of a prisoner. And, it was said, if he couldn't get a confession, he would secure a signature on a blank document, which he would later fill in as the charge demanded.

One of Seward's first assignments for Baker was the task of disrupting Confederate lines of communication in southern Maryland. The likes of Thomas Jordan, George Donellan, Thomas N. Conrad, Benjamin Franklin Stringfellow, and William Norris made this no simple task. Whereas Lincoln had sent William Alvin Lloyd on his mission without any thought given to communications, and General Scott had sent Baker on what he trusted would be a kind of round-trip reconnaissance exercise, Confederate espionage from the very beginning included couriers and, very soon after, the fairly sophisticated network of communications used by Conrad and Stringfellow use.

Neither Lafayette Baker nor his superiors, though they sniffed conspiracy everywhere, were fully aware of the depth and complexity of the rebel lines of communication. One of the Union's earliest counterespionage measures had been put into effect only a few days after the outbreak of war, when Union agents descended on telegraph offices in and about Washington and began to monitor transmissions out of the capital. These censorship efforts, though quite irritating to Northern telegraphers and anyone who wanted to send a message, legitimate or not, were largely ineffective in stemming the flow of information pouring into the South. Seward, complaining that the result of every cabinet meeting was being reported in Richmond within twenty-four hours, now suspected that the postmasters of lower Maryland were conveying sensitive information to Fredericksburg through blockade runners and spies, who relayed the intelligence by telegraph to Richmond. In November 1861, Seward and Secretary of War Stanton detached to Baker's command three companies of the Third Indiana Cavalry— three hundred men—with orders to make a sweep of Charles, Prince George's, and St. Mary's counties.

The expedition began on a comic note, as Baker entered the post office at Chaptico, about sixty miles outside Washington. The postmaster and all his family were ill, save for a twelve-year-old girl. Baker knocked on the door.

"Father told me I must not let any of the Yankee soldiers in."

"I am not a Yankee soldier," Baker replied, "but an agent of the Post-office Department."

Baker entered and asked where the office was. The girl pointed to a box of pigeon holes. Baker set about examining it and happened across a rough pine box with an iron hasp and hinges and a U.S. mail lock. It had a partition through the center, with a hole for letters on either side of the partition. One side was labeled "Southern Letters," the other "Northern Letters."

"What is this box for?" Baker asked the girl.

"Why, the letters put in that hole go to Richmond; and those in the other go to Washington."

By this time, the postmaster had risen from his sickbed. He overheard his daughter.

"No," he said, "that ain't so; why do you tell the gentleman such a story?"

"I guess the girl tells the truth."

Baker sent the box back to the Post Office Department as a curiosity, where, Baker observed in his 1867 *History of the United States Secret Service,* "it still remains."

Following this conquest, Baker—who, at the time, held no formal military rank—and the cavalry made numerous arrests with sufficiently clumsy arrogance to enrage the populace, who felt that their state was suffering an invasion. Baker's raid did nothing to disrupt the Confederate Secret Line; if anything, it served to turn more Marylanders against the Union.

It is very difficult to assess the career of Lafayette C. Baker. His own ghost-written *History of the United States Secret Service* is self-aggrandizing and defensive. It was written in the thick of the controversy and outrage that followed upon his activities prior to and during the impeachment proceedings against Andrew Johnson, on whom he and his agents illegally spied. Aside from his own first mission, Baker's National Detective Police did little espionage work. Mainly, his organization kept files on suspected Confederate agents, monitored the Post Office, and kept tabs on Confederate activities in Canada—all aspects of a counterespionage mission. Baker and his agents devoted even more time and energy to investigating wartime frauds and abuses. The trouble is that Baker was among the abusers. During his eight years as head of the National Detective Police, he accumulated eight to ten times his legitimate total salary as a civilian War Department employee, then as an army colonel, and, finally, brigadier general. Under his direction, his cousin Luther Baker tracked, and cornered John Wilkes Booth on April 26, 1865. And, even this coup of skillful detection was soon clouded by the darkest of suspicions.

It is true that many believed Baker to have been a scoundrel—"a miserable wretch . . . [who] held, . . . in the hollow of his hand, the liberties of the American people," according to *House Report No. 7* of the Fortieth Congress. Doubtless, he was both high handed and downright corrupt—though he operated in a wartime atmosphere that drove Abraham Lincoln himself to suspend habeas corpus and within a context of wholesale profiteering and corruption. Yet, in most of his wartime activities, Baker seems more of an overzealous gumshoe and self-important rascal than a truly sinister figure. After all, the worst thing that happened to most of the individuals he arrested—and, doubtless, many of them did, in fact, merit arrest—is that they were compelled to take a loyalty oath. Finally, despite the grandiose and self-bestowed designation as the National Detective Police, Baker's operation was never very large. Early in the war, his activities were formally transferred to the War Department, and Baker himself was made a provost marshal, but not a provost marshal *general*. One modern scholar, Edwin C. Fischel, has pointed out that *Colonel* Baker took most of his orders from *Major* Levi C. Turner, judge advocate of the War Department, who customarily addressed him as a judge might address "a none too bright deputy sheriff." Baker ran his "national" organization on a budget that never exceeded sixty-five-thousand dollars a year and commanded a total of perhaps thirty operatives, supported, to be sure, by an informal network of paid and volunteer informants.

Contemporaries may have believed that he was capable of anything, and the blackest suspicion against Baker was terrible indeed: complicity in the assassination of Abraham Lincoln. Few historians today place much credence in this charge. For one thing, it *is* hard to believe that this man, who so often behaved like a cloak-and-dagger equivalent of the local cop who is not above appropriating a few apples from the merchants on his beat, had it in him to participate in the murder of the president. Then again, it is also hard to believe that the life of the great commander in chief could be ended by a bullet from the derringer of a popular actor. Lafayette Curry Baker, desirous as he was of power and public acclaim, remains one of the most shadowy figures of the Civil War.

CHAPTER 11

THE WAR BETWEEN THE SPIES: THEATER EUROPE

W hen, on reading the news of South Carolina's secession, William Tecumseh Sherman, who had been enjoying a quiet life as superintendent of the Louisiana State Military Academy, exploded in rage at his Christmas Eve dinner companion, he remarked pointedly on the industrial weakness of the South: "where are your men and appliances of war . . . ? The North can make a steam engine, locomotive or railway car; hardly a yard of cloth or a pair of shoes can you make." Sherman overstated his case. Establishments like the Tredegar Iron Works, which transformed the USS *Merrimack* into the ironclad CSS *Virginia*, were as good as anything in the North. However, it was true that such factories were few and far between. The fact was that the South could not produce anywhere near all the arms, munitions, and ships the Confederacy needed. But the new Confederate government was not as blithely ignorant of this truth as Sherman seems to have thought. Directly after the fall of Fort Sumter, James D. Bulloch called on Confederate Secretary of the Navy Stephen R. Mallory, offering his services as a naval officer. Georgia-born Bulloch had been a sailor since age sixteen, when he joined the United States Navy as a midshipman. The U.S. military, both navy and army, presented a singularly unrewarding career, even to young men of promise. After fourteen years of service, Bulloch had attained nothing beyond the rank of lieutenant. He resigned his commission in 1853 to become skipper of a commercial mail steamer plying the waters between New York and New Orleans. Bulloch lived in the North, near New York City, where his half-sister was married to Theodore Roosevelt, Sr., father of the future twenty-sixth president of the United States. Despite his residence and relatives, when the war broke out there was no question where Bulloch's allegiance lay.

Secretary Mallory was less interested in Bulloch's seamanship than in his business sense, knowledge of naval architecture, and his discretion. Mallory wanted Bulloch not to command a vessel, but to travel to England to buy or commission to be built six commerce raiders, arm them, and recruit the crews to man them.

Although the Confederacy would later commission from an English yard examples of that most unprepossessing new weapon of naval warfare known as the ironclad, the decision to obtain a half-dozen commerce raiders first was significant. Within the opening weeks of the war, Winfield Scott unleashed his "Anaconda," an attempt to strangle the South with a total blockade of its ports. The blockade was intended to prevent the South from importing war materiel and from exporting its most abundant commodity, cotton, to pay for it. The term "anaconda," however, especially at the beginning of the war, reflected more wishful thinking than actuality. For, while the North had far more ships than the South, the U.S. Navy was hardly equipped to patrol thousands of miles of Southern coast. The Confederate plan was not to attack the warships of the blockade directly, but to raid northern commerce, attack commercial vessels, capture their cargoes, commandeer the ships themselves, and, in the process, divert Yankee ships from blockade duty so that Southern and other pro-Confederate blockade runners could carry in arms and carry out cotton.

To obtain the commerce raiders, Bulloch needed to work with the British for two compelling reasons. To begin with, England was a great shipbuilding nation. It was also, among all foreign powers, the South's most important trading partner. Its great textile mills fed on raw Southern cotton, making Scott's Anaconda almost as great a threat to England as it was to the South. Visitors to the major port city of Liverpool in the summer of 1861 reported seeing more Confederate flags flying there than in Richmond. Such a display must have been encouraging, but the South did have one serious problem with Great Britain. Officially, the country had declared itself neutral in the war between the American states. No one in Her Majesty's government wanted to provoke war with the United States—at least, not at this time. And that's where Bulloch's discretion was called for.

Bulloch hired a prominent attorney to find him a loophole in the Foreign Enlistments Act, which, among other provisions, prohibited the arming of ships to be used by foreign combatants. The act did not, of course, affect the construction of nonmilitary vessels. Even more important, Bulloch's lawyer discovered, it included nothing that forbade building *unarmed* ships in Great Britain that might be *armed* elsewhere. Insofar as any unarmed vessel could be defined as nonmilitary, Bulloch had found his loophole. Build, but do not arm, the required ships in England, then sail them elsewhere to be fitted out with guns. Accordingly, by early June 1861, Bulloch called on Charles K. Prioleau, partner in the banking house of Fraser, Trenholm & Company, and made the necessary arrangements for converting cotton into the cash needed to finance the first two commerce raiders. This accomplished, he presented his exacting specifications to the Liverpool shipbuilding firm of William Miller & Sons and, in nearby Birkenhead, the Laird shipyard.

Loophole or not, Bulloch was not about to flaunt the fact of the vessels' construction. The Confederate agent invented a cover story that the Miller & Sons craft was being built for a company with ties to Palermo, Sicily. The ship, he told all concerned, including the shipyard workers, was to be called the *Oreto*—a fine Italian name. Actually, she was to be christened CSS *Florida* and would prove to be a highly effective raider. As to the ship under construction at the Laird works, it was without name and was therefore known only by its shipyard designation of "Number 290." Near completion, while Bulloch prepared to slip it out of England and beyond the reach of federal diplomats, it would be called the *Enrica*, but it was as the CSS *Alabama* that it would eventually fight.

Armed though he was with a legal loophole, James Bulloch was hardly home free. Federal espionage and counterespionage, which was getting off to a sluggish start at home and would remain there the poorly coordinated province of amateurs throughout much of the war, was, by comparison, aggressive and thorough in England

and elsewhere in Europe. This was largely due to the efforts of Secretary of State William H. Seward and his chief agent in Europe, Henry S. Sanford. Officially minister to Belgium, Sanford was, in fact, at the center of a network of spies and paid informants. Anticipating all-out war, Seward, well *before* the attack on Fort Sumter, had given Sanford the assignment of counteracting "by all proper means" the efforts of the "projected Confederacy" to enlist the aid of European powers.

Sanford launched his intelligence offensive on four fronts. He placed agents—or hired informants—not only in shipyards and factories, but also in banking houses and in British textile mills. Through his shipyard and factory assets, he was able to monitor the building of ships and the manufacture of arms. By means of his people in the banking houses and textile mills, however, he managed to do more than merely monitor attempts to supply the Confederacy. By obtaining information on financial transactions and sales of cotton, he could *anticipate* Confederate purchases of ships and arms. Sanford's second front was diplomatically more hazardous. He had spies and informants in various agencies of the British government, especially in the postal service and the government's telegraph system. In this way, he intercepted Confederate communication with mills, factories, and shipyards, as well as Bulloch's communications with his network of spies. In July 1861, Sanford hired a private detective named Ignatius Pollaky, who, like Allan Pinkerton back in the United States, had his own team of "operatives." Pollaky identified seventeen Confederate agents and reported on their activities. His men monitored telegraph traffic and frequently intercepted messages—not through any means as technologically sophisticated as tapping the telegraph lines, but, rather, by befriending telegraph messengers, liquoring them up at local pubs, and rifling through their documents. Under Sanford's orders, Pollaky also bribed postmen, at the rate of a pound a week per man, to furnish lists of towns that appeared on the postmarks of letters received by the seventeen known Confederate agents. When any number of seaport postmarks turned up, Pollaky knew that he should send a man to investigate what, in all likelihood, was the presence of a ship being loaded with Confederate-purchased goods.

Typical of Pollaky's operations was the discovery, in October 1861, that Bulloch had purchased the new British steamer *Fingal*. This was not a commerce raider, but a blockade runner, according to Bulloch's 1884 account in his *Secret Service of the Confederate States in Europe,* loaded with the following:

> *On account of the Navy Department*—1,000 short rifles, with cutlass bayonets, and 1,000 rounds of ammunition per rifle; 500 revolvers, with suitable ammunition; two 4¹/₂-inch muzzle-loading rifled guns, with traversing carriages, all necessary gear, and 200 made-up cartridges, shot and shell, per gun; two breech-loading 2¹/₂-inch steel-rifled guns for boats or field service, with 200 rounds of ammunition per gun; 400 barrels of coarse cannon powder, and a large quantity of made-up clothing for seamen.
>
> *For the State of Georgia*—3,000 Enfield rifles.
>
> *For the State of Louisiana*—1,000 Enfield rifles.

Other sources put the total number of Enfields at fourteen thousand.

Through his network, Pollaky traced arms shipments from London, to Liverpool, to Greenock, Scotland, which would serve as a port of embarkation for many blockade runners throughout the war (the ill-fated *Condor*, bearing Rose Greenhow, set sail from Greenock at the end of August 1864). One of his agents installed himself at the Old Sailor's Home in that port town and wandered the docks; he discovered the *Fingal* and case upon case of Enfields ready to be loaded onto her.

The cases bore the name of Isaac Campbell & Company, which Sanford and Pollaky knew to be the purchasing agent used by one Caleb Huse, a Confederate major sent to England early in the war to procure arms and ammunition. Huse's activities were all too familiar to Sanford. For the third means by which the American spymaster sought to thwart Confederate efforts to acquire arms was to buy up available supplies before men like Huse could get at them. In his 1904 memoir, *Supplies for the Confederate Army,* Huse recalls:

> On arriving in London I went to what was then a favorite hotel for Americans—Morley's in Trafalgar Square. . . . My orders were to purchase 12,000 rifles and a battery of field artillery, and to procure

one or two guns of large caliber as models. A short time before the beginning of the war, the London Armory Company had purchased a plant of gun-stocking machinery from the Ames Manufacturing Company of Chicopee, Massachusetts. Knowing this, I went to the office of the Armory Company the day after my arrival in London, with the intention of securing, if possible, their entire output.

On entering the Superintendent's office, I found there the American engineer who superintended the erection of the plant. I had known him in Chicopee. Suspecting he might be an agent for the purchase of arms for the United States Government, I asked him, bluntly, if he was, and added, "I am buying for the Confederate Government." Such a disclosure of my business may seem to have been indiscreet, but at that time I thought it my best plan, and the result proved that I was right. He made no reply to my inquiry, but I was satisfied my suspicion was correct and resolved on the spot to flank his movement if possible.

The engineer was, in fact, under orders from Sanford to preempt a Confederate purchase by putting in a timely order on behalf of the United States. This strategy worked—almost. Huse sought a "price for all the small arms the company could manufacture." The Armory Company superintendent referred him to the president, who put him off for a day.

> On calling at his office the following day, he told me that the company was under contract for all the arms it could turn out, and considering all the circumstances, the directors felt they ought to give their present customer the preference over all others.

Undiscouraged, Huse—acting on his own authority—offered the Armory Company a substantial premium. "The Atlantic cable was not then laid, and correspondence by mail required nearly a month—an unreasonable time for a commercial company to hold in abeyance a desirable opportunity for profit. . . . Within a few days I succeeded in closing a contract under which I was to have all the arms the company could manufacture, after filling a comparatively small order for the United States agent."

Huse also bested Sanford in a subsequent deal with the Austrian government. Europe in 1861 presented a seller's market for desirable small arms. Antiquated smoothbore muskets were plentiful throughout the continent, but modern rifles were available only from England, though not in great quantity, and from Austria. Accompanied by an "intermediary," Huse went to Vienna and summarily purchased from the Imperial Austrian Arsenal 100,000 rifles "of the latest Austrian pattern," together with ten field artillery batteries, of six pieces each, including ammunition. Sanford ordered a protest from the United States minister to Austria. The reply to the protest was that the Austrian government had earlier offered to manufacture arms for U.S. export, but that the offer had been declined. The Confederate States of America was, in the view of the Imperial Austrian government, a nation and a belligerent and, therefore, as legitimate a customer for arms as the United States. Unburdened by anything like Great Britain's Foreign Enlistments Act, the Austrians shipped the rifles and ordnance through Hamburg to Bermuda, where the cargo was transferred to a blockade runner for delivery to the South.

In other cases, it was Sanford who got the better of his Confederate counterparts. His office bribed Belgian clerks to supply information on Confederate purchases and was able to preempt buys by outbidding Confederate purchasing agents on such items as saltpeter for gunpowder and explosives, guns, and cloth. In at least one instance, Sanford bought out from under the Confederate agents a contract for sixty thousand rifles. Now Sanford and Pollaky were determined to prevent the *Fingal* from sailing. The ship was to operate under a British flag, nominally commanded by a captain holding a British Board of Trade certificate and manned by a British crew in accordance with the Merchant Shipping Act. But, Pollaky learned, the real skipper was to be Bulloch himself. He sent more agents to shadow Bulloch in Greenock, but the Confederate, anticipating Pollaky's move, slipped out of town and fled undetected to Holyhead. After departing Greenock, the vessel would quietly touch port there, and Bulloch would board her. To the bewilderment of Pollaky's agents, when the *Fingal* left Greenock on October 9, Bulloch was not aboard.

Bulloch's successful stratagem, however, nearly cost him his ship and cargo. A severe storm blew up near Holyhead, and, at four o'clock on the morning of October 15, the second officer of *Fingal*, a Mr. Low, knocked loudly on the door to Bulloch's bedroom. "I was only half awake. . . . I was startled by a sepulchral voice which seemed to be mumbling under the breast of the peajacket, like the last tremulous quivering of a thunderclap. But my ear caught the sound of a few articulate words, among which 'Fingal,' 'brig,' 'collision,' 'sunk,' were fearfully jumbled together. . . . Before I could leap out of bed a painful scene of wreck and disaster passed vividly through my brain, and I fancied the *Fingal* at the bottom of Holyhead harbor."

It wasn't, however, quite so bad as that. In the storm, the *Fingal* had accidentally rammed and sunk the Austrian brig *Siccardi*. Since the *Fingal* was an iron steamer and the *Siccardi* a wooden sailing vessel, the *Fingal* suffered little damage. Of course, there was the very real problem of an investigation consequent upon the accident, which would mean customs inspectors, a lot of questions, and, quite possibly, the seizure of the ship and its cargo. Bulloch dispatched a quick message to Fraser, Trenholm & Company, asking them to find the owners of the brig and make "the best possible arrangement with them." In the meantime, Bulloch boarded the *Fingal* as planned and steamed for Bermuda, arriving on November 2. The United States consul at Bermuda did his best to keep the vessel bottled up at the island, but his efforts were to no avail. The *Fingal* evaded Sanford. Now there was the blockade itself to run.

Bulloch had sailed from a British port, under a British flag, and with a British crew, bound for another British port. Before setting off from Bermuda to run the blockade he

sent for all hands to come aft to the bridge. I told them very briefly that . . . I had no right to take them anywhere [other than a British port] without their consent, and I did not mean to use either force or undue pressure to make them do anything not set out in the shipping articles, but I thought they must have suspected that there was some other purpose in the voyage than a cruise to Bermuda and the Bahamas, and the time had arrived when it was both safe and proper for me to tell them the real port of destination, which was Savannah, and of course this meant a breach of the blockade, with the risk of capture and some rough treatment as prisoners-of-war. . . .

I had thought over what to say, and was prepared with a few exhilarating and persuasive phrases; but [instead] . . . I put the question plainly, "Will you go?" to which there was a prompt and unanimous consent. I thanked them, but said there was still something to explain, which I did to the following effect:

"The United States have been compelled to buy up steamers from the merchant service for blockaders. Many of them are neither so strong nor so efficient in any way as this ship, and they are not heavily armed. If we should fall in with any blockaders off Savannah at all, they are likely to be of that class. . . . the Confederate Government . . . [does] not feel disposed to give up this valuable and important cargo to a ship not strong enough to render resistance useless . . . . So long as the *Fingal* is under British flag, we have no right to fire a shot, but I have a bill of sale in my pocket, and can take delivery from the captain on behalf of the Confederate Navy Department at any moment. This I propose to do, if there should appear to be any likelihood of a collision with a blockader. . . ."

In fact, the *Fingal* met with no resistance and delivered its cargo to Savannah.

But the Union's Sanford was by no means always thwarted. The fourth front of his assault on Bulloch and his cohorts was a propaganda campaign. Much of Europe, and Great Britain in particular, was pro-Confederate. Newspaper editors willing to publish material sympathetic to the Union were hard to come by; but, Sanford discovered, they could be bought. A French writer by the name of A. Malespine was given a monthly stipend, financed out of a special secret service fund, for writing favorable articles. Sanford even tried to purchase a popular newspaper, and when Secretary Seward balked at this, he sought funding from private sources. Sanford failed to obtain the funds to buy a paper outright, but he did succeed in placing many stories in many venues. It may well have been Sanford who directed that a disquieting story detailing Bulloch's mission be published in *The Times* of London. The information revealed in *The Times* article, obviously based on the meticulous reports of Sanford's detectives, included the amounts of money allotted for Bulloch's mission, the banks involved, and so on. And all of this published *before* the mission actually got under way.

Both sides could play at the propaganda game. The Confederacy sent Henry Hotze, an editorial writer for the Mobile *Register*, to England to write and place pro-Confederate news articles. He also prepared speeches for sympathetic members of Parliament. On May 1, 1862, he even began publishing an English Confederate newspaper, *The Index,* which was avidly read by an influential coterie of British politicians and policy makers. Throughout the war, Hotze, like his federal adversary Sanford, cajoled or bribed British editors into publishing favorable stories. He managed to infiltrate the London papers by placing on staff no fewer than seven writers, paid by the Confederate States of America. As good as Sanford was at generating and disseminating propaganda, Hotze was even better. In the end, it was not Sanford who defeated him, but the unpalatable ideology of slavery. Hotze, who had once written a book justifying slavery on anthropological grounds, was good at his job, but he was not good enough to overcome England's professed political aversion to the outright ownership of flesh and blood. By the middle of the war, the Confederacy could still secure some supplies from British contractors, but it had become apparent that England would never officially support the South.

After successfully bringing the *Fingal* into Savannah, James Bulloch returned to England in March 1862 to look after the completion of the *Oreto* and "No. 290." By that time, the *Oreto* had drawn the attention of Thomas Dudley, the United States consul at Liverpool. He hired his own private detective, Matthew Maguire, who soon gathered enough evidence to convince Dudley that the ship was being built as a commerce raider. The consul passed Maguire's report on to Charles Francis Adams, U.S. minister in London. He presented the case to the British foreign secretary, Lord John Russell. Among other things, Adams pointed out, observers watched two gun carriages being loaded upon the vessel. It was a blatant violation of the British neutrality laws.

Russell went through the motions of an inquiry, but claimed to have discovered nothing incriminating—no powder and no guns. True, her bulwarks were pierced for guns, but that, according to Russell, was insufficient reason to find her in violation of the Foreign Enlistments Act. On March 22, 1862, flying British colors, *Oreto* set out for Nassau. There she was fitted out with guns and ammunition smuggled out of England by the steamer *Bahama* and was christened CSS *Florida.* Before she was captured in October

1864, this commerce raider had captured or sunk thirty-seven Northern vessels.

Dudley, frustrated and outraged by his failure to stop the *Oreto/ Florida*, turned his attention to "No. 290." A network of his detectives and spies furnished a mountain of affidavits of evidence indicating that she was a commerce raider. The documents were duly presented to Samuel Price Edwards, collector of customs at Liverpool. But he turned a blind eye, claiming that the evidence, though voluminous, was nevertheless inconclusive and insufficient. "No. 290" was given the name *Enrica* and launched from the Laird yards on May 15, 1862. She had to be towed, however, to a graving dock in Liverpool, where she would be fitted out with engines and masts. Dudley's detective, Matthew Maguire, owned a Liverpool boardinghouse frequented by sailors. There he learned from one of his boarders, a Southern sailor named Robinson, that the *Enrica* was indeed a raider. Robinson supplied details of armament and other appurtenances of war, and, once again, Dudley submitted affidavits to customs collector Edwards. And, once again, Edwards deemed the evidence insufficient.

In frustration, Dudley took the affidavits to Charles Francis Adams, who presented them directly to Lord Russell. Russell passed the matter on to the Treasury, which threw the case back into the lap of Samuel Price Edwards—who, of course, yet one more time deemed the evidence insufficient.

What neither Dudley nor Adams knew was that Edwards was strongly inclined to deem any and all evidence insufficient. For he had invested heavily in Southern cotton and had, therefore, a substantial stake in Confederate victory.

This time, however, Adams did not let the matter rest. As Bulloch had employed a prominent English attorney to render an opinion on the Foreign Enlistments Act, so Adams employed another, Robert R. Collier, who presented Russell with an opinion that, if the *Enrica* were allowed to sail, the United States would have a valid claim against Great Britain for any and all damages she might cause to American shipping. The threat of fiscal harm at last moved Russell to action. He turned the entire case over to Sir John Harding, a Queen's Law Officer, asking for an immediate opinion. As fate would have it, Harding was just then in the throes of nervous collapse, a condition the poor man's wife had covered up so well that no one in the Law Offices was aware of it. The delay and confusion Harding's incapacity created resulted in word leaking to Bulloch that the *Enrica* was in imminent danger of seizure. Bulloch ordered the *Agrippina*, a British steamer laden with the guns and munitions that were to be fitted to the *Enrica* at Terceira in the Azores, to sail immediately. In the meantime, he hurried the *Enrica* to completion and announced that she would put to sea for trials on July 29.

On that day, she set out—but did not return to Liverpool. Instead, she headed for Moelfra Bay on the Welsh coast, where Bulloch planned to board her and steal out of English waters and beyond the influence of U.S. diplomatic pressure. But Confederate naval secretary Mallory had a different commander in mind. Narrowly evading a federal steam sloop, *Tuscarora*, sent in search of her, the *Enrica* braved a storm in the Irish Sea to rendezvous briefly with the *Agrippina*, from which Captain Raphael Semmes, a fifty-three-year-old Maryland-born Alabamian destined to become the Confederacy's most celebrated naval officer, boarded her and took command.

By the narrowest of margins, and despite the best efforts of American spies and diplomats, Bulloch had succeeded in launching *Enrica*. As CSS *Alabama*, Raphael Semmes commanding, it would capture or destroy about sixty-five Union ships until it was sunk by USS *Kearsarge* on June 19, 1864. Robert R. Collier's opinion regarding the ultimate validity of United States claims against Her Majesty's government would prove accurate. In 1872, after lengthy litigation, an international tribunal would award the United States $15.5 million in gold for damages caused by vessels built in Great Britain or armed with weapons manufactured there. The *Florida* and *Alabama*, together with another ship commissioned in England by James Bulloch, the *Shenandoah*, were alone responsible for $12,498,033 of the damages awarded.

Although the settlement of what was popularly called "The *Alabama* Claims" was not made until seven years after Appomattox, by the end of 1862, Charles Francis Adams was already bombarding Her Majesty's government—and especially the slow-to-act Lord Russell—with claims, ever-mounting claims, for shipping taken or destroyed by vessels built in and around Liverpool. Both official Britain and the English public were beginning to turn against the

Confederacy by the spring of 1863, when James Bulloch was overseeing the completion of a pair of ironclads. Built at the Laird shipyards, the two vessels would be known as the Laird rams and were intended specifically for breaching the Union blockade. The persistence of Adams and Sanford, as well as the evolution of British opinion, imperiled the Laird rams. To make matters worse for the Confederates, Clarence Yonge, who, in the capacity of assistant paymaster, had recruited British sailors to man CSS *Alabama*, was discharged by Raphael Semmes on account of drunkenness. Embittered, Yonge returned to England, offering to sell to Adams information on the Laird rams, which would confirm, once and for all, that the Foreign Enlistments Act was being violated. The ever-vigilant Bulloch scrambled for a quick cover story, hastily transferring ownership of the rams to a French businessman and claiming that the ships were being built on commission from the Pasha of Egypt! Bulloch, who had proven himself skillful in the naming of vessels, christened the pair *El Tousson* and *El Mounassir*.

Despite this subterfuge, Lord Russell was at last prompted to move. He submitted all of Adams's affidavits concerning the rams to the Queen's Law Offices. Astoundingly, that department informed him that Adams's evidence was legally insufficient to justify seizure. At this juncture, the British consul at Cairo informed London that the ships had not, in fact, been commissioned by the Egyptians. Exercising particular care, Russell investigated the question of French ownership as well. The British ambassador to France reported that the vessels were no more French than Egyptian. By the end of summer 1863, one of the rams was about ready to be launched. Consul Dudley approached customs collector Samuel Price Edwards with all the evidence Adams *and* Lord Russell had gathered, but, of course, Edwards declined to seize the ram. Desperate, but also confident that circumstances were now very different from what they had been in 1862, Charles Francis Adams presented Lord Russell with an ultimatum: either the rams were to be seized, or a state of war would exist between the United States and Great Britain. As Bulloch groped for a means by which he might sneak the vessels out of Liverpool, Her Majesty's government seized the Laird rams on October 9, 1863. (They were ultimately appropriated for service in the Royal Navy, but proved so unseaworthy that they were soon decommissioned. It is, therefore, unlikely that they would have had much effect on the Union blockade; certainly, they would have done nothing approaching the damage inflicted by the commerce raiders Sanford, Adams, et al had been unable to intercept.)

Aggressive and inventive as both sides were in conducting clandestine activities in Europe, the Union, at least, proved that it was also capable, in some European operations, of the same poor judgment and blundering that often marked its secret service efforts at home. The best-known misadventure was the so-called *Trent* Affair, alluded to in earlier chapters. Late in 1861, Richmond sent two special commissioners, James M. Mason and John Slidell, to Europe with the assignment of persuading respectively England and France to recognize the Confederate States of America as a sovereign entity. The commissioners left Charleston at one o'clock on the morning of October 12; they arrived in Nassau two days later, then went to Cuba, where they were to board the British mail steamer *Trent* on November 7. The American consul in Havana informed Captain Charles Wilkes, skipper of the USS *San Jacinto*, of the commissioners' plans, and Wilkes decided to ambush the *Trent* as it steamed through the Old Bahama Channel enroute to St. Thomas. At 11:40 A.M. on November 8, Captain Wilkes fired two shots across the *Trent*'s bow. The steamer stopped, Wilkes sent an armed boarding party to take the commissioners and their secretaries prisoner, and he prepared to seize the *Trent* as a prize. The action of the boarding party was so clumsy that the commissioners were able to hand over their dispatches to a civilian, a Charlestonian, who took them to England. Worse, the lieutenant in command of the party persuaded Wilkes not to take the *Trent* after all; to do so, he argued, would leave the *San Jacinto* dangerously short-handed. Ironically, it was the failure to claim the ship—an arguably legitimate action in time of war—that constituted a violation of international law and outraged the British.

In the United States, initial reaction to the capture of the commissioners was jubilation, and Wilkes was fêted as a hero by a Union that had suffered a string of battlefield defeats. The British, however, saw things very differently. Analogous acts on the part of the Royal Navy had provided the rationale for America's declaration of war on England in 1812. Her Majesty's government now demanded the release of the commissioners and embarked eight thousand troops for Canada to back up the demand. On December 26, 1861, Secretary of State Seward agreed to release Slidell and Mason ("They will be cheerfully liberated," he wrote to Lord Lyons, British minister in Washington) and thereby averted an armed conflict with Great Britain that, during the disastrous early months of the Civil War, could well have meant doom for the Union. The price of peace, unfortunately, was a degree of humiliation. As to the erstwhile hero Wilkes, his fortunes precipitantly declined after the *Trent* Affair. Troublesome—a martinet to those he commanded, insubordinate to those who commanded him—he was court-martialed in 1864 and compelled to "retire."

Far less potentially damaging, albeit embarrassing enough and certainly more strange than the *Trent* Affair were three Quixotic attempts to recruit into the cause of the Union the Italian patriot Giuseppe Garibaldi. The scheme was the product of desperation both national and personal. Reeling from ignominious defeat at the first Battle of Bull Run, Lincoln and Seward were prepared to grasp at whatever straw presented itself to pull the Union out of its present slough of demoralization and despair. That straw was offered by one James W. Quiggle, the American consul at Antwerp, Holland. Having been appointed by James Buchanan, Quiggle was about to lose his job with the ascendancy of a new administration. He thought, however, that a brilliant idea might save his position, and one was not long in coming to him.

Giuseppe Garibaldi, having made a giant stride toward the unification of Italy through his leadership of a successful revolt against the reactionary governments of Sicily and Naples in 1860, had suffered a disappointing rebuff at the hands of the Sardinian monarch, Victor Emanuel II, who, through Garibaldi's efforts, was now also ruler of Naples and Sicily. The Italian freedom fighter wanted the king to march next against Rome, occupied by troops of Napoleon III, ostensibly present to protect the Pope. Victor Emanuel refused to move against the Vatican, and Garibaldi, in disgust, betook himself to voluntary semi-exile on the remote island of

Caprera, off the northeastern coast of Sardinia. Quiggle heard reports that Garibaldi had expressed interest in leaving Caprera for the United States in order to fight for the Union. Without consulting Secretary Seward, Quiggle wrote to the self-exiled patriot on June 8, 1861: "The papers report that you are going to the United States, to join the army of the North. . . . If you do, the name of LaFayette will not surpass yours. There are thousands of Italians and Hungarians who will rush to your ranks, and there are thousands and tens of thousands of American citizens who will glory to be under the command of the 'Washington of Italy.'" In his state of forced retirement, Garibaldi was not immune to such blandishments. He replied on June 27, informing Quiggle ("My dear friend") that the news reports were "not exact." However, he wrote, if the government of the United States believes "my service to be of some use, I would go to America, if I did not find myself occupied in the defense of my country."

Quiggle then contacted Seward, who consulted with the president. The prospect of a great guerrilla leader and symbol of national union coming to fight for the *American* Union was, in the dark days of 1861, utterly seductive. Quiggle did not, however, wait for Seward's reply, but told Garibaldi that he would soon receive an official invitation to come to the United States "with the highest Army Commission which it is in the power of the President to confer." This convinced the Italian that Lincoln intended nothing less than to make him supreme commander of the Union armies.

As for Seward, eager to proceed with negotiations, he was also anxious to cut the Democrat Quiggle out of the loop. He directed Henry Sanford to effect communication with Garibaldi and, if all was well, to offer him an immediate commission as major general. In sharp contrast to Quiggle, whom Sanford called "a low besotted Pennsylvania politician," Sanford was, for better or worse, a consummate diplomat. He did not dare begin by approaching Garibaldi directly, for fear that rejection would augment the humiliation the Union had already suffered at Bull Run and for fear of provoking outrage from the Vatican and Victor Emanuel, who were sure to resent foreign meddling in their domestic affairs. Accordingly, Sanford carefully strategized with George Perkins Marsh, United

States minister to the new kingdom of Italy, before taking any rash action.

Even practiced diplomats make mistakes, however, and Sanford's was to tell Quiggle that he was about to leave for Turin to meet with Marsh. The consul, wanting to steal Sanford's thunder, wrote directly to Garibaldi, again implying that he was to be given a position of great power. This flattering "news" could not have found Garibaldi in a more receptive mood. It is a fact that Garibaldi, who had lived in America for three years, was an enthusiastic abolitionist who spoke of the United States as his adopted country. He enjoyed tremendous popularity with the American public and was sincerely interested in fighting to preserve the great Union. But he also had an agenda of his own. Garibaldi wanted to free Rome from papal rule and the influence of Napoleon III; Victor Emanuel II refused the freedom fighter's demand for a march on the Eternal City. Having retired temporarily to Caprera, but believing that his continued support was indispensable to the king, Garibaldi saw, in threatening to accept the Union's offer, a chance to force the monarch's hand. Surely, Victor Emanuel would not want him to leave Italy.

In the meantime, Sanford and Marsh had determined that the most prudent course was to send a lower-level diplomat, Marsh's legation secretary, to sound out Garibaldi before either of them ventured to Caprera personally. If the freedom fighter's answer came in the negative, little face would have been lost, and by keeping as much distance possible at this point between Garibaldi and Lincoln, neither the Vatican nor the new Italian king would have much cause to complain about the U.S. meddling with Italy's internal affairs.

The plan seemed to work very well. Garibaldi replied to Giuseppe Artomi, Marsh's Italian-American secretary, that, if Victor Emanuel had no need of his services, he would be "immediately at [the] disposal" of the United States. This said, Garibaldi played his trump card, sending one of his trusted followers, Colonel Gaspare Trecchi, to inform Victor Emanuel of the American offer and to seek his permission to accept it. Now the king, Garibaldi reckoned, would have to see things his way. On September 6, however, Victor Emanuel II replied, not with a plea that Garibaldi remain, but with permission for him to leave Italy in order to accept the commission in the Union army. The very next day, Sanford set out for Caprera, and Garibaldi was eager to receive him.

The eagerness quickly dissolved into more disappointment.

Based on his initial communications with Quiggle, Garibaldi was prepared to come to America on two absolute conditions: that he be made supreme commander of the Union forces and that he be given authority to free the slaves. It was now Sanford's painful duty to tell him that he could promise nothing more than a commission as major general and that, as to emancipation, it was the sole prerogative of President Lincoln. Summoning all his diplomatic self-control, Sanford hoped to salve Garibaldi bruised ego by offering him an expenses-paid tour of the theater of war, so that he could make a decision based on firsthand knowledge of the situation. But the Italian patriot would not compromise, and Sanford returned from Caprera without "the Washington of Italy."

And so the matter died, only to be revived, briefly, in September 1862 by an individual even less adroit than Quiggle had been. He was Theodore Canisius, the American consul in Vienna, who enjoyed a particularly interesting relation to President Lincoln. Except for the fact that he spoke German, Canisius was not especially qualified for the post he occupied. His was, like so many government posts, a patronage appointment. Nothing unusual about that. It was, rather, the *nature* of the patronage debt Lincoln owed Canisius that was peculiar. Back in Lincoln's adoptive state of Illinois, Canisius had run a German-language newspaper. It was losing money, and Canisius sought a partner in Lincoln, at the time an aspiring politician. In return for Canisius's agreement to publish pro-Republican articles, Lincoln invested in the newspaper. After he became president, Lincoln persuaded a reluctant Seward to reward Canisius further by giving him the Viennese consular post.

This patronage hack, then, took it upon himself to write to Garibaldi on September 1, 1862, asking him directly if he would be willing to fight for the Union. Indeed, without bothering to consult Seward or anyone else, for that matter, Canisius offered him a commission in the Union Army. The Italian patriot, under arrest and convalescing from a wound he had received in an abortive attempt to seize Rome, replied that he was not presently free to accept a commission. "However," he continued, "I believe that, if I am set at liberty and if my wounds heal, the favorable opportunity will have arrived in which I shall be able to satisfy my desire to serve the great American Republic. . . ." Garibaldi made no allusion, this time, to either of his former requirements: that he be made supreme Union army commander and that he be given authority to emancipate the slaves. Optimistic that Garibaldi would accept his offer, Canisius expressed his enthusiastic support for the freedom fighter's attempted march on Rome and informed the press that the "Washington of Italy" would probably soon be fighting for the Union.

The newspaper stories produced precisely the result Sanford and Marsh had earlier worked so carefully to avoid. Victor Emanuel protested that the consul was meddling in Italian affairs, whereupon Secretary Seward summarily removed Canisius from his post. An official apology satisfied the Italian government, however, and the secretary general of the king's cabinet let it be known that his majesty had no wish to see Canisius, who had "acted only impulsively," lose his job. Doubtless Seward would have been just as happy to let him go, but Lincoln also interceded, and the consul was reinstated.

Almost simultaneously with the Canisius indiscretion, Minister Marsh tried his own hand, one last time, at enlisting Garibaldi into the cause. He proposed to a Neapolitan intermediary that a commission in the Union army would benefit the Italian government by providing Victor Emanuel with a face-saving means of setting the popular patriot free. Again, the way seemed reasonably clear for Garibaldi's acceptance of an offer. But, this time, no offer was forthcoming. By now, the close of 1862, Seward and, presumably, Lincoln were far less enthusiastic about creating the appearance of having to import a general to win a civil war. And thus, quietly, before it even began, ended Giuseppe Garibaldi's participation in the War Between the States.

CHAPTER 12

THE NORTHWEST CONSPIRACY

T he neatly printed pages of history tell us that the Union victories at Vicksburg on May 22–July 4, 1863, and Gettysburg on June 27–July 4 marked the turning point in the War Between the States. That a Northern triumph was now inevitable is clear enough to the hindsight of history, but was by no means apparent to Northern eyes that burned from two terrible years of black powder and tears. Discontent born of war weariness was epidemic even in a North approaching the threshold of victory. In what should have been the triumphant afterglow of Vicksburg and Gettysburg, that discontent flamed forth during one violent week in New York City.

From the beginning, New Yorkers never wholeheartedly rallied round the flag. Their mayor, Fernando Wood, proposed the secession of the city (and Long Island) as early as January 1861. The wealth of New York was bound to the South by the stout cords of trade, and Wood proposed that New York City, as an independent, neutral nation, become a free port trading equally with North and South. While the city did not finally pursue this radical course, it was, throughout the war, guided more by a cynical spirit of commerce than a love for the Union. The principles on which the North prosecuted the war were far less important in Manhattan than how one might profit from the war. Indeed, to some New Yorkers, at least one of the Union's principles was downright repugnant. To the mass of poor immigrants who called the city home—and especially to the 200,000 Irish who had fled the great Potato Famine of 1848—the prospect of a new wave of even more downtrodden immigrants, emancipated slaves coming up from the South, was a grim one. The Irish lived largely by supplying cheap common labor; African Americans would supply it cheaper. On April 13, race riots broke out in the city as Irish workers attacked blacks.

War weary, profit-driven at the top end of the economy, fearful at the bottom, New York was hardly jubilant over Vicksburg and Gettysburg. On the contrary, it was ready to explode. Congress itself had set match to fuse early in March when it passed an ill-conceived Conscription Act. The problem was not with the draft as such; most Northerners realized that the army needed the troops, and passage of the act even prompted a good many men to enlist, largely to avoid the stigma of being drafted. The real problem was that the law was fundamentally unfair. A draftee could avoid service by providing a (presumably paid) substitute or by paying a $300 "commutation fee"—a very large sum in an era when manual labor earned about a dollar a day. Men of means could avoid military service, but the poor, already oppressed by the specter of cheap black labor, could not. Worse, the unfair law was administered unfairly as well as obnoxiously. Provost marshal's agents, in the manner of old-time British press gangs, rousted young men and boys from their houses, conducting searches without benefit of warrant. Draftees who failed to report as directed were arrested as deserters and dealt with harshly. Demonstrations were branded "unlawful assemblies" and roughly quashed by armed troops.

The first uprisings occurred in the Old Northwest and the Ohio Valley—chiefly Iowa, Illinois, Indiana, and Ohio—but the worst violence broke out during a three-day period in New York. On Saturday, July 11, the draft commenced in the city. On Monday, "a ragged, coatless, heterogeneously weaponed army," in the words of journalist Joel T. Headley, "heaved tumultuously along toward Third Avenue. Tearing down the telegraph poles as it crossed the Harlem & New Haven Railroad track, it surged angrily up around the building where the drafting was going on. . . . The mob seized the wheel in which were the names, and what books, papers, and lists were left, and tore them up. . . ." Frustrated because they were unable to break open a safe, the mob next set fire to the building. Deputy Provost Marshal Vanderpoel was assaulted, and Police Superintendent John Kennedy was beaten beyond recognition. The Second Avenue armory was overrun and looted, as were jewelry and liquor stores. Squads of rioters chased blacks, some of whom were hanged from lampposts. On Tuesday, the rioting and looting continued, and the Colored Orphan Asylum was set ablaze; the rioters cheered the flames.

By Wednesday, with rioters actually tearing down the houses of blacks, it was evident that the mob had seized the city. President Lincoln and Secretary of War Stanton dispatched a detachment of General Meade's Gettysburg veterans to march on New York and restore order. They arrived Wednesday evening. "There was some terrific fighting between the regulars and the insurgents," a witness recorded, "streets were swept again and again by grape[shot], houses were stormed at the point of the bayonet, rioters were picked off by sharpshooters as they fired on the troops from housetops; men were hurled, dying or dead, into the streets. . . ." The introduction of Meade's regulars ended the bloody business, with casualties among the rioters and their victims estimated at anywhere from three hundred to one thousand. However, sporadic violence briefly flared in nearby Brooklyn, Jamaica, Staten Island, Jersey City, and Newark, then farther afield, in Albany and Troy, New York; Boston; and Portsmouth, New Hampshire. Columbia and Bucks counties, Pennsylvania, had trouble, as did parts of Kentucky. The governor of Wisconsin called in the militia to quell disturbances in Milwaukee and Ozaukee County.

Dixie greeted word of the Draft Riots with undisguised glee. J. B. Jones, a clerk in the Confederate War Department, noted in his diary on July 17: "But we have *awful* good news from New York: an INSURRECTION, the loss of many lives, extensive pillage and burning. . . ." Many Northerners saw in the riots the hand of Confederate agents, though nothing was ever proved, and whatever role *agents provocateurs* may or may not have played, all the provocation really necessary seems to have been amply supplied by the Conscription Act and its administration. However, there were those, both North and South, who saw the Draft Riots as only the most visible evidence of potential disloyalty in the Northern population. And there were those in the South who were eager to exploit it.

The most vocal among the Northern disaffected were the radical Democrats, who saw greater enemies in the ranks of diehard loyal Republicans than in the ranks of rebel Southerners. They opposed the Conscription Act, and they opposed the Emancipation Proclamation, arguing that it had changed the Civil War from a struggle to preserve the Union to a "war for the Negro." Even more, they opposed the radical Republican view, as expressed by Pennsylvania Congressman Thaddeus Stevens, that, after victory was won, the loyal North should "treat those states outside of the Union as conquered provinces and settle them with new men." Such "new men," of course, were not likely to be Democrats. In short, Northern Democrats were being asked to fight a war that would restore the Union but destroy their party. The only course to take, they argued, was neither conquest nor surrender, but armistice.

Among this radical group the most radical organized into secret societies either modeled on or an actual outgrowth of the Southern Rights clubs of the 1830s. In 1854, a medical practitioner of dubious credentials, George W. L. Bickley, founded the Knights of the Golden Circle. Headquartered in Cincinnati and replete with passwords, quasi-masonic rituals, secret signs and symbols, the Knights of the Golden Circle (later called the Order of the American Knights and, by February 1864, the Sons of Liberty) quickly spawned satellite lodges ("castles," they were called) throughout Kentucky, Missouri, Iowa, Illinois, Indiana, and Ohio. By way of identification, members wore on their lapels the head of Liberty cut from an old-style copper penny. Seizing on the lapel pins, their enemies called them Copperheads, a reference to the venomous snake.

If the Copperheads rallied around any one leader, that man was Clement Vallandigham, a brilliant individual, who at age two knew the alphabet, at twelve spoke Greek and Latin, at seventeen entered Jefferson College in Philadelphia, at nineteen became principal of Union Academy in Maryland, at twenty was editor of a radical Democratic newspaper called the *Western Empire,* and who gained renown in Ohio as an unbeatable, if eccentric, defense attorney.

After a term as lieutenant governor of Ohio, Vallandigham was elected to Congress as an anti-Abolitionist Democrat, but was defeated in 1862. His last speech before Congress, directly following passage of the Conscription Act, urged his countrymen to stop fighting. Republicans decried the address as treason; Copperheads heard it as a rallying cry.

Governor Oliver Morton of Indiana, fearing the spread of Copperhead influence in his state, appealed to Secretary of War Stanton to detach Colonel Henry B. Carrington from his Washington duties in the Adjutant General's Office to come to Indianapolis and organize a squad of detectives to infiltrate and, ultimately, destroy the Copperheads. Carrington arrived and, finding Copperhead activity widespread, appealed to headquarters of the Department of the Ohio to initiate a full investigation. The commanders had heard of the Copperheads—who hadn't?—but dismissed them as fanatics as harmless as they were windy. While headquarters declined to furnish Carrington a staff, it did authorize an investigation. Carrington next appealed to Governor Morton, who was more than willing to appropriate funds, but the Copperhead-dominated legislature would not permit it. Nevertheless, the colonel managed to piece together a small staff of amateur investigators. He and his men even secured a few indictments, and it was quickly becoming apparent that the Copperheads had graduated from mere defeatism—preaching the wisdom of armistice—to outright collaboration with the Confederates, aiding and abetting John Hunt Morgan, whose mounted "Raiders" were as famed and feared in the Old Northwest and Kentucky as John Singleton Mosby's men were in the war's eastern theater. On March 19, 1863, Carrington wired Lincoln with the intelligence that Morgan intended to "raise the standard of revolt in Indiana. Thousands believe this and his photograph is hung in many homes. In some counties his name is daily praised."

The understaffed Carrington did not realize at the time that Morgan was far more than a popular icon of rebellion. He could well precipitate a Northern revolt. For early in the summer of 1863, Confederate Captain Thomas Henry Hines called on the leader of Indiana's Copperheads, Dr. William A. Bowles, at his home in French Lick. According to a report Colonel Carrington would make more than a year later, Hines attempted to coordinate Morgan's raid with an uprising of "Bowles's army," a force Bowles claimed included ten thousand armed Copperheads, who would take over state and local government, seize arsenals, and assassinate whomever it was necessary to assassinate.

In the meantime, although Washington and the military generally dismissed the Copperheads, General Ambrose Burnside, smoldering from his ignominious defeat at Fredericksburg, was compelled to take cognizance of Confederate intelligence, which served the rebels so well at that battle. On April 13, 1863, he issued Order No. 38, which authorized the death penalty for couriers carrying secret mails and for enemy agents operating behind Union lines. The order also extended to "recruiting officers of secret societies." This last provision Clement Vallandigham took as a gauntlet flung in his face. On May Day Vallandigham addressed a mass Democratic meeting at Mount Vernon, Ohio. He not only spat on a copy of the order, but decried Burnside as a tyrant, a usurper of American freedom. Vallandigham asserted that the war could be ended by negotiation *now,* that the Republicans were prolonging the bloodshed for the purely political purpose of destroying the Democratic party. Burnside, who had sent soldiers in civilian clothes to report on the Mount Vernon rally, summarily ordered Vallandigham's arrest. Seeking neither authority from his superiors nor advice from his staff, the general sent his aide-de-camp, together with a company of soldiers, to Dayton. They knocked on Vallandigham's door at 2:30 in the morning of May 5. When the fiery Copperhead refused to admit them, barricading himself and his wife in a bedroom and even firing pistol shots out a window, the company of soldiers broke down the door and took the former congressman to Cincinnati, where he would be brought before a military commission.

Soon, rioting broke out in Dayton, and rallies—some violent and destructive, all threatening to become so—were staged across the country. A state of insurrection seemed clearly in the making. As for Vallandigham, he refused to plead before the military commission on the grounds that it had no jurisdiction over a civilian, a citizen of a state not—despite appearances—in the throes of rebellion. Although he was silent before the officials, he was tolerably loud in his public statements protesting the fact that he had been imprisoned for declaring his political beliefs. Even newspapers opposed to the radical Democratic party line rose to defend the right of free speech. Burnside had handled Vallandigham about as competently as he had managed Fredericksburg. The Ohio politician whom few outside his own state and party took seriously was now elevated to national prominence. Abraham Lincoln decided to intervene. He did not wish to countermand Burnside's authority publicly, but seized instead on something the general had said earlier: that violators of Order No. 38 might be banished to the "lines of their friends." After a two-day trial, Vallandigham was sentenced to imprisonment for the duration of the war and was confined at Fort Warren, Boston. On May 26, the President commuted the sentence to banishment, reasoning that he would do less harm behind enemy lines than as a vociferous martyr in a Northern prison.

As Burnside's act had been rash and foolish, so there was wisdom in Lincoln's strategy. However, he *was* sending the Copperhead leader into the hands of an enemy with whom, according to Carrington's early intelligence, certain Copperhead groups were already collaborating. A detachment of federal troops, operating under a flag of truce, escorted Vallandigham south of Murfreesboro, Tennessee, and thence to a Confederate outpost between Tullahoma and Shelbyville. Officially, Confederate authorities informed Vallandigham that he could not remain in the South if he still considered himself loyal to the Union. Indeed, he declared, he was loyal. Therefore, he traveled to Wilmington, North Carolina, traditional port of embarkation for blockade runners, and boarded a vessel bound for the West Indies. From there, he made his way to Nova Scotia, arriving on July 5. Despite his banishment, the Democratic party defiantly nominated him as its candidate for governor of Ohio. On July 15, he opened his campaign—in exile—by directing an address to the people of Ohio from the Canadian side of Niagara Falls.

So much is known for certain. But at least one historian, James D. Horan in his *Confederate Agent: A Discovery in History,* speculates that Confederate General Braxton Bragg, cavalry raider John Hunt Morgan, and one Captain Thomas Henry Hines had ample opportunity to confer—or plot—with Vallandigham at the Confederate camp between Tullahoma and Shelbyville.

Just who was Captain Hines? Few Civil War histories mention him. Certainly, his name is far less familiar than that of his friend, colleague, and sometime commander, John Hunt Morgan. Born in 1841, Hines was descended on his mother's side from the Dinwiddies of Virginia. A quiet, slightly built man—he never weighed more than 130 pounds—Hines was teaching on the faculty of Masonic University, La Grange, Kentucky, when the war broke out. Little known and never celebrated, he would become, according to a modern biographer of Morgan, "the most competently dangerous man in the Confederacy."

Hines and fourteen other men formed a troop of cavalry the day after Fort Sumter was fired on and dubbed themselves Buckner's Guides, after General Simon Bolivar Buckner, a Kentucky military hero. After staging raids throughout the state, the Guides were disbanded in January 1862. In Richmond, Hines heard stories about Morgan's exploits and, in May, enlisted in the 9th Kentucky as a private. With Morgan, who soon commissioned him a captain, Hines conducted brilliant raids throughout Kentucky, Indiana, and Ohio. Although Hines and his men frequently posed as federals, their guerrilla sorties were not primarily espionage missions, but acts of military banditry, most often aimed at liberating stores of supplies and obtaining gold and greenbacks.

As Colonel Carrington had forewarned in his March 19 wire to President Lincoln, Morgan and Hines, operating in conjunction with Copperhead forces, were now terrorizing Indiana, where they easily outmaneuvered an emergency militia force of eleven hundred men. But a full-scale rebellion never materialized. The Copperheads not only lacked effective military organization, but Morgan and Hines alienated potential support by failing to distinguish between Copperhead and loyalist when it came to appropriating whatever money, supplies, or valuables they needed. They simply robbed *everyone,* and that policy was hardly conducive to recruiting partisans. By July 26, federal troops had run Morgan and Hines, who were operating separately, to ground. Hines and his men were taken at Buffington Island in the Ohio River and Morgan and his command near the village of East Liverpool, Ohio.

Hines and his command were quickly transported downriver to Cincinnati, where, except for a few troopers who managed to escape by jumping overboard and swimming to shore, enlisted men were confined at Camps Morton and Douglas and officers were deposited in the city jail. Morgan and his men were sent directly to the penitentiary at Columbus. After three days in Cincinnati, Hines and his men were moved to Johnson's Island in Lake Erie. Here they made escape plans, which were foiled by an informer, and they, too, were shipped on to Columbus. With time on his hands, Hines began reading Victor Hugo's *Les Miserables.* The story of Jean Valjean gave him an idea and, with infinite patience, Hines planned another escape.

Using a wooden prop that supported his bed, Hines carefully tapped across the floor of his cell. Each thump resounded hollowly, from which Hines concluded that the cell floor did not rest directly on a solid foundation, but had beneath it an air chamber. He decided to cut a hole in the concrete floor of the cell and tunnel his way to freedom. After procuring mess knives from two officers, who were ill and whose meals were therefore brought to them in their cells, he and several others, including Captains Hockersmith, Bennett, Taylor, Sheldon, and Magee, began digging. Hines, in the role of lookout, sat on edge of his bed reading Gibbon's *Decline and Fall of the Roman Empire,* advising his diggers with a set of signal taps when to dig and when to stop. Rubble was carefully hidden behind Hines's bed tick and smuggled out into the yard at every opportunity. When a guard approached too closely, the men "spontaneously" broke into song to cover the sound of digging.

On November 13, after almost two weeks of digging, they broke through the foundation of the prison. Now it remained to tunnel under the yard and to the wall, which the escapees would scale with a rope. Accounts of the escape vary. One version puts the completion of the tunnel at the very end of November; another at Thanksgiving Day, November 20. Yet another version claims that no tunnel was dug at all; the prisoners escaped not by dint of brain and brawn, but bribery. Most likely, the escape did involve a tunnel—as well as a few judicious bribes. Whatever the precise day of completion, Hines, the other captains, and General Morgan used shirts and underwear to fashion dummies that were neatly laid out in their bunks. With a flourish more typical of John Hunt Morgan than himself, Hines pinned a note to his dummy memorializing the tunnel:

Castle Merion, Cell No.20.

Commencement November second, 1863. Number of hours per day; five. Tools, two small knives. *La patience est amère mais son fruit est doux.* By order of my six honorable Confederates.

T. H. Hines,
Captain, C.S.A.

Once outside the prison walls, the men—seven including Hines—split into pairs, except for Captain Magee, who went off alone. Hines and Morgan traveled together. At the Columbus depot, they boarded a Cincinnati-bound train, taking care not to sit together. A federal colonel also boarded and took a seat next to Morgan. He offered the Confederate general a nip from his bottle of peach brandy.

"Will you join me, sir?" the colonel offered.

"Certainly, sir," Morgan replied.

As the train passed the penitentiary, the colonel remarked, "This is the hotel at which Morgan stops, I believe."

"And will stop, I hope," Morgan replied. "He has given us his fair share of trouble and will not now be released. I drink to him. May he ever be as closely kept as he is now."

Twice, while making his way back to Confederate lines, Hines was captured by Home Guard patrols, and twice he overpowered and outdistanced them.

As early as 1862, a Missourian named Captain Longuemare, had outlined a grand conspiracy to Jefferson Davis. Copperhead societies would rise throughout the North, political officials would be overthrown or murdered, Chicago and New York would be razed, Confederate prisoners of war would be liberated. According to Longuemare, Davis jumped "to his feet with the quick nervous motion peculiar to him" and exclaimed: "It is a great plan. . . . You show me that this conspiracy is engineered and led by good men. I want military men: men that were connected with West Point. Give me some, even if only one or two, and I will have confidence in it."

Yet nothing came of the plan in 1862, and despite the Draft Riots, despite Copperheads and secret conspiratorial orders, and despite raiders like Morgan and Hines, the year 1863 ended without any offer of armistice from the North, let alone a revolution there. To even the most hopeful of Confederate leaders it was becoming apparent that, provided the North remained willing to hurl men into battle, the region's greater population and far more substantial economic and industrial base would inexorably prevail. Worse, Northern policy makers were themselves well aware of their advantages. After July 1862, realizing that the South was chronically short of manpower, the North generally suspended prisoner exchanges. Captive Northerners could be replaced, but Southerners were in shorter and shorter supply.

Early in 1864, then, the Confederate administration, in well-founded desperation, was anxious to strengthen and to capitalize on relations with the Copperheads, despite the earlier failure of "Bowles's army" to materialize. Perhaps Davis and Confederate Secretary of War James A. Seddon were thinking specifically of Longuemare's plan when they summoned Hines to Richmond in February and March 1864. According to Hines, they discussed the idea of fomenting a general uprising. Secretary Seddon's formal orders to Hines were not so explicit, but the agent's assignment was ambitious enough, and there is plenty to be read between the lines:

Confederate States of America
War Department
Richmond, Va., March 16, 1864

Captain T. Henry Hines:
Sir—You are detailed for special service to proceed to Canada, passing through the United States under such character and in such mode as you may deem most safe, for the purpose of collecting there the men of General Morgan's command who may have escaped, and others of the citizens of the Confederate States willing to return and enter the military service of the Confederacy, and arranging for their return either through the United States or by sea. You will place yourself, on arrival, in communication with Hon. J. P. Holcomb, who has been sent as special commissioner to the British Provinces, and in his instructions directed to facilitate the passage of such men to the Confederacy. In passing through the United States you will

confer with the leading persons friendly or attached to the cause of the Confederacy, or who may be advocates of peace, and do all in your power to induce our friends to organize and prepare themselves to render such aid as circumstances may allow; and to encourage and animate those favorable to a peaceful adjustment to the employment of all agencies calculated to effect such consummation on terms consistent always with the independence of the Confederate States. You will likewise have in view the possibility, by such means as you can command, of effecting any fair and appropriate enterprises of war against our enemies, and will be at liberty to employ such of our soldiers as you may collect, in any hostile operation offering, that may be consistent with the strict observance of neutral obligations in the British Provinces. . . .

> Respectfully,
> James A. Seddon,
> Secretary of War

Seddon's orders stressed the liberation of Morgan's men in particular since, in February 1864, Morgan's cavalry had been reactivated. Once again, the plan was to coordinate his raids with an uprising of Copperheads.

To Lieutenant General Leonidas Polk, Seddon gave instructions that would facilitate the financing of an ambitious operation:

> . . . I shall have occasion to send Capt. T. Henry Hines, an enterprizing officer, late of Gen. Morgan's command, who was so efficient in aiding the escape of that General and others from the Ohio penitentiary, on special service through the lines of the enemy. To provide him with funds for the accomplishment of the purpose designed, it will be necessary *that I shall have transferred to Memphis some two hundred (200) bales of cotton,* which I have ordered an officer of the Bureau to have purchased at some convenient point in North Mississippi.
>
> Capt. Hines will himself arrange the agencies by which the cotton can be transferred and disposed of, so as to place funds at command in Memphis, and I have to request that facilities, in the way of transportation and permission to pass the lines, may, as far as needful, be granted him and the agent he may select. You will please give appropriate instructions to effect these ends to the officers in command on the border.

Two hundred bales of cotton were worth somewhere near a hundred thousand 1864 dollars, and there is evidence to suggest that, by the time the war ended, perhaps a million dollars had been invested in what came to be called the Northwest Conspiracy.

During April, Hines made his way to Toronto. Family legend has it that, at a banquet given in his honor just before he left on his mission, Hines bet a fellow officer that, his pockets stuffed with the bonds needed to finance his activities in Canada, he would shake hands with President Lincoln himself as he passed through Washington on his way north. Hines's single modern biographer, James D. Horan, not only gives this story his credence, but speculates that Hines may have gained access to the president by presenting himself as the famous actor he so strikingly resembled—John Wilkes Booth. Maybe, maybe not. But such a gesture was not beyond Thomas Hines. Recall the note he pinned to the dummy in his cell at the penitentiary in Columbus. Or consider that, on March 28, 1864, in the wake of his top secret discussions with Jefferson Davis and Secretary Seddon and on the threshold of his mission to Canada, Hines wrote a letter to his father in which he enclosed papers intended for a Lexington, Kentucky, historian—a Dr. Blanton—who was planning to write "a book," presumably about the exploits of Tom Hines. But there is even more. "I have written to *Atlantic* [the Boston-based magazine] for the sale of the escape." Hines was selling the story of the Ohio penitentiary escape to a Yankee magazine.

Hines reached Toronto on April 20. Officially neutral, Great Britain and its provinces were actually pro-Confederate, and Toronto served as a virtually open market for military secrets. It was also to be the headquarters of a so-called Confederate "peace commission," officially charged with identifying influential citizens and officials of the United States through whose aid the Union and the Confederacy might conclude a peace that would recognize the independence of the Confederate states. In August, the commission would organize a peace conference on the Canadian side of Niagara Falls, with the influential New York newspaper editor Horace Greeley in attendance. Unofficially, the commission was to orchestrate rebellion in the Old Northwest.

Captain Hines was the military commander of the commission.

The War Between the Spies

Jacob Thompson, a Mississippian who had served in the Buchanan administration as secretary of the interior, was appointed chief of the commission. Clement Clay, former United States senator from Alabama, and James P. Holcomb, a Virginian, also served as commissioners. A Kentucky friend of Hines's, William W. Cleary, was appointed secretary to the commission. Holcomb was already in Montreal; Thompson, Clay, and Cleary made the journey to Canada early in May 1864 by blockade runner to the Bermudas, whence the commissioners boarded a British mail packet to Montreal. William Cleary wrote an article for a collection of reminiscences called *Southern Bivouac,* published after the war by Morgan cavalry raider Basil Duke. It is a good account of the risky business of running the Union blockade:

> We left on the morning of the 6th of May, 1864, and slowly steamed down Cape Fear River to [Confederate] Fort Fisher, reaching the fort about four p.m. We waited until it was quite dark, and then started to run out of the harbor. We could plainly discern the United States blockading squadron, thirteen ships in number. The *Thistle* was very fast. It was said she could make nearly fourteen knots an hour. She was a long, narrow side-wheel steamer, lying low in the water, painted gray or nearly white, so that she could scarcely be seen at night. White has been defined as the absence of color, so that I may say she was colorless. All of the blockade runners were so painted. Her machinery was perfect and in exquisite order. It was a pleasure to visit her engine-room. Everything was clean and tidy, and the brass and steel burnished until they looked like gold and silver. All the parts of the machinery were kept well oiled, so that they worked noiselessly. When we began our run every light was extinguished. We burned anthracite coal and made little or no smoke, and a sort of hood was put over the furnace to prevent any reflection of its fires being seen.
>
> . . . [A]bout eight p.m. [we] were creeping along and twisting our devious and perilous way through the huge blockaders. . . . It seemed at times as if a stone could have been pitched from our vessel into one of these dangerous neighbors. If we were detected we might expect a broadside. Our Captain said, however, that the real danger would come with daylight—just at daylight —when we could be seen, and, not far away from the harbor, might find our ship close to some war vessel ready to give chase.

Then we would have to run for it. A blockade-runner was not built to fight, but intended to trust to her heels. . . . About seven a.m. on the 7th, the lookout gave notice that he had sighted a steamer. Our course was at once changed. The stranger immediately changed her course; and so on again and again, until it was plain that we were being pursued. We could see the black smoke pouring out from the chimneys of the pursuer, and our Captain said she was gaining on us—in a few hours she would be near enough to fire into us. This was pleasant intelligence to gentlemen going out on diplomatic business. I thought I might as well have remained and have been shot in the regular way on land. The Captain thought this pertinacious steamer the United States war steamer *Connecticut,* reputed to be very fast. We made all arrangements to burn our mail and papers, and to distribute the money. Each passenger began to prepare his little story, that he might be able to properly entertain his captors.

. . . The chase lasted five hours. We were taking in more courage [i.e., "some excellent 'Dutch courage' furnished from the Captain's stores"] during all that time. The Yankee seemed to gain on us rapidly. All at once our Captain got excited for the first time, and announced that we were running away from the enemy. He supposed that some part of her machinery had failed. At any rate, we got away. . . .

Captain Hines traveled to Montreal to meet the commissioners when they arrived on the morning of May 29. To Hines's dismay, the men fell to bickering almost immediately. Commissioner Clay wanted to spend the night in a Montreal hotel. Thompson argued, quite rightly, that, whereas Toronto was virtually an open city, Montreal crawled with federal detectives. It was dangerous to stay.

"I'm not going to do any more traveling, Jacob," Clay declared. "I'm tired. I want a hotel suite right here in Montreal."

Thompson replied: "We must move to Ontario."

"And I say I'm going to stay here!"

The chief backed down. They would spend the night and leave early the next morning. But there was more. Clay demanded that Thompson deposit ninety-five thousand dollars of the mission's money in the Bank of Montreal in a *personal* account payable to Clement C. Clay. To this, remarkably, Thompson also agreed.

They set up shop in an obscure boardinghouse in an out-of-the-way street. Once they were settled, Thompson outlined their mission with no small measure of bombast. First and foremost, they were to exercise all diplomatic means to gain peace. Failing that, they were to "adopt measures to cripple and embarrass the military policy of the Federal Government." The destruction of military and naval stores, the disruption of expeditions against the Confederacy, and the hindrance of supply were all within the mission's purview. The kind of guerrilla "warfare" waged by Morgan and Hines, which included robbery, was not to be permitted, Thompson declared. That restriction, Hines realized, would mean failure. To make matters worse, Secretary of War Seddon sent a dispatch to Canada at the end of May informing the mission that Hines was to subordinate himself to Thompson. Hines also found disturbing the presence of George N. Sanders, a Confederate agent, a member *ex-officio* of the Confederate Mission, but also a loose cannon and a meddler.

Despite these disappointments and impediments, Hines went about the completion of an important part of his mission, identifying, rounding up, feeding, and clothing escaped Confederate prisoners. Some he recruited for undercover work in Canada, but to most he gave fifty to a hundred dollars to finance their journey back to Dixie and Confederate military service. Thompson, in the meantime, was squandering funds on cranks. Word had spread throughout Toronto that a Confederate commission was paying men just for coming to them with schemes of sabotage and destruction. Thompson did not inquire very deeply into the qualifications of those who presented themselves, but blithely doled out money by the thousands. Even when he did ask for credentials, he seems to have gotten duped. A man asked him for ten thousand dollars for arms, claiming that he had authorization from Richmond. When Thompson demanded to see the official papers, the man replied that he had forgotten them—in Richmond. For three thousand dollars, he would travel back to the capital, fetch the papers, and return. Thompson paid, and thereby the Confederate States of America lost three thousand dollars.

While the Confederate Mission was doing its work in Canada, Colonel Henry B. Carrington, U.S.A., was still struggling to monitor

Copperhead activity in Indiana without benefit of adequate funding and sufficient personnel. In desperation he turned to an old friend of his, the provost marshal of Tennessee, asking the official to recommend the services of a good man. The provost marshal sent him Felix Stidger.

Carrington had been acquainted with the thirty-year-old, brown-eyed, mild-mannered clerk when both men were stationed at the War Department offices in Washington. Stidger was subsequently transferred to Tennessee, and Carrington asked him to volunteer as a "mole," to go to French Lick and seek out Dr. William Bowles, leader of the Indiana Copperheads. He was to introduce himself as a "Peace Democrat" and offer his services to the cause.

Stidger undertook the mission, setting out across Indiana in May, posing as a Kentucky Copperhead and stopping frequently for a friendly drink with this or that citizen to denounce Lincoln and advocate peace at any cost. At Salem, he found a drinking companion who was particularly vocal in his expression of Copperhead tenets. The agent befriended him, and even stayed the night in his home. The next morning the man asked Stidger if he wished to join the Order of the American Knights.

Agent Stidger was as good as in. Almost.

Dr. Bowles cross-examined the candidate closely, but Stidger was one of those natural spies, like Lafayette C. Baker or Timothy Webster, who could be convincing without trying very hard. He earnestly discussed with Bowles the situation in Kentucky, where U.S. Court of Appeals Chief Justice Joshua Bullitt was Grand Commander of the Order of American Knights and, consequently, the state's leading Copperhead. Soon Stidger had convinced Bowles to send him to Kentucky to assist Judge Bullitt in more effectively organizing his forces there. It was in Louisville that the federal agent took the second-degree oath, which admitted him to the order's secret councils. Publicly, the Copperheads demanded armistice—which, as staunch Republicans saw it, was in itself treasonable—but, Stidger discovered, in secret they were plotting nothing less than revolution. Moreover, the Copperhead army was to be armed by the Confederate States of America.

Felix Stidger filed his first report with Colonel Carrington on May 11, outlining the Northwest Conspiracy. A Copperhead army of some 600,000 would rise; cities would be burned; government officials assassinated. Rebel prisoners held in camps throughout the Old Northwest would be liberated to augment the Copperhead forces and those fighting in the South. Indeed, secret agents had already passed the word to the prison camps. Before long, Ohio, Indiana, and Illinois would become the Northwest Confederate States.

While in Kentucky, Stidger also attended a secret demonstration of a home-brewed concoction called Greek fire. It was to Confederate insurgents what the Molotov cocktail would be to Communist partisans. It looked innocent enough. A clear liquid resembling water but smelling like rotten eggs, it was put up in four-ounce jars that, when hurled against a wall, produced a muffled explosion and ignited with a flash. The chemist who demonstrated it to the Order of American Knights allowed that he could produce it in great quantity.

A meeting in Indianapolis a few weeks later yielded more intelligence, including the names of various conspirators, and brought news that terrified Felix Stidger. One of Carrington's other agents, a man remarkably enough named Coffin, had been found out and was to be *eliminated.* Dutifully, Stidger alerted Carrington to remove Coffin, but Stidger was also badly shaken on his own account. At least once, his own allegiance to the order had been called into question. Bowles not only stood up for him, but when the Doctor was named secretary of the Indiana Copperheads, he nominated Stidger as his assistant. Still, the agent now took to carrying a dagger and a pistol in his boot, and, as he wrote to Carrington, he feared that he would be "murdered in my sleep." We know more about the careers of Timothy Webster, Lafayette Baker, Thomas N. Conrad, and Rose Greenhow than we do about Felix Stidger's. Yet, of all these, it is Stidger who has left the most sympathetic, most *human* trace. Webster, Baker, Conrad, even the Rebel Rose must have known fear, but only Felix Stidger left a record of it. A small man, war office clerk by vocation, he was now a lone spy among conspirators who, as far as he could tell, numbered in the hundreds of thousands and who were backed by the Confederacy itself. No wonder his reports to Carrington were scrawled in a nervous hand, which one modern scholar describes as "spidery." Well aware of the stakes for himself, Stidger was terrified. But he also knew what was at stake for his country, and he mastered his fear. He stayed with the job.

It was well for the Union that he did. For in Louisville that June he met Captain Hines, who had come down from Toronto to confer with Dr. Bowles on new plans for the Copperhead uprising, set, with obvious symbolism, for July 4. As with the abortive "revolution" that had been plotted in 1863, the uprising was to be coordinated with new raids John Hunt Morgan—reinforced, in part, by Confederate escapees Hines had sent from Canada—was planning for Kentucky. Hines was as impressed with Stidger as Bowles had been, and as for Bowles, he was so taken with Hines that he had him initiated into the order. To all appearances, they were one big, happy, conspiratorial family. Couriers were spreading the word of the uprising throughout Indiana, Illinois, Kentucky, and Ohio. Others would coordinate activity in Chicago and New York.

In the meantime, the Confederate commissioners extended peace feelers from Toronto. By continually holding forth the prospect of peace, they hoped at the very least to erode the Union's resolve to continue fighting. They also hatched a scheme, first proposed by Confederate Secretary of State Judah P. Benjamin, to create a financial panic in the North by buying up gold and exporting it, thereby undermining the basis of the Union dollar. An agent named Porterfield was dispatched to New York with fifty thousand dollars, and through a complex series of maneuvers he exported the gold to England and sold it for sterling bills of exchange, which he converted to U.S. currency, and which he then used to buy more gold, managing to send out of the country some five million dollars in bullion. Porterfield claimed to have induced others to do the same, and, according to commission chief Thompson, the scheme had actually begun to have a "marked effect" on the federal economy just when General Ben ("Beast") Butler put a stop to it by arresting an associate of Porterfield. Porterfield himself was forced to flee back to Canada.

Early in June 1864, Hines sent Secretary of War Seddon a report outlining the planned Copperhead uprising. Two regiments, Hines wrote, were forming in Chicago and were preparing to move against Camp Douglas, a prisoner of war facility on the outskirts of the city.

Simultaneously with the attack on Camp Douglas, "a force of 3,000 Democrats under a competent leader" would attack Rock Island, Illinois, where some seven thousand Confederate prisoners were kept. Other elements of the Copperhead army would attack Chicago proper and Springfield, the state capital. The governments of Illinois, Indiana, and Ohio would be seized, "and their executives disposed of." Within ten days of the first attacks, Hines thought that his army of Copperheads and liberated Confederate prisoners would number some fifty thousand. The grandiose plan was, in fact, more imagination than plan. It was so haphazardly conceived that Hines neglected to mention in his report the role to be played by John Hunt Morgan's latest raid on Ohio and Kentucky. The plan was for Morgan's raiders to join forces with the Copperheads.

Morgan began the raid on June 2, 1964. On June 11, he attacked the town of Cynthiana, where he prevailed against a detachment of five hundred federals and, subsequently, against additional Union cavalry. It was at this critical point that he expected to be joined by the Copperheads. Together they would lay the ground work for the July 4 general uprising.

As had happened in 1863, the Copperhead army failed to materialize. The efforts of Colonel Carrington and Felix Stidger had finally begun paying off. Detachments of Federal soldiers trooped through Kentucky, arresting Copperheads and confiscating arms and ammunition. Next, Brigadier General Stephen G. Burbridge, Union commander of the District of Kentucky, turned his attention to Morgan, whom he outnumbered three-to-one. By the time Burbridge was done, he had pushed Morgan out of the state and sent him retreating to Virginia minus about half his men.

It was a terrible setback for the Northwest Conspiracy, but the Confederate commissioners pressed ahead as best they could. They dispatched the mission's secretary, William Cleary, to New York City to buy guns, ammunition, and the all-important Greek fire, and to make one additional purchase: the influence of the New York *Daily News*. Fernando Wood, the city's ex-mayor who in 1861 had urged the secession of New York, owned the paper with his brother. These two Copperheads employed a leader of the Sons of Liberty, Phineas Wright, as editor. For the sum of twenty-five-thousand-dollars, Wright put the paper's editorial pages at the disposal of the commissioners as a means of propagandizing for peace. Apparently, it never occurred to Chief Commissioner Thompson to question why a newspaper owned and run by Copperheads would require a twenty-five thousand dollar bribe to publish the Copperhead party line. But, then, as we have seen, Thompson troubled himself little when it came to spending the Confederacy's money.

With the failure of Morgan's raid and the federal disruption of Kentucky Copperhead activity, Hines, the commissioners, and their men turned their attention to other fronts. To begin with the most bizarre, there was the so-called "pestilence weapon." During the trial of the Lincoln assassination conspirators, held in the spring of 1865, a witness testified that the Confederate Mission has appropriated $200,000 "for the introduction of pestilence" in the North. The witness testified that he had delivered to Washington a large quantity of clothing and blankets that a Confederate doctor had "infected" with yellow fever. The immediate object was to infect Lincoln and his cabinet, but, of course, the disease would spread beyond them.

The plot seems too sinister for the nineteenth century and more befitting the world of Adolf Hitler or, perhaps, Saddam Hussein. However, germ warfare was not an innovation of the Civil War. In the Middle Ages, Muslims deliberately spread bubonic plague among invading Crusaders, and in America, during the so-called Pontiac conspiracy that immediately followed the French and Indian War, Simeon Ecuyer, defending Fort Pitt against a siege by Delaware Indians, refused a demand for surrender and sent the Indian attackers a "present" of two blankets and a handkerchief from the fort's smallpox hospital. Not only did the Delawares, fully comprehending this gesture, withdraw on June 24, 1763, a rescued white captive later reported that smallpox was sweeping the tribe. At the end of the year, even though Pontiac had agreed to peace in October, Major General Jeffrey Amherst considered effecting the wider dissemination of smallpox among the Indians by distributing infected blankets in quantity. He abandoned the scheme when he realized the danger of infecting his own people as well, especially in the heat of close combat.

Ironically, the Confederate scheme, however far it may have gone, would never have worked. As Dr. Walter Reed and his coworkers demonstrated in 1901 during the building of the Panama Canal, yellow fever is not transmitted by person-to-person contact or by contact with contaminated articles of clothing, but by *Aedes aegypti,* the "domestic" mosquito.

Early in the summer, Hines conferred with Copperheads in Chicago. Clearly, they were shaken by Morgan's defeat and decided to push the date of the uprising back from July 4 to July 20, 1864. The uprising in Chicago would be coordinated with a revolt in Louisville. Thousands were to gather at a so-called barbecue just outside the city and, at a given signal, start the revolt. After the fall of Louisville, they would march on Cincinnati and St. Louis. Chief Justice Bullitt, the Kentucky Copperhead leader, claimed a following of three hundred thousand.

It was, however, at this very moment that, acting on Felix Stidger's intelligence, Colonel Carrington moved against Bullitt and again conducted sweeping raids through Kentucky. The chief justice, returning from Toronto with Confederate funds for buying arms, was arrested at the Louisville ferry, where he had rendezvoused with Stidger. In best undercover fashion, Stidger was also taken into custody. Bullitt carried a valise full of greenbacks, but also pockets full of checks drawn on a Toronto bank and signed by Jacob Thompson. By failing to cash the checks immediately, Bullitt had obligingly supplied the federals with documentary evidence of fifth-column activity based in an officially neutral nation. Next, using Stidger's detailed reports, Carrington dispatched soldiers to seize some thirty thousand rifles and small arms, which had been cached in barns, haystacks, and the like throughout Kentucky, and to make arrests. As news of the Kentucky fiasco reached Indiana, the fires of Copperhead enthusiasm there were doused. For good measure, Carrington had Stidger put in prison with the captured Copperheads, from whom he continued to gather intelligence. For now, one thing was certain, there would be no revolution in Kentucky or Indiana.

CHAPTER THIRTEEN

OF TERROR AND GREEK FIRE

Despite the failure of Morgan and the collapse of Copperhead support in Kentucky and Indiana, the Confederate Mission launched attacks in New England, New York, and, as planned at the time of the Kentucky raid debacle, Chicago.

In May, June, and July 1864 folks who lived or fished along the coast of Maine reported seeing "artists" sketching the coastline. In fact, they were a team of fifty Confederate topographers who had run the Union blockade, landed at New Brunswick, Canada, and worked their way south to Maine. They were making careful maps of out-of-the-way coves and inlets that two armed steamers, the *Tallahassee* and *Florida*, could use as places of refuge, resupply, and refueling as they shelled the coast in a combined naval and land action. Confederate troops transported in blockade runners to Canada would descend on the terror-stricken state and seize control of it. The attack was meant to inspire terror, to give the North a taste of what Union troops were doing to the South, and to divert federal forces as far as possible from the war's primary fronts. In the meantime, Captain Hines visited discontented factions in Boston in an attempt to organize some manner of uprising there, and Francis Jones, the courier working on the Secret Line, delivered messages between Toronto, Maine, and the rest of New England in an effort to coordinate the operation.

Jones, as we have seen earlier, was a remarkable courier. But he was a moody man, sensitive and scholarly, given to introspection. His mother, a solid Unionist, begged him to come home to St. Louis, where he also had a sweetheart waiting for him (his wife and child had recently died). On the eve of the operation in Maine, Jones wrote to U.S. Secretary of War Edwin Stanton, asking that he be allowed to take the oath of allegiance to the Union and return home. Stanton refused. Worse, someone in the Confederate command discovered Jones's attempted defection. Inexplicably, Jones was not confined or punished in any way, but sent to St. Johns, Quebec, where he was ordered to join Captain William Collins, who, with a man named Phillips, was gathering escaped Confederate prisoners for a raid into Washington County, Maine.

Even without the blatant security risk posed by Jones, the raid was doomed from the start. For Collins and Phillips, fond of drink, boasted about the mission ceaselessly. Word of it reached the ears of the American consul in St. Johns, who notified the War Department, which alerted the Home Guard. When the raiders hit the Calais (Maine) National Bank late in July, guardsmen, police, and the Portland marshal were ready for them. Collins, Phillips, and Jones were jailed.

While imprisoned, Jones revealed to his jailer, a Sheriff Brown, the scope of the plans directed against Maine. Brown sent a letter to Secretary of State Seward, who directed Secretary of War Stanton to act on the matter. Stanton had Assistant Secretary of War Charles Dana send an assistant judge advocate, L. C. Turner, to Maine to get a complete confession from Francis Jones. The resulting document revealed not only the details of the plot against Maine, it also listed the names of conspirators the well-traveled courier knew of, as well as the location of armament caches in New York, Cincinnati, Indianapolis, St. Louis, Brooklyn, and elsewhere.

With the capture of Collins, Phillips, and Jones, the raid was canceled, and from the end of July 1864 to November 23, when Stanton examined a summary of Jones's confession, nothing more was heard of it. The *Tallahassee,* instead of bombarding Maine's coast, worked its way up from Wilmington, North Carolina, preying upon shipping off the shores of New York and New England. The *Florida* likewise continued to ply her trade as a successful commerce raider. There was, perhaps, a certain wisdom in Stanton's having delayed action on the rich intelligence Jones had supplied. The months that elapsed must have lulled into a false sense of security the more than twenty key operatives he named in Maine, Massachusetts, New York, Pennsylvania, Maryland, Illinois, Missouri, Kentucky, Tennessee, and Ohio. On November 24, Stanton ordered arrests in all of those states, together with the confiscation of arms, ammunition, and supplies. As to Jones, Collins, and Phillips, their fate is unknown. No judicial records attest to trials or sentences.

During the summer of 1864, as the Maine scheme died aborning, Thomas Hines, Jacob Thompson, and Clement C. Clay met with Clement Vallandigham in an effort to rally the Copperheads. The uprising set for July 4 had been pushed to the 20th, and was again postponed, the day of action now set for August 29, 1864, when the Democratic Convention would open in Chicago. For the August operation, Hines resolved to take a strong hand in providing the Copperhead forces with sorely needed military organization.

The Copperheads set up regimental headquarters in the Invincible Club at Randolph and Dearborn streets under the command of a Cook County political boss and member of the Sons of Liberty, "Brigadier General" Charles Walsh. To supply Walsh's men with the necessary military leadership, Hines returned to Toronto, selected fifty Confederate soldiers recruited there, and appointed as his second in command Captain John Breckinridge Castleman, the company commander under whom Hines had first served with Morgan's Raiders. Already stationed in Chicago was Colonel George St. Leger Grenfel, an aging but experienced and able Confederate guerrilla. By the time the squadron was ready to depart for Chicago, its numbers had grown to seventy. The additional twenty men had not been handpicked by Hines, but by Jacob Thompson and the ever-meddlesome George N. Sanders on account of their "high connections"—whatever that meant. The squadron departed Toronto two men at a time beginning on August 10. In Chicago, they established headquarters at the Richmond House, identifying themselves as the Missouri delegation to the Democratic Convention.

A primary target of the uprising was Camp Douglas, the prisoner of war facility just outside the city. The plan was to work from without and within to effect the escape of the prisoners and then to arm them. Their release would swell the ranks of the army of insurrection, and, surely, Chicago would fall to the combined forces of Copperheads and freshly liberated Confederate soldiers.

Camp Douglas was eminently vulnerable to a massive jail break. Five thousand prisoners were crowded into the space of seventy acres bounded only by a twelve-foot-high board fence. With a garrison of just sixteen hundred Union troops to guard them, prisoner-trusties served as auxiliary guards. And while many of the men were in rather seedy condition after long confinement, a good many of them were battle-hardened Texans and raiders from Morgan's command. Well aware of his precarious position, Colonel Benjamin Jeffrey Sweet, Eighth Regiment, Veterans' Corps, commandant of Camp Douglas, practiced a high degree of vigilance. He became suspicious, early in the summer of 1864, when the volume of letters issuing from the prisoners dramatically increased. The letters seemed harmless enough: the usual sentiments expressed to wives, family, and sweethearts. But there was a peculiar uniformity about them. They were written on long sheets of paper, but each sheet bore only a few lines. The peculiarities were more than enough to prompt a hunch, and Sweet made an experiment. He took one of the letters, held it before the open door of a stove, and characters written in invisible ink blackened before his eyes: "The 4th of July is going up like a rocket and an all-fired sight of powder is going to burn" and "The 4th of July will be a grand day for us. Old Sweet won't like it."

Sweet wired for reinforcements, but was told, in effect, that there was a war on, and he'd have to make do. With the postponement of the Democratic Convention to the end of August, the date of the prison break and the uprising was also pushed back. For the Confederates, it proved to be a fatal delay, as a Confederate major, identified only as attached to Captain Thomas H. Hines's command, came forward to Union authorities in mid-August offering information on the planned breakout and uprising in exchange for money and an opportunity to sign a loyalty pledge. The ultimate fate of the major is unknown. According to Hines's biographer, James D. Horan, the captain's son revealed in 1933 that his father had pursued a "traitor" from Detroit to Niagara Falls and hurled him therein. Probably this was the treacherous major, but there is no way of ascertaining with certainty the truth of the story.

Armed now with the major's revelation, Sweet secured reinforcements of three thousand troops to guard Camp Douglas and patrol the city. Worse for Hines and his plan, although Walsh claimed to command a hundred thousand Copperheads, he reported to Hines on the night before the convention opened that the couriers who were to spread word of the strike to Copperhead contingents in Indiana and Ohio had failed to do so. Then the fateful day came, the convention opened, and the revolt in Chicago evaporated.

Still, Hines refused to give up. There was an arsenal and a prison camp at Rock Island, on the Illinois side of the Mississippi, yet to be assaulted. All he needed, Hines said, was five hundred men. With captured arms and liberated prisoners, he could return to Chicago, take the city, and then march on Springfield as well. The telegraph office would be seized and the message flashed to the Copperhead bands in Indiana, Ohio, and the rest of Illinois, as well as to New York City. Walsh, who had promised one hundred thousand men, now demurred at five hundred. *Two* hundred, then. Walsh and other Copperhead leaders promised to return with that number. In fact, they came back with twenty-five volunteers. The revolution in the Old Northwest had failed.

Following this disappointment, the Confederate Mission turned to political means to achieve its ends, funding the candidacy of Democrat James C. Robinson for governor of Illinois in return for his pledge of support. Robinson implied that, if elected, he would turn over the state's militia and arsenal to the Sons of Liberty. Not that military measures were altogether abandoned. Confederate raiders commanded by Hines burned some federal warehouses in Mattoon, Illinois, and his second in command, Castleman, conducted an incendiary raid on some seventy steamers docked at St. Louis. It was partially successful, though Castleman was disappointed by the relatively light degree of damage. Out of seventy vessels, five to ten were destroyed or damaged. The raid had worse consequences for Castleman, however. John P. Maughan, a Toronto bank clerk and one of the men Thompson and Sanders had foisted on Hines, got drunk and boasted in a Mattoon barroom how he had participated in the burning of the warehouses. Maughan was promptly arrested and soon made a full confession. Hines managed to elude the federals who, on the basis of the information Maughan supplied, were sent after him, but Castleman was apprehended. Hines made an abortive attempt to free his former commanding officer as he was being transported to prison in Indianapolis, but it was no use.

The Confederate Hines, though, was nothing if not persistent. Castleman was put in solitary confinement at Indianapolis, but Hines found a guard willing to be bribed and smuggled to the prisoner a small saw, with which he cut a hole in the wooden floor of his cell. Castleman tunneled out to the prison yard—only to be caught by the captain of the guards as he emerged. The saw having been confiscated, Hines smuggled in thirteen more, made of watch springs that had been serrated. He secreted them in the binding of a Bible, which, in best prison-break fashion, was delivered to Castleman by his elderly mother. When she told her son who had sent the Bible, Castleman knew it was no ordinary edition of the Good Book, and, for extra measure, Hines had underlined such passages as, "And if I go and prepare a place for you, I will come again and receive you unto Myself; that where I am, there ye may be also" and "I will not leave you comfortless; I will come to you." But, even with the saws, Castleman decided that escape was impossible. Charged with the dire crimes of spying in Ohio, Indiana, and Illinois, of plotting to "lay waste" Chicago, of plotting to free prisoners in Rock Island, Camp Morton, and Camp Douglas, and of conspiring to burn the steamers at St. Louis, Castleman, like so many other spies, was (astoundingly enough) exiled—not, however, to the South, but to Canada, where Captain Thomas Hines was waiting for him.

In the meantime, federal authorities swept up the remaining shards of the shattered Northwest Conspiracy. Acting on information supplied by the indefatigable Felix Stidger, Colonel Carrington ordered the arrest of Indiana's leading Copperheads, including Doctor William A. Bowles. It was at the trials of Bowles and his fellow conspirators that Stidger's identity was finally revealed; for he was the government's star witness. Although one of the conspirators, Harrison H. Dodd, escaped from prison before he was brought to trial, all of the men—including Dodd in absentia—were found guilty of treason. Unlike Castleman, who could claim to be a Confederate soldier doing his duty, Bowles and the others were civilians, citizens of an ostensibly loyal state. They were sentenced to hang.

Ironically, the death sentence almost made Doctor Bowles, at long last, an effective leader of insurrectionists. Copperheads throughout Indiana were again calling for revolt, this time to avenge their condemned chief. Indiana, according to many observers, was a powderkeg, but then Washington cut the fuse by commuting the death sentences to life imprisonment.

The Northwest Conspiracy had yet one more act to play out before the conspirators turned their attention back east. The Great Lakes, which seemed to lie safely outside the theater of war, were patrolled by only one Union gunboat, the USS *Michigan*. John Yates Beall, serving as acting master of the Confederate Navy, proposed to Hines and the Confederate commissioners a plan to capture the vessel, use it to liberate Confederate prisoners held at Johnson's Island, on Lake Erie, near Sandusky, Ohio, and then, in a combined water and land attack, hit the principal cities on the lake. It was yet another grandiose plan, but, unlike the blowhard Copperhead bosses, Beall had impressive credentials earned in desperate battle.

He had fought, on land, with Stonewall Jackson and was so severely wounded that he was invalided out of the army. Convalescing from his wound and afflicted with tuberculosis, Beall decided to go for broke. As early as 1862, he proposed the capture of the *Michigan,* but the Confederate Navy decided that the scheme was too risky. Instead, Beall was offered a commission as a privateer plying the waters of Chesapeake Bay. There he captured several vessels as Confederate prizes and managed quite handily to outwit the Union navy until late 1863. At that time, one of his officers was captured and revealed Beall's whereabouts. He, too, was apprehended and, with his men, convicted of piracy and condemned to die. The Confederacy repeated its threats of the first year of the war when the men of the privateer *Jeff Davis* were captured and sentenced to death. Richmond threatened to retaliate by executing federal prisoners. In the end, Beall and his men were exchanged.

On his return to Richmond, Beall again broached his *Michigan* plan and was again turned down. He reenlisted in the army briefly and then offered his services directly to Commissioner Thompson in Canada. There he was joined by Captain Charles Cole, and the pair set off for Sandusky to confer with Thomas Hines. At Sandusky they were joined by Lieutenant Bennett Young, and together they secured Hines's approval to reconnoiter the Great Lakes in general and the *Michigan* situation in particular. What they discovered was that Buffalo was weakly garrisoned but rich in government stores, including an arsenal. Cleveland, Milwaukee, and Chicago were similarly vulnerable, with Chicago's Fort Douglas easily attacked from the lake. Based on the report, Hines approved a plan to capture the *Michigan.*

Captain Cole volunteered to ingratiate himself with the officers and men of the *Michigan.* His plan was to arrange a party on board the vessel and get the men so liquored up—there was mention of drugged champagne—that Beall could simply board and take the ship. The *Michigan*'s guns could then be used against the lake cities in an attack coordinated with the liberation of Confederate prisoners at Johnson's Island and Camp Douglas. Cole, handsomely supplied with funds from Commissioner Thompson's apparently inexhaustible coffers, seems to have had a high time implementing his mission. In Buffalo, he "befriended" a young woman who introduced him to the skipper of the *Michigan.* Cole and Carter quickly became drinking companions in the barroom of the West House in Sandusky. At last, Cole was invited aboard the *Michigan* for a fine dinner on September 19.

The plan appeared to be working remarkably well. On the night of the dinner, Beall appropriated the lake steamer *Philo Parsons* in a bloodless and remarkably efficient operation. Beall had recruited twenty-eight seamen and waited with them at Sandwich, on the Canadian shore of Lake Erie. Bennett G. Burley, who had been one of Beall's Chesapeake privateers, booked passage on the *Philo Parsons* at Detroit. He asked the captain if the ship stopped at Sandwich. No, he was told, but an exception could be made. When the vessel put in at Sandwich, Beall and his men boarded her and claimed her as a Confederate prize.

With passengers and crew still on board, the *Philo Parsons* made for Middle Bass Island. Beall sighted the large steamer *Island Queen,* cut across her bow, and boarded her. The raiders took as prisoners thirty-five unarmed officers and men of the 130th Ohio Infantry, who were on their way home to Toledo. Their imprisonment was brief, however, as Beall took it upon himself to "parole" them. After depositing the soldiers and others on the American side of the lake, Beall scuttled the *Island Queen.* He continued, on the *Philo Parsons,* to his rendezvous with the *Michigan.*

Captain Cole was to have fired a signal rocket to indicate that the *Michigan* was fully compromised and ready to be boarded. Beall approached. There was the *Michigan.* If all went well, the vessel would be taken, signals would be given, and the eight thousand plus prisoners at Johnson's Island, assisted from the outside by a force of Copperheads, would break out. In attacks coordinated with the *Michigan,* this newly constituted Confederate army would do to the lake cities of the North what Sherman and other federal commanders were doing to the cities of the South.

But there were no rockets.

Beall, aching for glory and doomed, in any case, by tuberculosis, ordered the assault on the *Michigan* to commence. To his men, however, it was obvious that they had been betrayed. They refused to proceed. Faced with mutiny, Beall backed down—but not quite all the way. He demanded that his men compose and sign a "memoir of your treachery and cowardice":

> On Board the *Philo Parsons,*
> September 20, 1864.
>
> We, the undersigned crew of the boat aforesaid, take pleasure in expressing our admiration of the gentlemanly bearing, skill, and courage of Captain Beall as a commanding officer and a gentleman, but believing and being well convinced that the enemy is informed of our approach, and is so well prepared that we cannot possibly make it a success, and having already captured two boats, we respectfully decline to prosecute it any further.

Beall turned back, though he would soon return.

What went wrong? To begin with, Cole had not been altogether unsuccessful. Through bribery he had effected serious sabotage of the *Michigan*'s engines, and she was dead in the water. Neither Beall nor his crew knew this, of course, though it wouldn't have changed much. An attempt to board the *Michigan* would still have been suicidal. There was, after all, nothing wrong with her guns, whereas the *Philo Parsons* was unarmed. Moreover, the crew of the *Michigan* outnumbered the privateers, and, unlike the soldiers captured from the *Island Queen,* they were well armed.

But Cole himself never made it to his dinner party aboard the *Michigan,* because he was arrested in his Sandusky hotel room while dressing for it. Accounts vary as to how he was betrayed. One version proposes that he played his role as merrymaker all too well, got drunk, and told somebody much more than he should have. Another version holds that the scheme was revealed by a Confederate turncoat named Godfrey Hyams—who, as we shall see, also sabotaged even bigger operations—in return for seventy thousand dollars in gold. Cole was tried, found guilty on twelve counts treason, and sentenced to death. At the last minute, however, he made a full and revealing confession, on the strength of which he was allowed to take a loyalty oath and was released. His subsequent fate is not known.

Beall, on orders from Commissioner Thompson, did his best to exploit what damage Cole had managed to do. With the *Michigan* temporarily out of action, Beall, together with Morgan alumni Colonel Robert Martin and Lieutenant John W. Headley (no relation to the New York journalist, Joel T. Headley), *purchased* rather than purloined the lake steamer *Georgiana.* The vessel was fitted out with guns and sent out to bombard Buffalo. The attack would be coordinated with a rebel guerrilla operation directed at the capture of the federal arsenal and the burning of ships moored at the Buffalo wharf. Finally, after reducing Buffalo, Beall was determined to turn his attention back to the *Michigan.* Its capture would be the signal for a riot at Johnson's Island.

Again, victory seemed well within Beall's grasp. Buffalo was in a panic. The Home Guard there, consisting of boys and old men, posed no threat. It all seemed ripe for the taking.

But, again, word had leaked to the federals. Lafayette Baker's agents were on hand, and New York troops rushed in to garrison Buffalo. The United States government had pressured the Canadians into enforcing their own neutrality regulations, so that the

Georgiana was interned. Canadian officials arrested Burley and seized caches of arms and ammunition intended for the raid.

Beall, foiled again, again eluded capture. It was the last time, though. His death, at the end of a hangman's rope, would come on February 24, 1865.

After all he had been through, the circumstances of Beall's capture were anticlimactic, even comic. In December 1864 he had hatched a plan to liberate some Confederate generals and colonels who were being transferred by train from Johnson's Island to Fort Lafayette, New York. Beall and his men, including a local boy named Anderson, who had been recruited because he knew the country-side, waited for the train at the Dunkirk, New York, depot, a few miles outside Buffalo. They would board, hijack the train, kill the guards, and liberate the prisoners.

The trouble was that, when the train finally pulled in, the Confederate prisoners were not aboard. The word now was that they would be transported on the Buffalo Express, which did not stop at Dunkirk. Not to be daunted, Beall decided to derail the train outside of Buffalo, rescue the prisoners, and spirit them into Canada on sleighs. Remarkably, no one seems to have considered the possibility that the derailment might kill passengers, especially Confederate prisoners helplessly bound in irons.

Beall and his men laid a rail across the tracks, the train roared through, caught the rail on its pilot, and tossed it harmlessly off the tracks. The engineer stopped—he knew he had hit *something*—and the would-be liberators ran off at the approach of the conductor's lantern. Everyone managed to slip back into Canada, except for young Anderson and Beall. It seems that, exhausted, they fell asleep in the Niagara Falls depot restaurant. A local cop, seeing vagrants snoozing on a bench, tapped Beall's feet with his night-stick. Whereupon a panic-stricken Anderson revealed everything.

Just before Beall was hanged at Governor's Island, in New York Harbor, his hat blew off. The hangman bent to get it, but the doomed prisoner stopped him.

"Never mind, hangman, I won't need it where I'm going."

To the minister who pronounced the prayer for the dead, Beall smiled: "As some author has said, Reverend, we may be as near God on the scaffold as elsewhere."

The War Between the Spies

One after the other, the operations authorized by the Confederate Mission collapsed. On October 19, 1864, mainly at the behest of the shadowy George Sanders, Lieutenants Bennett Young and William Hutchinson led a team of about twenty men on a lightning raid of three banks in the border town of St. Albans, Vermont. The operation netted almost a quarter of a million 1864 dollars and resulted in the death of one citizen and the wounding of another. Several of the town's principal buildings were set ablaze by hurled bottles of Greek fire. The raiders fled to Canada. Eight, including Young, were captured on Canadian soil by a Vermont posse, but officials forced the posse to remand the men to Canadian custody, and skillful lawyers successfully fought extradition. Young not only survived the war, he returned to the United States after Appomattox to become president of the Monon Railroad, the Louisville Southern Railroad, and finally, the Kentucky and Indiana Bridge Company. He even served as a delegate to the Constitutional Convention of 1890–91.

In terms of the profit it made and the terror it inspired, the St. Albans raid was probably the Confederate Mission's most successful operation. Frightened New Englanders predicted that it was merely the vanguard of a general terrorist invasion. Sanders himself boasted to the correspondent of the St. Albans *Messenger* that the raid was "the starting point in inaugurating our frontier warfare against the North." But the Confederate Mission could not command the resources to capitalize on the raid, and the northeastern border remained quiet for the balance of the war.

Not so in Chicago and much of the Midwest—or so Thomas Hines hoped. The uprising in these places, so often postponed, was now firmly set for November 8, 1864, election day. More exciting was the fact that, this time, New York was also a target. The greatest cities of the North would rise in simultaneous revolt. "Brigadier General" Charles Walsh, leader of the Sons of Liberty, promised that, this time, his Copperheads would not falter. Chicago would be burned, and the prisoners at Camp Douglas and Rock Island, some fifteen thousand of them, would be liberated and armed. Similar uprisings would take place in Cincinnati, and throughout Missouri and Iowa. In New York, plans called for arson everywhere and for the seizure of the U.S. Sub-Treasury. The great stone wall of Fort Lafayette, a prisoner of war camp, would be breached with explosives, the prisoners liberated and armed.

At the beginning of November, Hines, Colonel Vincent Marmaduke, one of Commissioner Thompson's favorites, but a man whom Hines distrusted, Richard T. Semmes, brother of Raphael Semmes, senior officer of the Confederate navy, and Lieutenant J. J. Bettersworth, among others, set off from Toronto for Chicago, where Colonel George St. Leger Grenfel was already in residence. Colonel Robert Martin and Lieutenant John W. Headley, with eight other men, made for New York City, where they would join James McMasters, editor of the virulently Copperhead *Freeman's Journal,* and Captain Longuemare, the man who had originally proposed the Northwest Conspiracy to Jefferson Davis.

What Hines and the others did not count on was that, at this late stage of the war, Northern counterintelligence had become comparatively sophisticated, and, even worse, plenty of once-loyal Confederates, having decided that the cause was hopeless, were prepared to sell their secrets and their services. One such former Confederate soldier, otherwise unidentified, had found work as a federal detective. On November 5, he heard from a paid informer that Hines was in Chicago, intending to burn the city on election day. The detective approached Doctor Edward W. Edwards, known in Chicago as a Copperhead leader, who boasted that Colonel Marmaduke was staying at his house. Apparently Marmaduke had known the detective when he was a loyal Confederate soldier, for the colonel unfolded to him the planned assault on Camp Douglas. The detective informed the camp's commandant, Colonel Sweet, who questioned two prisoners, Lieutenants Maurice Langhorn and James Shanks, offering them freedom and amnesty in exchange for information. Langhorn at last revealed the plan in detail.

Next, Sweet went to work on prisoner Shanks. The commandant knew that he had something on the young Confederate lieutenant. When Shanks served with Morgan's Raiders, he had captured a federal colonel named De Land. The colonel was subsequently exchanged and became Sweet's predecessor as commandant of Camp Douglas. In September 1864, Shanks ended up a prisoner at Camp Douglas, and De Land became quite cordial toward him, probably employing him as an informant. Camp Douglas was subject to visits by a local ladies' aid society, which brought fruit and other luxuries to the ill-fed and ill-housed prisoners. When a romance developed between Shanks and one of the ladies, Colonel De Land gave the lieutenant leave to visit the lady at her home twice a week. After Colonel Sweet took over as commandant, he continued the privilege. Now Sweet was able to confront Shanks: "Do you love your friends more than your lady and your country?"

Shanks had not the will to resist. He turned informant, and his primary assignment was to locate Hines.

Sweet staged the lieutenant's "escape" from Camp Douglas in a garbage collector's wagon. Shanks called on Marmaduke and asked him where Hines was. But Marmaduke was not the man to whom Hines would have given that information. In the meantime, prisoners at Camp Douglas had become suspicious of Shanks and his escape. Why, they wondered, would a prisoner who enjoyed such favored treatment risk escape? They warned Hines and Marmaduke, but had failed to reach Lieutenant Bettersworth before Shanks got to him. Shanks invited Bettersworth to the house of his inamorata, and the couple plied him with peach brandy. Drunk, Bettersworth reeled off strategies and names. Shanks reported to Sweet, and the colonel dispatched men throughout the city to arrest the conspirators.

Once again, a Hines operation died aborning, but Hines himself slipped through Colonel Sweet's net. He hid out in the house of Dr. Edwards. As one of Sweet's patrols drew near, Hines asked: "Doctor Edwards, have you a large box mattress?"

Yes, the Doctor answered, but his wife, ill with diphtheria, was sleeping on it.

So much the better, Hines must have thought. Hines slit the mattress with his side knife and crawled into it. He told the Doctor to admit the patrol. Marmaduke was arrested in the next room, but they failed to find Thomas Hines.

With the failure of the Chicago uprising, the planned revolts elsewhere likewise fizzled. Hines managed to slip out of the city and worked his way to Brown County, Ohio. Amid the collapse of his schemes, this man, now actively sought by federal authorities across the nation, decided to marry his long-time sweetheart, Nancy Sproule. He picked her up at the Dunville Institute, an Ohio convent school, and took her to Covington, Kentucky, where they were wed. After a week's honeymoon, Hines was off to Indiana for a meeting with Dr. Bowles, whose Copperheads he still hoped to stir to action.

As election day came and went without incident in Chicago, so it passed in New York. Not only were the New York conspirators discouraged by events in Chicago, they were intimidated by the arrival of General Butler, with ten thousand federal soldiers, bent on enforcing martial law. Obviously, Copperhead security leaks had spread beyond Chicago. The conspirators decided to postpone the New York operation until Thanksgiving Day, November 25, 1864.

Then, at the last minute, James McMasters, the *Freeman's Journal* editor, announced that his Copperheads were withdrawing "from any further connection with the proposed revolution."

It was a thunderbolt, but the contingent from Toronto did their best to shake off its effects. Martin, Headley, Longuemare, and their eight subordinates resolved to carry out an incendiary attack on their own. Their plan was to check individually into the city's most prominent hotels—a New York *Herald* story places the number at nineteen—go up to the room, set it on fire, and calmly walk out. For this purpose, they would rely on Greek fire. Captain Longuemare knew a chemist who had set up a secret laboratory in a basement off Washington Square. He commissioned from the man 144 four-ounce bottles of the combustible fluid, instructing him to pack them in a valise, which Lieutenant Headley would call for.

Twelve dozen bottles of anything are heavy. Twelve dozen bottles of highly combustible liquid packed into a clumsy valise, four feet long by two or three feet high, are both heavy and terrifying. Headley picked up the valise at the chemist's basement and was then faced with the task of transporting the cargo uptown. He could walk only a few steps before he had to lay his burden down to get a fresh purchase on it. He tried to hail a carriage hack—the nineteenth-century version of a taxi—but, this being New York, when Headley really needed a cab, he couldn't get one.

So this spy, saboteur, and arsonist lugged the valise several long blocks to the horsecar line and boarded a crowded, uptown-bound car. He was able to get a seat behind the conductor, and he tucked the valise between his legs.

His relief was short-lived. Soon, he detected the rotten-egg stench of hydrogen sulfide. He looked down, expecting to see a horrible spreading stain or, worse, an accumulating puddle of Greek fire. But, no. Nevertheless, the sniffs and wry faces of Headley's fellow passengers soon made it clear that he was not alone in having detected the odor.

"Something smells dead here," a woman said. Then, worse: "Conductor, something smells dead in that man's valise." But, again, this being New York, the conductor did nothing. When, at last, the car reached Central Park, where Headley disembarked, the terrorist tipped his hat to the lady and said, "Madam, I assure you I don't carry dead bodies in my valise. Good day."

In late 1864, the vicinity of the newly established, but far from completed Central Park was dotted with ramshackle cottages. In one of these the conspirators unpacked their bottles of Greek fire and agreed to meet again in the cottage on the following evening, November 25, and then check into the hotels. None had much hope of starting anything like a revolution. Their motive now was revenge, pure and simple, and Colonel Martin instructed his operatives that, if captured, they were to give their correct name and rank, declaring that what they had done was in retaliation for the depredations Sherman and Sheridan had committed against the cities and towns of the South.

By zero hour, two of the terrorists had backed out, failing to show up at the cottage. Despite their absence, Headley checked in at the Astor, City Hotel, and the United States Hotel; Martin at the Hoffman House, Fifth Avenue Hotel, and the St. Denis; and Lieutenant Philip Ashbrook at the St. Nicholas, LaFarge, and St. James. Beginning about seven o'clock in the evening, each man registered at the desk, received his key, walked up to his room, and closed the door. Headley later related what he had done at the Astor House: "I hung the bedclothes loosely on the headboard and piled the chairs, drawers of the bureau, and washstand on the bed, then stuffed some newspapers about among the mass and poured a bottle of turpentine over it all." Instead of hurling one of his bottles of Greek fire against the wall—which would have shattered and exploded, thereby attracting attention—he merely spilled it, quickly, on a "pile of rubbish. It blazed up instantly and the whole bed seemed to be in flames before I could get out. I locked the door and . . . left the key at the office as usual." He walked through the lobby with calm deliberation, having told the desk clerk that he was off to dine with friends. Actually, he was off to register at the City Hotel, his next target. And so it went in hotel after hotel.

In addition to the hotels, the arsonists hit Barnum's Museum on lower Broadway, a blaze made all the more terrifying by the roar of the showman's lions and tigers and the trumpeting of his elephants, which were trapped in their cages. Reports claimed that the flames had driven Barnum's seven-foot-tall giantess to a frenzy so wild that it took five firemen and a physician's sedative to restrain her. Several people were injured or killed in the general panic. The audience at Niblo's Garden, a popular theater then playing *The Corsican,* panicked when, amid the clangor of fire bells outside, someone yelled *Fire!* The theater's manager, a Mr. Wheatley, mounted the stage and shouted instructions to ushers. They ran up and down the aisle, holding above their heads placards on which the words "NO FIRE" had been written. The combination of the placards and Mr. Wheatley's calming words, settled the audience back into their seats, and *The Corsican* resumed. Actually, there *was* a fire, albeit a small one, in the theater's basement. It was easily extinguished. At the Winter Garden Theater, next to the La Farge Hotel, smoke was seen coming up from under the stage. There are at least two versions of how panic was narrowly averted. One report says that the superintendent of firemen, a Mr. Leonard, happened to be in the audience that night. When the cry of "fire" was heard, he rose from his seat and affably shouted, "That's only a drunken man. Go on with the play." However, he did slip out to investigate and helped extinguish a blaze in the basement. Another version has it that the evening was saved by the quick thinking of the three principal players in *Julius Caesar.* They stepped out of character briefly, reassured the audience, and then resumed the play. In fact, it was the only time these three actors had ever appeared on the stage together. The performance was a special benefit to raise money for a statue of Shakespeare in Central Park. They were the Booth brothers, Edwin, Junius, Jr., and John Wilkes.

Finally, Headley also hurled Greek fire at ships tied up along the west side wharfs. A hay barge, the *Marie*, was sunk, and one other merchant vessel was declared a loss. A few other ships were damaged. But there was no catastrophic conflagration, not along the wharfs, nor, really, in the city itself. It is true that the epidemic of fires sparked panic and rumors of an imminent rebel invasion, and it is true that two floors of the Belmont Hotel and the Metropolitan were destroyed, and the St. Nicholas was a complete loss. A dry goods firm, Halsted and Haines, located on Broadway and White Street, was also completely destroyed. It was not on the Confederate raiders' original hit list, and the incendiary devices the fire marshal found there—bottles of turpentine and phosphorous sealed with plaster of Paris—were different from the Greek fire Headley had delivered. Most likely, the blaze was set by some Copperheads acting independently both of their faint-hearted leaders and Colonel Martin's Raiders. Despite the terrorists' best efforts, damage to the rest of their target hotels was slight. In the case of the Astor, for instance, it was a mere $100.

What had gone wrong? To begin with, Greek fire, which rebel terrorists so favored, produced an intense blaze, but one of very brief duration. It ignited on contact with air and then, almost as quickly, burned itself out. For this reason, Captain John Breckinridge Castleman, disappointed by the results of his attempt to set the St. Louis wharves ablaze, later said that the Copperheads would have done better with a box of "old-fashioned matches" than the Greek fire they used. Secondly, the arsonists had neglected one additional ingredient essential to fire—oxygen. Each man set his blaze and left, closing the door behind him. None thought to open a window first. Most of the fires quickly ignited, consumed the available air in the room, and thereby extinguished themselves.

There was worse news to come. Extra editions of the *New York Times* and the *Herald*, which hit the streets late that very night, printed full descriptions of the Confederate arsonists! The morning papers printed a full account of the plot as revealed by Godfrey Hyams, the very man who had foiled John Yates Beall's attempt to seize the USS *Michigan*. Martin and his men had all they could do to slip out of New York as quickly as possible. Probably with the aid of bribes judiciously placed in the hands of a few willing railroad conductors, they made their way, by train, to Albany and, from there, across the Canadian border.

As the fires died in New York, so died the great Northwest Conspiracy, the most ambitious project of espionage in the Civil War. Before the Confederate surrender, Hines engaged in a few more guerrilla expeditions, and, at the very end of 1864, Headley and Martin were sent on a mission to kidnap U.S. Vice-President-elect Andrew Johnson as he passed through Louisville. They failed simply because Johnson took an early boat out of the city instead of the later train he had originally planned to use. Months earlier, in August or September 1864, John Wilkes Booth, who belonged to no official Confederate organization, had hatched a scheme to kidnap Lincoln. Like Headley and Martin's mission to abduct Andrew Johnson, it came to nothing.

But, of course, Booth didn't give up.

That resulted in tragedy for the nation—and nearly in the death of Thomas Hines, who, two days after the assassination of the president, was in Detroit, making his way back to Canada after raiding Kentucky. He had been mistaken for John Wilkes Booth before, when Booth was nothing more than a popular actor. After Lincoln's death, in a Detroit barroom, the shout of "That's John Wilkes Booth, I saw him many times in Baltimore and New York" resulted in a melee and a manhunt. Hines escaped by hijacking at gunpoint a ferry to Windsor. He holed up in Toronto until a few months after President Andrew Johnson signed a general amnesty on May 29, 1865.

Two of the men associated with Thomas Henry Hines, Captain Robert Cobb Kennedy, who admitted to setting Barnum's Museum ablaze, and John Yates Beall, were hanged. Others served prison sentences. But, remarkably, most of the men involved in the Northwest Conspiracy survived the war, were never punished, and enjoyed lives such as are rarely the lot of former spies. As we have already seen, Bennett Young, who led the raid against the banks in St. Albans, Vermont, became president of three major companies. Robert Martin became a prosperous tobacco merchant, as did John W. Headley, who also served the state of Kentucky as secretary of state. John Breckinridge Castleman rejoined the United States

The War Between the Spies

Army at the time of the Spanish-American War and was eventually commissioned a brigadier general. He later became prominent in Kentucky politics. Thomas Hines, military commander of the conspiracy, became a brilliantly successful lawyer and, eventually, chief justice of Kentucky's Court of Appeals.

CHAPTER FOURTEEN

ASSASSINS AND RESURRECTIONISTS

From the very beginning on that Christmas Eve 1860 when he exploded in horror and disbelief at the news of South Carolina's secession, William Tecumseh Sherman entertained no illusions about the nature of war and warriors. Not so Brigadier General Judson Kilpatrick, a twenty-eight-year-old West Pointer, whose dreams of glory were limitless. Short, slight, sporting ginger-colored side whiskers, he affected a particularly rakish uniform: a jaunty hat, a smartly tailored cutaway uniform coat, and buff-colored cavalry trousers tucked into high boots. His men were not impressed, one of his officers declaring that it was "hard to look at him without laughing." And there was worse. Before the war was over, Brigadier Kilpatrick hoped to become Major General Kilpatrick, and, after the war, he wanted to be governor of New Jersey, then president of the United States. To achieve his ends, Kilpatrick was ruthless in sacrificing his soldiers. At Gettysburg, he ordered Elon Farnsworth, a brigadier junior to him, to charge against a rebel position that was protected by a stone wall. Farnsworth protested that it was suicide. "If you are afraid to lead this charge," Kilpatrick bellowed, "I will lead it." Whereupon Farnsworth, muttering "I will obey your orders," rode off to slaughter as certain as it was futile. After that, Judson Kilpatrick's men nicknamed him Kilcavalry. William Tecumseh Sherman simply called him "a hell of a damned fool."

But Judson Kilpatrick had an idea. It was early in 1864, and he had heard that the Confederates, acutely short of men and material, had left Richmond largely defenseless, or, rather, defended only by aged and ill-equipped Home Guardsmen. Kilpatrick wanted to stage a lightning cavalry raid against the rebel capital with the purpose of harassing Confederate lines of supply and communication, disrupting government, and liberating the five thousand Union prisoners languishing in the hell holes that were Libby Prison and Belle Isle. If he pulled the raid off, promotion was assured, and, after the war, well, the voters would remember.

Kilpatrick would not easily get approval for such a daring scheme. He feared that his superior, Alfred Pleasonton, would usurp the assignment for himself, and if he, the brigadier general, went over Pleasonton's head to seek permission from Major General George G. Meade, a commander known for his caution, the plan would certainly be rejected out of hand. Kilpatrick bypassed both men and communicated with friends who were known to have the president's ear. On February 11, 1864, Lincoln sent a laconic telegram to Pleasonton: "Unless there be strong reason to the contrary, please send Gen. Kilpatrick to us here, for two or three days." Both Lincoln and Secretary of War Stanton readily approved the notion of dashing into Richmond, especially with the goal of freeing the inmates of the rebel capital's military prisons. The horror stories coming out of those places were not only personally difficult for Lincoln to endure, they were bad for national morale. And there would be a bonus. Lincoln had just issued a Proclamation of Amnesty and Reconstruction—in effect, surrender terms he hoped a war-weary Southern populace would persuade its leaders to accept—and he specified that each of Kilpatrick's cavalry troopers would carry a hundred or so copies of the proclamation to distribute behind the lines.

Over the objections of Pleasonton and Meade, the plan was put into motion. Indeed, Lincoln's orders to Kilpatrick were "preemptory." He was to be given whatever he needed to carry out his mission. Word of the exciting project reached the ears of Ulric Dahlgren, at twenty-one the youngest colonel in the Union army. He was the son of Rear Admiral John A. Dahlgren, chief of naval ordnance and inventor of the familiar bottle-shaped gun that the federal navy found so effective. It was not, however, Ulric Dahlgren's family connections alone that earned him his colonelcy. Like Kilpatrick, he was bent on achieving glory and showed such zeal that Edwin Stanton himself commissioned Dahlgren captain at age nineteen. He served with distinction under Generals Sigel, Burnside, Hooker, and Meade. With the latter, on July 6, 1863, in the aftermath of Gettysburg, Captain Dahlgren was shot in the foot at Boonsboro. Too gallant to yield to what seemed a relatively minor wound, the young officer remained in his saddle until he collapsed from the loss of blood. His leg was amputated above the knee three days later. After convalescence aboard his father's flagship outside Charleston, Dahlgren returned to Washington, where the youthful hero was jumped in rank to colonel. It was in the capital that he heard of Kilpatrick's proposed raid. Impatient with his invalidism and capable now of stumping about on an artificial leg, he sought and secured Pleasonton's permission to speak to Kilpatrick about joining the raiding party. In Dahlgren, Kilpatrick saw two things: a daring young officer, who—in contrast to the unfortunate Farnsworth—would need no prodding to risk death, and the son of a renowned admiral. That connection alone would bring added attention and honor upon the raid. Kilpatrick eagerly took on the volunteer. Overjoyed at the prospect of striking the rebel capital, Dahlgren wrote to his father: "If we do not return, there is no better place to 'give up the ghost.'"

It began beautifully, without a single difficulty, one hour before midnight on February 28, 1864. At dawn, Kilpatrick mustered his 3,585 troopers behind Ely's Ford, on the Rapidan, which they quickly crossed, reaching Spotsylvania, fifteen miles south of the river. So far, they had met no challenge from the enemy. At Spotsylvania, Dahlgren was detached with five hundred men to proceed to the vicinity of Goochland, on the James River upstream from Richmond. While Kilpatrick and the main force approached the city directly from the north—it was only fifty miles distant now— Dahlgren would come roundabout from the southwest. They would enter the capital simultaneously in order to force the Home Guard to divide and spread out so that the federal cavalry might punch more easily through their lines. The advance of both Dahlgren and Kilpatrick would be further aided by a diversionary expedition under the command of another boyish cavalry officer, George Armstrong Custer. He and his fifteen-hundred-man brigade raided Lee's left rear, occupying Jeb Stuart's cavalry by deliberately drawing them off in pursuit.

As for Kilpatrick, he couldn't have been more pleased with his own progress. By noon, February 29, his command had crossed the North Anna River, burned the Virginia Central Railroad depot at Beaver Dam, and was making camp near the South Anna River by nightfall.

At one o'clock on the morning of March 1, as Kilpatrick roused his raiders from sleep, the weather turned nasty. Kilpatrick shot off rockets to signal Dahlgren that all was ready for the attack, and he gazed through the curtain of an icy rain in search of an answering rocket.

There was none.

Kilpatrick pressed on through the worsening ice storm over the Chickahominy by daybreak, close to Ashland by 10 A.M., and subsequently within sight of Richmond's outer fortifications, five miles from the very center of the capital, where he came under fire.

No worry, though, as his opponents were nothing but Home Guardsmen, who could be quickly brushed aside. Home Guard they were, but Kilpatrick had not reckoned on their grit. Defending their homes, they fought well, skillfully, and with determination. It was reported that Kilpatrick exploded with anger: "They have too many of those damned guns!" The impetuosity that had earned him the epithet "Kilcavalry" suddenly abandoned him. Dahlgren was nowhere in evidence. Certainly, Kilpatrick heard no guns to the southwest, which would have indicated that Dahlgren, as planned, was engaged with the enemy there. Yet Kilpatrick was just outside of the rebel capital with the bulk of his command. He could fight it out now, punch through, and carry out the raid on Richmond himself. After all, if he succeeded, the liberation of the men at Libby Prison and Belle Isle, unarmed though they were, would augment his force by some five thousand troops. Or he could wait, continuing to engage the Home Guard in a limited fashion, until Dahlgren and his five hundred materialized. Kilpatrick chose the latter course, fighting for six or seven hours, thereby giving the Confederates ample time to reinforce the Home Guard with regular troops.

"Feeling confident that Dahlgren had failed to cross the river," Kilpatrick stated in his official report, "and that an attempt to enter the city at that point would but end in a bloody failure, I reluctantly withdrew."

In the process of withdrawal, he was attacked by Confederate regulars. Kilpatrick resisted successfully, but he continued his retreat to the northeast. At a place called Tunstall's Station, near the Pamunkey River, he finally met up with Dahlgren's detachment—or what remained of it, 260 men and a captain. They had, the men reported, reached Goochland at daybreak on March 1. To continue on to Richmond, thirty miles upriver, it was necessary to ford the James, and Dahlgren found Martin Robinson, a local plantation slave, who offered to show them a fording place. Things were going fine.

Then they reached Jude's Ford, the place to which Robinson had guided them. Two days of hard rain had swollen the river and rendered the ford impassable. The mood of the one-legged colonel instantly turned sinister. Robinson expressed surprise at the condition of the ford, but Dahlgren, fully aware that he would not only be delayed, but would have to approach Richmond from a different direction, decided that the slave had deliberately sabotaged his mission. If he could not reach Richmond with alacrity, he could play judge, jury, and executioner with dispatch. Dahlgren ordered Robinson hanged then and there. The irony, of course, was terrible, and, later, Southerners would make the most of it. The Union colonel, serving a cause dedicated to the liberation of the slaves, cold-bloodedly murdered one.

Dahlgren and his five hundred proceeded down the north bank of the James, heading east toward Richmond in search of a passable ford. Apparently having abandoned all hope of salvaging anything of his schedule, Dahlgren vented his frustration by setting fire to whatever mills and buildings he encountered. Eight miles outside of the capital he heard guns. At the sounds, though his horses and men were exhausted, he poured on the speed, but he met with the same surprisingly stiff resistance the Home Guard had offered Kilpatrick. Through the engagement, it was becoming increasingly apparent that Kilpatrick had withdrawn. Dahlgren decided to abort the mission and make his way back to federal lines through Fredericksburg.

It was a miserable and disorderly retreat. The troops were exhausted, and the icy rain became heavy enough to reduce visibility so badly that Dahlgren's column split, about three hundred men losing sight of the two hundred in the lead. Some forty of the former were killed or captured. The rest met up with Kilpatrick at Tunstall's Station. Dahlgren and the two hundred troopers still with him crossed the Pamunkey River and then the Mattaponi. Shortly after, at a place called King and Queen Courthouse, they were ambushed by Confederate regulars.

Badly outnumbered and completely surprised, Dahlgren fell back on the streak of fantastic bluster that came so naturally to him.

"Surrender, you damned rebels," he thundered, leveling his revolver, "or I'll shoot you!"

The reply was a volley of shots, at least four of which hit Dahlgren. One report says his body was "riddled" with buckshot. The remnant of the colonel's command panicked and ran. Some were killed, some escaped, others were captured. Indeed, instead of liberating rebel prisons, the Kilpatrick-Dahlgren raid augmented their population by about three hundred, all told. But the futile attack on Richmond was just the beginning of the story.

In hot pursuit of Dahlgren's command, none of the rebels stopped to examine the colonel's body. William Littlepage, a thirteen-year-old boy from Stevensville, found it lying in a ditch, the feet—one of flesh, the other of wood—against a tree and rail fence bordering the road. Littlepage had been harvesting souvenirs, guns, haversacks, and so on, that the fleeing Yankees had abandoned along the road. The officer's corpse was a real find. Littlepage rifled Dahlgren's pockets. Edward W. Halbach, the lad's schoolmaster, tells what happened:

> The little fellow wanted to own a watch, and as the Yankees had robbed me, his teacher, of a gold watch a short time before, I suppose he concluded that there would be no harm in his taking a watch from a 'dead Yankee;' but his teacher always discouraged any feelings of this kind in his pupils. Littlepage failed to secure the prize by not

looking in the overcoat pockets and the watch (for there was really one) was found afterwards by Lieutenant Hart. But in searching the pockets of the inner garments, Littlepage *did find* a cigar-case, a memorandum-box, etc. [Another source reports that he *did* find the watch.]

The youngster brought the contents of Dahlgren's pockets to Halbach, who read the papers in the "memorandum-box." There was, first of all, a speech, Dahlgren's address to his troops, written—in red ink, no less—on official Third Division stationery:

You have been selected from brigades and regiments as a picked command to attempt a desperate undertaking—an undertaking which, if successful, will write your names on the hearts of your countrymen in letters that can never be erased, and which will cause the prayers of our fellow soldiers, now confined in loathsome prisons, to follow you and yours wherever you may go.

We hope to release the prisoners from Belle Island first, and, having seen them fairly started, we will cross the James river into Richmond, destroying the bridges after us, and exhorting the released prisoners to destroy and burn the hateful city, and do not allow the Rebel leader, Davis, and his traitorous crew to escape. The prisoners must render great assistance, as you cannot leave your ranks too far or become too much scattered, or you will be lost.

. . .

Many of you may fall; but if there is any man here not willing to sacrifice his life in such a great and glorious undertaking, or who does not feel capable of meeting the enemy in such a desperate fight as will follow, let him step out, and he may go hence to the arms of his sweetheart, and read of the braves who swept through the city of Richmond. . . .

On another sheet of stationery, together with some "detached slips," was a series of special orders:

Guides—Pioneers (with Oakum, turpentine, and torpedoes)— Signal Officer—Quartermaster—Commissary—Picket.
Scouts and pickets—men in rebel uniform.
. . . All *mills* must be *burned* and the *canal; destroyed,* and also

everything which can be used by the Rebels must be destroyed including the boats on the river. . . . We will try and secure the bridge to the city (one mile below Belle Island), and release the prisoners at the same time.

. . .

. . . The bridges once secured, and the prisoners loose and over the river, the bridges will be secured and the city destroyed. The men must keep together and well in hand, and once in the city it must be destroyed, and *Jeff Davis and Cabinet killed.* . . .

Other papers included an itinerary, from the start of the mission to and through Richmond and back, and a letter addressed to the Provost Marshal General's Office reporting the "execution" of the slave, Martin Robinson. There was also a folded facsimile of a hundred-dollar bill, a joke, bearing as its issuer the "Plantation Bank" and good for one bottle of "Plantation Bitters."

Lieutenant James Pollard, in command of the unit that had ambushed Dahlgren, Company H, Ninth Virginia Cavalry, better known as Lee's Rangers, persuaded Halbach to allow him to take the papers to Richmond. These he delivered to the headquarters of General Fitzhugh Lee, together with Dahlgren's artificial leg. After hurriedly reading the papers, Lee took them to Jefferson Davis, who was in conference with Secretary of State Judah P. Benjamin. Davis read the documents aloud, laughing when he reached "Jeff Davis and Cabinet killed."

"That means you, Mr. Benjamin," he said.

Davis and Benjamin also took considerable interest in Dahlgren's artificial leg. (Littlepage had reported to Halbach and Pollard that the Yankee officer whose pockets he had searched had a wooden leg. "How do you know he has a wooden leg?" Pollard asked, "greatly agitated." "I know he has, because I caught hold of it and tried to pull it off.") After the president and secretary of state finished examining the leg, it was placed on display in a Richmond store window. Its career did not end there, either. One source reports that it was sent over to army medical headquarters as a model for rebel military surgeons. Another reports that for "nine or ten months" it was worn by John N. Ballard, a Confederate amputee, who received it from Lieutenant Pollard himself. Pollard, according to this source, lost his own leg shortly after the Dahlgren encounter and took the colonel's prosthesis to "Mr. John Wills' Leg Factory" at Charlottesville to have it fitted for his own use. Finding it too small, however, he presented it to Ballard. On November 8, 1865, the wooden leg was returned to Ulric Dahlgren's father.

The documents were immediately made available to the Richmond newspapers, which, in righteous indignation, published them in their entirety. Publication immediately triggered denials from the government and military of the United States along with accusations that the documents were fabrications and forgeries. Fully a generation of partisans on both sides debated the authenticity of the Dahlgren papers for years after Appomattox had settled the military contest between North and South.

At the end of March, Jefferson Davis also sent the original documents, together with four sets of photographic copies, to General Fitzhugh Lee, who was instructed to communicate with Union General George G. Meade and ask him point-blank whether "the Government of the United States sanctions the sentiments and purposes therein set forth." On April 1, Lee sent a letter to Meade, together with photographic copies of the Dahlgren papers. Heavy rains made delivery across the lines impossible until the 16th. Meade forwarded the packet to Washington and ordered Kilpatrick to report to him. Kilpatrick issued a statement: "The photographic papers referred to are true copies of the papers approved by me, save so far as they speak of 'exhorting the prisoners to destroy and burn the hateful city and kill the traitor Davis and his Cabinet,' and in this, they do not contain the indorsement referred to as having been placed by me on Colonel Dahlgren's papers. Colonel Dahlgren received no orders from me to pillage, burn, or kill, nor were any such instructions given me by my superiors." In turn, Meade officially replied to Fitzhugh Lee: "neither the United States Government, myself, nor General Kilpatrick authorized, sanctioned, or approved the burning of the city of Richmond and the killing of Mr. Davis and Cabinet, nor any other act not required by military necessity and in accordance with the usages of war," and he enclosed a copy of Kilpatrick's statement. Privately, Meade confided in a letter to his wife:

> This was a pretty ugly piece of business, for in denying having authorized or approved 'the burning of Richmond, or killing Mr. Davis and Cabinet,' I necessarily threw odium on Dahlgren. I, however, enclosed a letter from Kilpatrick, in which the authenticity of the papers was impugned; but I regret to say Kilpatrick's reputation, and collateral evidence in my possession, rather go against this theory. However, I was determined my skirts should be clear, so I promptly disavowed having ever authorized, sanctioned or approved of any act not required by military necessity, and in accordance with the usages of war.

Just what the "collateral evidence" was we do not know, but Meade's letter to his wife makes it clear that his official reply was meant, at the very least, to cover his—skirts. Provost Marshal General Marsena Patrick recorded in his diary a conversation with Captain John McEntee, one of the survivors of Dahlgren's command. "He has the same opinion of Kilpatrick that I have," Patrick wrote, "and says he [Kilpatrick] managed just as all cowards do. He further says that he thinks the papers are correct that were found upon Dahlgren, as they correspond with what D[ahlgren] told him."

In fact, the original documents have disappeared. Perhaps they were burned up with many other Confederate documents in the blazes that swept through Richmond when Grant took the city. They are known only through their appearance in the Richmond newspapers and in a single photographic copy in the National Archives and Records Administration, a document so faded as to be virtually unreadable. Pointing to the fact that the address to the troops was signed "Dalhgren" instead of "Dahlgren" and that the signature included only the initial "U" instead of the full first name that Dahlgren customarily used in signing documents, partisans of the North have labeled the papers a forgery. Some have claimed the documents were planted on Dahlgren. In view of Kilpatrick's statement that the papers were authentic (except as he indicated), this is highly unlikely. That is, Dahlgren probably *was* carrying the papers. The question then becomes whether they were, in fact, subsequently altered. In 1885, J. William Jones published a compilation of the documents in volume 13 of the *Southern Historical Society Papers*, together with a host of supporting documents and affidavits of authenticity that convincingly demonstrate there was no opportunity for forgery. The question concerning the authority on which Dahlgren acted when he wrote the documents is still very much open.

If the story ended even here, with the tantalizing possibility that Judson Kilpatrick and Ulric Dahlgren were agents of a federal conspiracy to assassinate Jefferson Davis and company, the narrative of the failed raid on Richmond would, like the unconventional cavalry exploits of Mosby and Morgan, lie beyond the scope of a book on Civil War espionage and counterespionage. But, in death, the body of Colonel Ulric Dahlgren seems to have taken on new life. It is a tale that savors of Southern gothic and that the William Faulkner of *As I Lay Dying* might well have appreciated. More important for our purposes, the saga of Dahlgren's corpse hints at the organization and operation of the federal underground movement in the Confederate capital.

Young William Littlepage was not the last person to subject the body of Ulric Dahlgren to indignity. With no small dash of ghoulish relish, the Richmond *Examiner* reported on March 8:

DAHLGREEN'S [sic] *BODY* was boxed up at Walkerton on Sunday and brought to Richmond, with the object we understand of positive identification, and establishment of the fact of the finding of the infamous documents upon it, all of which has been attested by witnesses. . . . It would seem something of the curse he came to bestow on others lighted upon his own carcass, when it fell riddled by avenging Southern bullets. Stripped, robbed of every valuable, the fingers cut off for the sake of the diamond rings that encircled them, when the body was found by those sent to take charge of it, it was lying in a field stark naked, with the exception of the stockings. Some humane persons had lifted the corpse from the pike and thrown it over into the field to save it from the hogs. The artificial limb worn by Dahlgren was removed, and is now at General [Arnold] Elzey's headquarters. It is of most beautiful design and finish.

Yesterday afternoon the body was removed from the car that brought it to the York River railroad depot and given to the spot of earth selected to receive it. Where that spot is no one but those concerned in its burial know or care to tell. It was a dog's burial, without coffin, winding sheet or service. Friends and relatives at the North need inquire no further; this is all they will know—he is buried, a burial that befitted the mission upon which he came. . . .

In spirit, the *Examiner* account was accurate enough, though some of the details are wrong. The Richmond *Whig*, in a report confirmed by various witnesses, noted that Dahlgren lay in a pine box, "clothed in Confederate shirt and pants, and shrouded in a Confederate blanket." Only one finger—"the little finger of the left hand"—had been cut off. No one, the *Whig* concluded, "knows, or is to know, where" Dahlgren had been buried.

Admiral John A. Dahlgren was heartbroken, both by word that his son had been killed in action and by the reports he had heard—and read, in the Richmond newspapers brought to him—concerning the abuse and indignities to which Ulric Dahlgren's remains had been subjected. Particularly cruel was the thought that his son's body, heaped into an unmarked, secret grave, would not be returned. Admiral Dahlgren appealed to Major General Benjamin F. Butler, commander of the Eighteenth Army Corps and Federal Commissioner of Exchange of Prisoners. Butler, on March 18, 1864, wrote to his Confederate counterpart, Robert Ould, agent for exchange, requesting the return of the body, by way of a flag-of-truce boat, all expenses to be defrayed by the federal government. On March 23, despite its original intention never to reveal the burial site, the Confederate government assured Butler that the body would be returned. The body was due to arrive on March 29, and Admiral Dahlgren went out to meet the flag-of-truce boat. But his son's remains were not aboard. Communications passed back and forth until April 17, when General Butler sent Dahlgren a telegram quoting Robert Ould: "That upon going to the grave of Colonel Dahlgren it was found empty, and that the most vigorous and persistent search fails to find it; that the authorities are making every exertion to find the body, which shall be returned and found."

It was bizarre, embarrassing to the Confederacy and painful to Admiral Dahlgren. Just three days later, however, Butler was able to telegraph the Admiral: "I have reliable information from Richmond that Colonel Dahlgren's body has been taken possession of by his Union friends, and has been put beyond the reach of rebel authorities." However, Butler went on to explain in a subsequent message, it was impossible for *him* to direct Ould to the remains "because that will show such correspondence with Richmond as will alarm them [the Confederate government], and will redouble their vigilance to detect my sources of information." Butler's "sources" were none other than the agents of the underground, the so-called Richmond Ring, whose principal coordinator—perhaps even leader—was Elizabeth Van Lew. In order not to compromise them, Admiral Dahlgren would be made to endure at least another year without further word of his son's remains. On April 5, 1865, just two days after Grant took Richmond, Butler wrote a letter to Colonel James A. Hardie, requesting a pass for Arnold B. Holmes and John Newton Van Lew—Elizabeth Van Lew's brother—both Union loyalists who had fled Richmond in the spring of 1864 and who now wanted to reenter the federally occupied city. Butler vouched for Van Lew's loyalty by pointing out that his sister "was my secret correspondent in Richmond and furnished valuable information during the whole [of Grant's] campaign [against the Confederate capital]. She is now the repository of the secret burial place of *Col Dahlgren* whose remains were taken by the Unionists of Richmond from a dishonored grave and put in a place of safety known to her." It would be November 1, 1865, before Ulric Dahlgren's body was finally laid to rest in Laurel Hill Cemetery, Washington, D.C.

Elizabeth Van Lew's fellow operatives in this case were William S. Rowley, the Lohmann brothers (Frederick William Ernest and John A.), Almond E. Graham, Robert Orrock, and Martin Lipscomb.

Rowley was a forty-five-year-old farmer, of modest means, married with three sons. A native of New York state, he declared in a postwar petition for compensation that

> When the Rebellion broke out my sympathies were with the Union side. I did not vote on the question of secession. I thought the presence of soldiers at the polls made the election an imposition & mere pretence. I solemnly declare that from the beginning of the war till its close, my sympathies were constantly with the Union cause. I never did anything to injure it, & I constantly did everything in my power to aid it, frequently risking my life & liberty to do so. I never owned a slave.

In an 1869 letter to President Grant, Elizabeth Van Lew called Rowley the "bravest of the brave, and the truest of the true."

The Lohmann brothers were sons of a Prussian immigrant who settled in Richmond during the early 1840s. Frederick William

The War Between the Spies

Ernest (called William) and John A. Lohmann were carpenters by trade, but in 1860 William and his wife Angelina expanded the grocery store of Angelina's father, Anton Gude, to include a restaurant. It was located near the terminal of the Richmond, Fredericksburg, & Potomac Railroad and, therefore, the office of the railroad's superintendent, Samuel Ruth. It is reasonable to assume that Ruth frequented the restaurant, not only to meet with Lohmann on "secret service" matters, but to trade on the black market. In a 1964 article for *The Virginia Magazine of History and Biography*, Meriwether Stuart speculates that Ruth and Lohmann, together with Christian Burging, a Unionist saloon owner whose establishment was adjacent to Lohmann's restaurant, may have conversed in the Pennsylvania "Dutch" dialect to insure the security of their conferences together. William Lohmann seems to have become active in the underground at about the same time as Ruth, clandestinely distributing money to "families of deserving and necessitous Union men in Richmond." Unlike Ruth, Lohmann had military experience. He was a second lieutenant in the Virginia Rifles, Company K, First Virginia Regiment, before the war and served through December 27, 1861. Apparently he was, at least for a time, commanding officer of the company. For much of the war, William Lohmann was active in transporting Union sympathizers north across the lines. That he performed this service for a fee earned him at least the partial censure of Elizabeth Van Lew. With Rowley, he also aided in the escape of several secret agents, including a Captain Harry S. Howard of General Butler's command, who was imprisoned in Richmond.

Almond E. Graham, a native of Vermont, was a stencil cutter by trade and thirty-one years old at the time of the Dahlgren incident. Little else of relevance is known about him. Robert Orrock, a farmer, had emigrated from Scotland with his wife. His farm was located near Hungary Station in present-day Laurel, Virginia, an area inhabited by numerous foreign-born families. Orrock was the brother-in-law of Isaac Silver, who, with Samuel Ruth, was charged with treason toward the end of the war. (Ruth and Silver were acquitted.) Orrock appears on the payroll muster of the Union army as a "guide"—a euphemism for spy—at the rate of two dollars per day.

All that apparently united this group of Richmond and Rich-mond-area residents, besides an allegiance to the Union, was the fact of either Northern or foreign birth. While it is true that Miss Van Lew had been born in Richmond, both her parents were Northerners, and her education had been conducted in the North, so that the only full-blooded Southerner in the group was Martin Meredith Lipscomb, who was not only a native of Virginia, but a member of a very old Virginia family. Like Elizabeth Van Lew, he was an "eccentric." By avocation he was a perennial and always unsuccessful candidate for political office, who ran for mayor of Richmond in 1864 even as he was operating in the Richmond Ring as a Union agent. By vocation, he was a bricklayer, but the exigencies of the war had prompted him to go into the business, as he said, of "pickling pork and burying dead Yankees." That is, Lipscomb was victualer to the Confederate army and also contracted with the Confederate government to bury enemy war dead. Unlike the others of Van Lew's circle, who, in petitioning for compensation after the war, claimed with justification to have been true partisans of the Union, Lipscomb ascribed his role in the Dahlgren affair to retaliation for breach of contract. When Confederate soldiers seized Dahlgren's body and buried it, Lipscomb argued, the government violated its contract with him.

Perhaps this explanation of his motive should be chalked up to yet another of Lipscomb's eccentricities. It is true that, when William Lohmann asked Lipscomb to aid in finding Dahlgren's grave, he at first refused. But it is also true that he had a history of association with pro-Union men, and after he became convinced that Lohmann's motives were humanitarian and patriotic, he joined in the search. By good fortune, Lohmann and Lipscomb found a black man who had been at the burying ground the night Dahlgren was taken there in a coffin borne on a four-mule government wagon. For reasons known only to himself—perhaps the secret midnight burial intrigued him—the black man marked the grave. On April 6, a stormy night, William Lohmann, his brother John, and Martin Lipscomb went to Oakwood Cemetery, disinterred the body, and loaded it on a spring wagon. They planned to deposit it temporarily at Rowley's farmhouse until Martin Lipscomb could secure a metal coffin, which everyone felt was far more befitting a

Union officer than the plain pine box to which his remains had been so rudely consigned. After Lipscomb found a suitable casket, the Lohmann brothers delivered it to Rowley's farm. There, the body was transferred to the casket, as Miss Van Lew records in a handwritten account oozing with a mid-Victorian blend of ghoulish gore and sentimental treacle:

> A few Union friends saw the body. Sad and sorrowful were their hearts and tender wailing fell from their lips. Col. Dahlgren's hair was very short, but all that could be spared was cut off and sent to his father before Richmond fell. Gentle hands and tearful eyes examined his breast to see if there was any wound there, but nothing of the kind could be perceived. [All of Dahlgren's wounds were in the back.] The body, except the head, was in a perfect state of preservation, fair, pure and firm the flesh; here and there a purple spot of mildew. This was remarkable, considering the length of time of the burial, unless, as was thought, it was becoming adipocere, the ground in which he was buried being very damp. The comeliness of the young face was gone, yet the features seemed regular and there was a wonderful look of firmness or energy stamped upon them. His dress was a shirt of the coarsest kind, not even fastened; pantaloons of dark blue cloth; a fine cotton sock was on his left foot, the right leg was wanting beneath the knee, his right hand was carelessly thrown across his person, the left, robbed of its little finger, was resting on his left thigh. I know a gentleman who saw a man cutting away this little finger. Around the body was wrapped a blue military blanket.

All was in readiness to transport the enshrined body to the farm of Samuel Orrock, when one of the resurrectionists suddenly recalled that it was necessary to seal the coffin lid lest seepage corrupt the remains. The trouble was that, in wartime Richmond, putty was virtually impossible to come by. William Lohmann, assisted by Almond Graham, improvised with a compound of chalk and oil. The sealed coffin was loaded on Rowley's wagon, which, Van Lew continues:

> was then filled with young peach trees packed as nursery men pack them, the coffin, of course, being covered and concealed. The horses being attached, Mr. Rowley took the driver's seat and drove all that remained of brave young Dahlgren through several pickets, one of

which was then the strongest around Richmond, for the reason that twice before this had the Federal forces been within the outer line of batteries, and at this very place the night before his death had Dahlgren fought for hours. Wary and vigilant were our pickets and if one had run his bayonet into this wagon only a few inches, death would *certainly* have been the award of this brave man; and not only death; but torture to make him reveal those connected with him—his accomplices. The forged papers said to have been found on Colonel Dahlgren's body had *maddened the people;* and Southern people, when maddened . . . stop not at trifles. . . .

When Mr. Rowley approached this strong post he realized, for the first time, his peril. He drove up to the tent, stopped before it and let fall his reins with the appearance of perfect indifference. The Lieutenant, being present, ordered the guard to examine the wagon and passed on into the tent. It so happened that at this moment a wagon was passing into the country on the opposite side of the road, and the guard seeing Mr. Rowley at leisure, proceeded to search this first. Then coming up to Mr. R. he said, "Whose peach trees are those?" observing at the same time, "I think, I have seen your face before." "Yes," replied Mr. R., "and I have yours." "Where" asked the guard. "At your own house at—" said Mr. R. "Ah, yes, at such and such a time," was the rejoinder and then the friendly talk and greeting. "But whose peach trees are those?" again inquired the guard. "They belong to a German in the country, to whom I am carrying them," said Mr. R. By this time, another cart or wagon had come up and required examination, which was thoroughly done. Then the man returned and the conversation was resumed in reference to the peach trees; about the lateness of the season to transplant them &c. Another cart, then a relapse to the culture of peach trees, with cementing friendship. In this way, from twenty to thirty minutes passed, during which time at least ten or twelve wagons were examined, this being the principal road to the city from that direction, until the Lieutenant sang out from the tent, with an oath to the man "to get through searching that wagon and let the man go on, not to keep him there until night." The guard said, "it would be a pity to tear those trees all up, when you have packed them in there so nicely." "When I packed them I did not expect them to be disturbed; but as it is, being a citizen I know a soldier's duty and expect him to do it." Then another wagon to be examined, and the Lieutenant called to him a second time to let the man go on. The guard said, but not loud enough for the Lieutenant to hear, "I don't want to hinder you any longer. I think it all right, at any rate your honest face is guarantee enough for me—go on."

And the body was taken to Orrock's farm, where it remained buried until it was transported back to Washington—and Admiral Dahlgren—late in the fall of 1865.

The affair of Dahlgren's corpse was an admixture of gallantry, futility, and the grotesque. On one level, it was a remarkably successful operation. The Richmond underground was so effective that its agents were able to disinter the body and then hide it from Confederate authorities for a year. Ironically, however, in carrying out the operation, the underground kept a grieving father in added sorrow for that same year. Even worse, the Richmond Ring seriously risked capture, which would have entailed possibly dire consequences to its members as well as to the Union cause. An important source of military information might well have been cut off. The best one can say about the operation is that, for better or worse, it did work, and it attests to the efficiency of the Richmond underground. It also attests to the dedication of Elizabeth Van Lew and her associates, who, clearly, did not act from vainglorious motives. Indeed, the story is so obscure that it would not have come to light at all were it not for references to the affair in petitions for compensation submitted to the United States government after the war.

If the Richmond Ring was moved to action by a selfless sense of patriotism, so much cannot be said of the self-serving Judson Kilpatrick or, alas, even the glory-struck Colonel Ulric Dahlgren.

The Dahlgren episode also makes clear that the Union spy ring in Richmond endured, intact, until the very end of the war. Indeed, it is ironic that the most sustained and fully documented evidence of the successful and efficient operation of the ring was occasioned by a failed raid and abortive assassination attempt. To the end of the war, and even beyond, the Confederate apparatus of espionage likewise continued to function in and around Washington. This we know, in part, because of another assassination scheme—unlike Dahlgren's, a scheme brought to tragic completion—and the very nearly successful escape of the assassin. Thus the final mission of the Union's Richmond Ring was carried out in service to a corpse, while the final function of the South's Secret Line was to aid a doomed and demented partisan of a dead cause.

Americans would always find it hard to accept that their chief executives were the targets of lone, lonely assassins. But, alas, there was no grand conspiracy pulling the strings of Charles J. Guiteau, the disappointed seeker of office who shot President James A. Garfield. President William McKinley's wild-eyed assassin, Leon Czolgosz, claimed to be an anarchist, but the notion of his having acted in a deliberate anarchist conspiracy is a contradiction in terms. Despite the conclusions of the Warren Commission, the question of conspiracy in the assassination of John Fitzgerald Kennedy is still very much subject to debate. Most bizarre of all, perhaps, is John Hinckley, a bland young man and consummate loner, who lived a Hollywood-inspired political-sexual fantasy in which, by killing President Ronald Reagan, he would win the heart of movie star Jodie Foster.

Various politicians, investigators, and writers, both immediately after Lincoln's murder and well into the succeeding century, have attempted to prove that John Wilkes Booth acted as part of a grand conspiracy, either as an agent of the Confederate "secret service," the Confederacy in general, or even as a tool of the Union's Radical Republicans, or Secretary of War Stanton and/or Vice-President Johnson! The thought that the president, in whom resides the collective will of the people, could be felled by the likes of an actor named Booth, or such ciphers as Hinckley, Oswald, Czolgosz, or Guiteau, is somehow more disturbing than the notion that the chief executive might become the object of an organized political conspiracy. Such a thought was as true in 1865 as it is in our own century. Allan J. Pinkerton successfully defended President-elect Lincoln against a small army of would-be assassins who, on the eve of civil war, were clearly agents of a conspiracy. Throughout the war, many officials, chief among them Edwin M. Stanton, expressed concern for Lincoln's safety. The secretary saw to it that, to the extent possible, the swarms of office seekers and petitioners who loitered in the halls of the White House were cleared out. Toward the end of the war, Stanton repeatedly cautioned Lincoln against venturing out at night. He even sought specifically to dissuade

Lincoln from attending the theater, which Mrs. Lincoln so loved. After the fall of Richmond, when the president announced his intention to visit the city, Stanton sent him a message congratulating him "and the nation" on the glorious victory, but, he concluded, "Allow me respectfully to ask you to consider whether you ought to expose the nation to the consequences of any disaster to yourself in the pursuit of a treacherous and dangerous enemy like the rebel army." The warnings were all prudent, of course, the last one particularly so. They were also revelatory. Stanton did not use the word *assassin*, but alluded instead to "a treacherous and dangerous enemy," intending the collective sense of that term. In the years, months, and days before that Good Friday evening at Ford's Theater, Stanton and others feared attack by agents of the Confederate government or high command. Lincoln was just one more potential military target. No one had anticipated a lone assassin.

Abraham Lincoln's tendency to melancholy is well known, as is the dream he reported to Mrs. Lincoln, Ward Hill Lamon (U.S. marshal for the District of Columbia), Iowa Senator James Harlan, and a handful of others assembled in the Red Room of the executive mansion on Tuesday evening, April 11, 1865. "I had been waiting up for important dispatches," the president related. "I could not have been long in bed when I fell into a slumber, for I was weary. I soon began to dream."

> There seemed to be a deathlike stillness about me. Then I heard subdued sobs, as if a number of people were weeping. I thought I left my bed and wandered downstairs.
>
> There the silence was broken by the same pitiful sobbing, but the mourners were invisible. I went from room to room. No living person was in sight, but the same mournful sounds of distress met me as I passed along. It was light in all the rooms; every object was familiar to me, but where were all the people who were grieving as if their hearts would break?
>
> I was puzzled and alarmed. What could be the meaning of all this? Determined to find the cause of a state of things so mysterious and so shocking, I kept on until I arrived in the East Room, which I entered. There I met with a sickening surprise. Before me was a catafalque, on which rested a corpse in funeral vestments. Around it were stationed soldiers who were acting as guards; and there was

a throng of people, some gazing mournfully upon the corpse, whose face was covered, others weeping pitifully.

"Who is dead in the White House? I demanded of one of the soldiers.

"The President," was his answer. "He was killed by an assassin."

Then came a loud burst of grief from the crowd, which awoke me from my dream. I slept no more that night, and, although it was only a dream, I have been strangely annoyed by it ever since.

"Annoyed"—but he comforted himself with this thought: "What does anybody want to assassinate me for? If anyone wants to do so, he can do it any day or night, if he is ready to give his life for mine." Yes, in the first place, an assassination attempt now, when the South had nothing to gain from the President's death, would be foolish; worse than foolish, it would be unnecessary. And, in the second place, while an assassin might well succeed in killing the President, he would surely die in the attempt or immediately thereafter. It would be suicide, purposeless suicide. No government would order such a thing. Only a madman would seriously contemplate it.

Was John Wilkes Booth a madman? After four years of battle, brother against brother, as the cliché went, in which half a million died, the question seems an odd one. Suffice it to say that the best evidence indicates that Booth's contribution to the madness of the Civil War was made without official sanction. As Booth himself put it in a letter he left with his sister, he was "a confederate doing duty upon his own responsibility." In this he was no different from any number of Southern ladies who took it upon themselves to dabble in espionage. Nor was he very different from the Union's Lafayette C. Baker, who would direct the manhunt that ran Booth to ground. At the beginning of the war, Baker, a vigilante from California, walked into General Winfield Scott's office and simply asked for a job as a spy. The nature of rebellion, of *civil* war entailed little respect for "official" credentials and invited *ad hoc*, improvised, individual action. Despite the efforts of contemporary investigators and later writers—most notably Otto Eisenschiml in his 1937 *Why Was Lincoln Murdered?*—we can be more confident that Booth acted on his own initiative than we can be that Ulric Dahlgren was about to act without the knowledge or approval of some superior in the government of the United States. Indeed, except for service in a Virginia volunteer company that took part in the capture of the abolitionist John Brown, Booth did not fight in the Civil War. Some have said that the actor was fearful of scarring his face in battle.

We have already seen that, late in 1864, Booth unsuccessfully plotted to kidnap Lincoln. He gathered about him two friends from his Maryland boyhood, Michael O'Laughlin and Sam Arnold, in addition to George A. Atzerodt, David Herold, and John Surratt. Of these men, only Surratt was regularly associated with the Confederate "secret service." He was a courier, his family's Maryland tavern served as a safe house for other couriers, and his mother's Washington boardinghouse harbored Confederate agents and sympathizers. Atzerodt, a Port Tobacco, Maryland, carriage maker, earned extra money during the war years ferrying Southerners—as well as Northerners—across Pope's Creek, but he was by no means an official operative in the Confederacy's Secret Line. Booth, Atzerodt, Herold, and Surratt met periodically in Mary Surratt's boarding house, where they discussed their plans. Without doubt, Mrs. Surratt's sympathies lay with the South; however, she seems to have been wholly unaware of the nature of Booth's schemes.

Booth planned to kidnap the president at Ford's Theater on January 18, 1865. He had sent Herold to Maryland to arrange for relays of horses along the escape route, and Atzerodt was to lease a flatboat to cross Pope's Creek for the getaway. Surratt was stationed at the master gas valve beneath the stage at Ford's. At a signal, he would turn the valve, plunging the theater into darkness. Booth, his gun held on the president, would gag and bind Lincoln, tie a rope to him, and lower him from his box onto the stage. Booth would follow down the same rope. He would bundle Lincoln into a waiting wagon and spirit him off to Richmond through Maryland, along the often-used route of Confederate couriers and spies, which had been developed in the earliest days of the war, when espionage was steeped in the romance of seductive ladies and dashing young men.

The trouble was that Lincoln chose not to attend the theater that evening. Disappointed, the conspirators dispersed until February, when Booth found a new addition to his band, a former Confederate soldier who called himself Lewis Paine, but whose real name was Louis Thornton Powell. By the middle of next month, the actor was ready with another plot.

President and Mrs. Lincoln were scheduled to attend a matinee performance of *Still Waters Run Deep* to be given at Campbell Hospital, just north of the city. John Surratt called at the tavern in Surrattsville that his father had once owned and that his mother then leased to a dipsomaniac innkeeper named John M. Lloyd. Against Lloyd's wishes, Surratt secreted in the tavern two army carbines, some rope, and a monkey wrench. The plan was to waylay the president's carriage as it passed out of the city. It is possible that, in his abduction scheme, Booth came closest to committing an officially sanctioned Confederate act. Thomas N. Conrad, as we have seen, aborted his own plan to abduct Lincoln along the very same road the year before. We have speculated that Surratt, a courier for Conrad, may well have inspired Booth's plan by discussing Conrad's with him. In one memoir, Conrad claimed that his own plan was sanctioned by Confederate Secretary of War Seddon. In a later memoir, however, he denied having acted on such authority.

Booth, Surratt, Paine, Atzerodt, Arnold, and O'Laughlin waited in ambush. At last, a carriage approached. Booth and Surratt, riding out to overtake it, peered inside. There was a passenger, all right, but he was *not* the president. At this turn of events, the conspirators fell to arguing. Arnold and Surratt believed that the vehicle was, in fact, the president's carriage, which the federals, having somehow learned of the plot, were using as a decoy. Booth said that it was certainly not the president's carriage, but that it would be along any minute.

After a quarter-hour the six conspirators lost their nerve, gave up, and dispersed. Once again, Lincoln had decided not to attend a performance.

Booth, who had been supporting his small band of would-be kidnappers, was running out of money. He was depressed and desperate. The black mood born of his defeat was mocked by the mounting din of celebration throughout Washington. Richmond fell, then Lee surrendered. The curtain was ringing down on the great drama, and John Wilkes Booth had yet to play his part. His chief rationale for the kidnapping scheme was to force the release of Confederate prisoners. With the armies of the Confederacy now surrendering, there was no longer any point in that. Besides, it was more difficult to kidnap the president than simply to kill him, and that is what Booth decided to do.

Mary Surratt was going to the Surattsville tavern. Her intention was to call on a boarder there, John Nothey, who owed her a debt of $479 plus thirteen years' interest. John Wilkes Booth added to her errand by asking that she pass on to Lloyd a message: "Have the guns ready." Or was it, "Have the *things* ready"? Later, when Mrs. Surratt stood trial for conspiracy in the murder of Abraham Lincoln, her life would depend as much on that questionable word as on anything else. She claimed to have known nothing about "guns." Booth had said only "things." Others, including John Lloyd, recalled the word as *guns,* and Mary Surratt was hanged. John Lloyd subsequently recanted his testimony, claiming some two years after her execution that he could not say for certain whether the word had been *things* or *guns.*

In the two or three days prior to Good Friday, April 14, Booth began drinking heavily. Of his original small band of conspirators, only Paine, Herold, and Atzerodt were left. Atzerodt was assigned to kill Vice-President Andrew Johnson. Paine and Herold would do in Secretary of State William H. Seward, who was convalescing from serious injuries sustained in a carriage accident. Booth would kill Lincoln.

This page is not the place to rehearse yet again the details of the assassination of Abraham Lincoln. For the story is both familiar and complex. Atzerodt backed out and didn't try to kill Johnson. While Herold held his horse, Paine attacked Seward, failing to kill him, but making a bloody mess of the assignment nonetheless. Seward was clubbed and stabbed. His son Augustus was injured, as was his daughter Fanny. A State Department messenger named Hansell was stabbed, along with Sergeant Robinson, a male nurse.

As for Booth, he entered the president's box at Ford's theater about 10 P.M. The lock on the door of the box had been broken only a few days earlier. Nobody bothered to report it, let alone fix it. Nor had Booth met with any challenge from the men who should have been guarding the President. He leveled his derringer between Lincoln's left ear and spine. He squeezed the trigger.

Not everyone among the 1,675 members of the audience heard the shot from the diminutive weapon. Even Mrs. Lincoln, seated next to her husband, and Major Henry Rathbone, seated in the presidential box with his fiancée, were not much startled by the dull report of the derringer. Booth, who knew the script of *Our American Cousin* well, had timed his shot to coincide with the play's biggest laugh—just after Harry Hawk, playing Mr. Trenchard, says, "Wal, I guess I know enough to turn you inside out, you sockdologizing old mantrap!" Booth's own infamous line—"Sic semper tyrannis!"—was even less audible. Those seated just below the presidential box failed to hear it. The assassin leapt to the stage, catching his right spur in the Treasury Regiment flag that festooned the box. As a consequence, his left leg took the full shock of his fall. It broke just above the instep. Booth limped into the wings, fell, recovered, and lopingly ran offstage.

He rode off toward the Anacostia River and the Navy Yard Bridge, which would put him on the road to Surrattsville and the safety of the tavern. The bridge was guarded, of course, and at 10:45 P.M. Sergeant Silas T. Cobb challenged a rider.

"Who are you, Sir?"

"My name," the assassin answered, "is Booth."

"Where are you from?"

"The city."

"Where are you going?"

"I am going home."

"And where would that be?"

"Charles."

"What town?"

"No town."

"Come now."

"Close to Beantown, but I do not live in the town."

"Why are you out so late? You know the rules," admonished the sergeant, alluding to the wartime curfew. "No one is allowed past this point after nine o'clock."

"That is new to me. You see, I had to go somewhere first, and I thought that I would have the moon to go home by."

"Go ahead."

A few moments later, Sergeant Cobb also allowed David Herold to cross the Navy Yard Bridge.

If Sergeant Cobb proved a tragically inept sentry, the ensuing pursuit of Booth was conducted to little more effect. Like most other Americans, Secretary Stanton could not bring himself to believe that President Lincoln's death was the work of single man, an actor, no less. He directed all his energies to uncovering a vast Confederate plot, and, in so doing, neglected such essentials as closing the Navy Yard Bridge. So ineffectively did Stanton direct the pursuit of the president's assassin that some contemporaries and later historians believed that he *wanted* Booth to escape.

Booth and Herold reached Surrattsville and the tavern shortly past midnight. The actor's leg, which had not at first hurt him much, was now excruciatingly painful. John Lloyd was drunk and responded with dazed inattention when Herold shouted for him to "make haste and get those things." At last, the innkeeper produced the carbines, a pair of field glasses, a box of cartridges, and some whiskey, which Booth drank to dull the pain. The actor inquired after a doctor, but Lloyd answered that the local physician, Doc Hoxton, no longer practiced.

"We killed the President and Seward," Booth announced.

Lloyd was too drunk to care.

"Don't you want to hear the news?"

"Use your own pleasure about that," the innkeeper replied.

Upon which Herold handed him a silver dollar, and the pair, equipped with their "things," rode off.

Lloyd's alcoholic indifference must have galled the actor as sharply as the pain in his leg. One last time, Surratt's tavern served its purpose along the Confederate Secret Line. But the function was performed dumbly now, without glory, almost unconsciously. Lloyd was no Confederate patriot. He was a besotted innkeeper who, as he had been asked to do, hid two guns and some other equipment until they were claimed by their owner. The Secret Line functioned, but the life had gone out of it. The entire Confederacy was in much the same condition.

The plan had been to set off from Surratt's tavern to Port Tobacco, eighteen miles south, where the conspirators could cross the Potomac into Virginia. It was a route familiar to any number of

Confederate couriers, but also to the Union army. Federal authorities could have closed it down long before, but they did not. In part, this may have been a failure of patchy counterintelligence. But the Line had also come to serve the Union. Federal spies used it. Lafayette C. Baker himself, on his first mission to Richmond, took this route. Knowledge of the Secret Line also made it possible to intercept dispatches, read them, then pass them on. Of course, on this occasion, federal authorities *should* have focused their pursuit of Booth on this road to Port Tobacco. But they did not.

In any event, Booth and Herold were forced to change their plan. The actor needed a doctor, and the only one he knew of was at Bryantown, ten miles out of the way to the southeast. His name was Samuel A. Mudd, the man who had introduced him to John Surratt on December 23, 1864. Like many citizens of Maryland, Mudd was wholly loyal neither to the North or South. Certainly, Booth did not trust him. As the two conspirators approached Mudd's house, Booth sent Herold ahead to knock on the door and awaken the doctor. When Mudd inquired who was knocking, Herold replied: "Two strangers riding to Washington."

It was a little after four in the morning. Mudd did not know David Herold. Later, Mudd claimed that in the early morning gloom, he did not recognize John Wilkes Booth, who, he said, was wearing false whiskers. Herold introduced himself as Henston, and Booth as Mr. Tyler. Although Mudd had not practiced for some time—he lived as a farmer—he set and splinted the leg with skill. He gave the two men beds and, after breakfast, satisfied Herold's request for the loan of a razor. It seems that Herold's injured friend, who had not come down from his room, wanted to rid himself of his beard and mustache. "It will make him feel better," Herold explained to Mudd. The doctor furnished the razor and then went out to work his five hundred acres. By the time he returned, his two guests had departed. At least, that is the substance of Mudd's testimony, when he was put on trial for his life as a conspirator in the murder of President Lincoln. It is difficult, though not impossible, to believe that Mudd failed to recognize Booth, and we are left to wonder if Samuel Mudd was nothing more than a Good Samaritan or, like Surratt's tavern, one more vestige of the Secret Line.

It was slow going, but they crossed the Potomac at Port Tobacco on April 22 after an unsuccessful attempt the day before and without the aid of the ferryman George Atzerodt. Atzerodt was supposed to meet them, but on April 15, he had simply boarded a stage for Rockville, Maryland, and worked his way home. Two days after Booth and Herold crossed the Potomac, they made it over the Rappahannock, about twenty miles below Fredericksburg.

In the meantime, a motley assortment of military and police squads were swarming across the countryside in fruitless pursuit. There were forces under Major James R. O'Beirne, provost marshal of the District of Columbia; Lieutenant David D. Dana, described as a "lesser provost marshal"; Captain John Kennedy, New York City chief of police, who, leading four detectives, joined in the manhunt at the request of Edwin Stanton; Colonel H. S. Olcott, who led a New York squad of "secret service" men; Colonel H. H. Wells, leading the troops of Major General Christopher C. Augur, commander of the Department of Washington, Twenty-Second Corps; and Major A. C. Richards, superintendent of the capital's police. In addition to these, General John P. Slough, headquartered at Alexandria, was ordered to bottle up the capital, and other commanders in Virginia and Maryland were told to seal their cities and towns. Stanton added another man to the dragnet:

Washington, April 15, 1865.

Colonel L. C. Baker:
Come here immediately and see if you can find the murderer of the President.

Edwin M. Stanton
Secretary of War.

On his arrival, despite the secretary's summons, Baker was met with an icy reception at General Augur's headquarters. As the operatives of Pinkerton and Baker had tripped over one another during the early years of war, so now the array of forces searching for the assassins worked at cross purposes. If anything, the one hundred thousand dollars in reward money offered for the capture of the assassins further discouraged cooperation and coordination among the manhunters. It was not until April 24 that Baker was empowered by Stanton to draw a twenty-five-man cavalry force from Major General Winfield Scott Hancock's command. Baker put the detachment, from the Sixteenth New York Cavalry, under the orders of his cousin, Lieutenant Luther B. Baker, who shared command with Everton Conger, a member of Baker's National Detective Police.

"You are going after Booth," Lafayette Baker told Cousin Luther. "Lieutenant, we have got a sure thing."

There are those who attach great significance to this remark, believing that the wily detective had access to inside information as to the whereabouts of Booth and Herold. For, in the period between April 15 and the 24th, Lafayette Baker's own detectives had been scouring the Maryland peninsula quite independently from the other manhunters. In a later investigation of the pursuit of Booth and Herold, Lafayette Baker claimed that his operatives turned up "a colored man," who had seen the conspirators "entering a small boat in the vicinity of Swan's Point. . . . This information, with my preconceived theory as to the movements of the assassins, decided my course."

The trouble is that the "colored man" was not identified and never presented a claim for the reward to which his information would have entitled him. Some years later, Albert Gallatin Riddle, a lawyer who successfully defended Baker when he was charged with "false imprisonment" and robbery in 1867, lauded the detective for his brilliant work in running the assassins to ground. But, Riddle pointed out, "The old negro informant . . . was a pure creation of the genius of L. C. Baker." Why did Baker invent him? And if the "colored man" did not exist, how did Baker know where to send his cavalry detachment? While at least fourteen hundred troops combed the countryside in vain, these few men located the fugitives holed up in the tobacco shed of the Garrett family farm near Port Royal, Virginia.

Some have ascribed the find to good luck. Others to the skill and intuition of Lafayette Baker. In his rambling autobiography, Baker included an engraving of himself with Cousin Luther and Lieutenant Colonel Conger. With a map of Virginia spread out before them, Lafayette Baker lays out the plan of pursuit. Riddle reported that the engraving, which also appeared in contemporary magazine articles, was accurate. "Before the starting of the party," Riddle wrote, "the Chief spread out a map of Virginia and designated the crossing-place of the fugitives and the place where they had probably landed; then, taking a compass, he placed one point at Port Conway, where a road crossed the Rappahannock, and drew a circle, which he said included a space of ten miles around that point, and within which that territory they would find the fugitives."

Still others have concluded that Lafayette C. Baker was a key figure in a conspiracy involving Edwin M. Stanton and Vice-President Andrew Johnson, both of whom, they contend, stood to profit by the death of Abraham Lincoln. Stanton, tremendously unpopular, was a ruthless asset to Lincoln during the war. With peace, however, many expected that the president would succumb to mounting pressure to divest himself of Stanton. Johnson, of course, had the most to gain from Lincoln's death. It would make him president.

The grand conspiracy theory, developed most fully by Otto Eisenschiml in *Why Was Lincoln Murdered?*, received what seemed to many overwhelming validation in 1961 when Ray A. Neff, a professional chemist and amateur Civil War buff, published an extraordinary discovery in *Civil War Times*. Perusing an 1864 bound volume of *Colburn's United Service Magazine*, a British military journal he had purchased for fifty cents in a second-hand bookstore in Philadelphia, Neff discovered two handwritten cipher messages. He decoded them, and what they said was astonishing enough. Then this chemist examined the rest of the volume for more messages, but found only some brownish spots. These he examined under ultraviolet light. One of the spots now glowed purple, and Neff applied a solution of tannic acid to it. The faded signature "L. C. Baker" emerged, indicating that he had been the owner of the volume.

"I am constantly being followed," the first message begins.

They are professionals. I cannot fool them. 2-5-68 In new Rome there walked three men, a Judas, a Brutus and a spy. Each planned that he should be the kink [presumably, king] when Abraham should die. One trusted not the other but they went on for that day, waiting for that final moment when with pistol in his hand, one of the sons of Brutus could sneak behind that cursed man and put a bullet in his brain and lay his clumsey corpse away. As the fallen man lay dying, Judas came and paid respects to one he hated, and when at last he saw him die, he said, "Now the ages have him and the nation now have I." [When the President was pronounced dead, Stanton, at his bedside, was heard to say, "Now he belongs to the ages."] But Alas fate would have it Judas slowly fell from g[r]ace, and with him went Brutus [if Stanton is Judas, Johnson must be Brutus] down to their proper place. But lest one is left to wonder what has happened to the spy, I can safely tell you this, it was I. Lafayette C. Baker 2-5-68.

There is more, as the ciphered message gives details of a conspiracy that unmistakably involved Stanton, Johnson, and "at least eleven members of Congress, . . . no less than twelve Army officers, three Naval officers and at least 24 civilians, of which one was a governor of a loyal state. . . . There were probably more that I know nothing of." The message specifies that eighty-five thousand dollars was "contributed by the named persons to pay for the deed" and promises that "these known conspirators" are listed by name in "Vol. one of this series." (Alas, that volume has never turned up.) The second of the two messages concludes: "I fear for my life. LCB."

Subsequently, Neff found a transcript of a hearing, held in Philadelphia in 1872, on the codicil to the last will and testament of Lafayette Curry Baker. According to the transcript, William Carter, who had served under Baker, stated that he saw the detective shortly before his death. "When I came into the room, he had a stack of books by his bed and had one open and was making marks in it. I asked him what he was doing and he said, 'I'm writing my memoirs.' . . . 'But General, them books is already wrote,' and he said, 'Right, they are going to have to get up early to get ahead of old Lafe Baker.' . . . I saw that he was writing cipher [in the book]. . . . It was an English military journal."

The hearing transcript also contained the testimony of Baker's physician, who reported that the detective was being followed during the last months of his life and that several attempts had been made to kill him. A servant in Baker's employ had almost been hit by a bullet shot through the window. Baker told the man something to the effect that they would get him yet. Who? the servant asked. "My old friends," Baker answered. While Baker's death in 1868 had been attributed to meningitis, the physician testified that it could have been caused by arsenic poisoning.

The evidence seems compelling and partakes more of the cloak-and-dagger than just about anything else involved with the Lincoln assassination. Most historians even accept the testimony of handwriting experts as to validity of the signature on the journal volume. It is Lafayette C. Baker historians do not trust. If the ciphered messages were written by him, a dying man, his reputation shattered by his illegal activities in framing the impeachment case against Andrew Johnson as well as by myriad charges of corruption (he was even compelled to return a portion of the reward money collected for having found Booth), they were likely fabricated to settle a score with Stanton and Johnson by implicating them in a heinous conspiracy.

But the end of a book on Civil War espionage is no place to investigate the convolutions of this conspiracy theory, let alone the many others that followed in the wake of Lincoln's murder. (For excellent discussions of them all, see Thomas Reed Turner's *Beware the People Weeping: Public Opinion and the Assassination of Abraham Lincoln* [Baton Rouge, 1982] and William Hanchett's *The Lincoln Murder Conspiracies* [Urbana and Chicago, 1983].) The fact is that we will never know for certain how Lafayette Baker located Booth and Herold. Certainly, his reputation was unsavory enough. If a conspiracy offered opportunity for profit, it is quite possible that Baker would have seized the main chance. But, as we have observed, it is also difficult to picture him as a conspirator in anything so sinister as assassination. In any case, no matter how thick the lurid atmosphere of conspiracy on the one hand, or how bumbling the counterintelligence on the other, it is well to remember that "Old Lafe" Baker was intimately familiar with the routes used by Confederate spies and couriers. It could well be that the single salient difference between him and those who commanded the hundreds of other men searching for the assassins was that Baker, through personal experience as one who had crossed Confederate lines himself, *knew* where to look. The other men pursuing Booth did not.

After midnight on April 26, the detachment under Luther Baker and Everton Conger laid siege to the Garrett tobacco barn. William

Garrett, formerly of the Confederate cavalry, was sent into the tobacco shed for a parley intended to coax the men into surrender. Herold emerged, but Booth resolved to shoot it out. Whereupon the troopers set fire to the shed.

They all could see the silhouette against the flames: a crippled man, with crutch and carbine. Someone—the soldier who claimed credit was Sergeant Boston Corbett—fired a shot that passed through the actor's neck. Others say Booth shot himself.

They dragged him out of the burning structure and laid him on the porch of the Garrett house. The bullet having severed his spinal cord, Booth was paralyzed.

"I thought I did for the best," he gasped out. Then he asked that someone lift his lifeless hands for him, so that he might look at them. This was done. He gazed at his hands.

"Useless, useless."

They were his last words.

It was sunup of a day at the end of a long war, a day haunted by a few more names in a dreadful litany of the dead and the dying. Near Richmond, Ulric Dahlgren's unquiet corpse lay now beneath the farm of Samuel Orrock. In a few months, it would be moved a final time. In Washington, the president also lay dead.

Now his assassin joined him. On this day, too, near Durham Station, North Carolina, the surrender terms agreed to between Grant and Lee at Appomattox were formalized and signed. The Confederate States of America ceased to exist, and the Civil War was ended.

SOURCES

Alexander, Edward Porter. *Military Memoirs of a Confederate.* New York: Charles Scribner's Sons, 1907.

Bakeless, John. "Lincoln's Private Eye." *Civil War Times Illustrated,* October 1975.

_____. *Turncoats, Traitors and Heroes.* Philadelphia: Lippincott, 1959.

_____. *Spies of the Confederacy.* Philadelphia: Lippincott, 1970.

Baker, Lafayette C. *History of the United States Secret Service.* Philadelphia: King and Baird, 1868.

Bates, David Homer. *Lincoln in the Telegraph Office.* New York: Century, 1907.

Beach, Thomas. *Twenty-five Years in the Secret Service: The Recollections of a Spy.* London: Heinemann, 1892.

Benton, Elbert J. *The Movement for Peace without a Victory during the Civil War.* New York: Da Capo, 1972.

Bishop, Jim. *The Day Lincoln Was Shot.* New York: Harper and Brothers, 1955.

Blackford, W. W. *War Years with Jeb Stuart.* New York: Scribner's, 1946.

Boyd, Belle. *Belle Boyd in Camp and Prison.* South Brunswick, N.J.: Thomas Yoseloff, 1968.

Brennan, John C. "The Confederate Plan to Abduct President Lincoln," *Surratt Society News,* March 1981.

_____. "Confederate Spy—Captain Thomas Nelson Conrad," *Surratt Society News,* June 1977.

_____. "General Bradley T. Johnson's Plan to Abduct President Lincoln," *Chronicles of St. Mary's* 22 (November and December, 1974).

Brown, R. Shepard. *Stringfellow of the Fourth: An Amazing Career of the Most Successful Confederate Spy.* New York: Crown, 1960.

Bulloch, James D. *The Secret Service of the Confederate States in Europe.* 2 v. New York: Thomas Yoseloff, 1959.

Butler, Benjamin F. *Butler's Book.* Boston: A. M. Thayer, 1892.

Campbell, Helen Jones. *Confederate Courier.* New York: St. Martin's, 1964.

Canan, H. V. "Confederate Military Intelligence." *Maryland Historical Magazine,* March 1964.

Catton, Bruce. *Glory Road.* New York: Doubleday, 1952.

_____. *Mr. Lincoln's Army.* New York: Doubleday, 1952.

_____. *A Stillness at Appomattox.* New York: Doubleday, 1953.

_____. *This Hallowed Ground.* New York: Doubleday, 1956.

Clarke, Asia Booth. *The Unlocked Book. A Memoir of John Wilkes Booth by His Sister.* New York: G. P. Putnam's Sons, 1938.

Cleary, W. W. "The Attempt to Fasten the Assassination of President Lincoln on President Davis and Other Innocent Parties." *Southern Historical Society Papers* 9 (July and August 1881).

Cleaves, Freeman. *Meade of Gettysburg.* Norman: University of Oklahoma Press, 1960.

Conrad, Thomas. *A Confederate Spy.* New York: S. J. Ogilvie, 1892.

_____. *The Rebel Scout.* Washington, D.C.: The National Publishing Co., 1904.

Cullop, Charles P. *Confederate Propaganda in Europe.* Coral Gables: University of Miami Press, 1969.

Cummins, Edward H. "The Signal Corps in the Confederate States Army." *Southern Historical Society Papers* 16.

Cuthbert, Norma B., ed. *Lincoln and the Baltimore Plot.* San Marino, California: Huntington Library, 1949.

Davis, Curtis Carroll. "The Civil War's Most Over-Rated Spy." *West Virginia History,* October 1965.

Davis, William C. "Behind the Lines," *Civil War Times Illustrated,* November 1981.

Dean, Henry Clay. *Crimes of the Civil War.* Baltimore: Wm. T. Smithson, 1868.

Doherty, Edward P. "Pursuit and Death of John Wilkes Booth: Captain Doherty's Narrative," *Century Magazine,* January 1890.

Duberman, Martin B. *Charles Francis Adams.* Boston: Houghton Mifflin, 1960.

Dye, John Smith. *History of the Plots and Crimes of the Great Conspiracy to Overthrow Liberty in America.* 1866; reprint ed., Freeport, New York: Books for Libraries, 1969.

Edmonds, S. Emma. *Nurse and Spy in the Union Army.* Hartford: W.F. William and Company, 1865; originally published as *Unsexed, or the Female Soldier.* 1864.

Eisenschiml, Otto. *Why Was Lincoln Murdered?* Boston: Little, Brown, 1937.

Fishel, Edwin C. "The Mythology of Civil War Intelligence." *Civil War History,* December 1964.

Foote, Shelby. *The Civil War: A Narrative.* 3 vols. New York: Random House, 1958.

Fowler, Robert H. "New Evidence in [the] Lincoln Murder Conspiracy," *Civil War Times Illustrated,* February 1965.

_____. "Was Stanton behind Lincoln's Murder?" *Civil War Times,* August 1961.

Frank, Seymour J. "The Conspiracy to Implicate the Confederate Leaders in Lincoln's Assassination," *Mississippi Valley Historical Review* 40 (March 1954).

Freeman, Douglas Southall. *R.E. Lee: A Biography.* 4 vols. New York: Charles Scribner's Sons, 1935.

Freese, Jacob. *Secrets of the Late Rebellion.* Philadelphia: Crombarger, 1882.

Gaddy, David W. "Gray Cloaks and Daggers." *Civil War Times*, July 1975.

_____. "The Surratt Tavern—A Confederate 'Safe House'?" *Surratt Society News*, April 1979.

_____. "William Norris and the Confederate Signal and Secret Service." *Maryland Historical Magazine*, Summer 1975.

Garrett, Richard Baynham. "A Chapter of Unwritten History. . . . Account of the Flight and Death of John Wilkes Booth." *Virginia Magazine of History and Biography* 71 (October 1963).

Glenn, William Wilkins. *Between North and South. A Maryland Journalist Views the Civil War*, ed. Bayly Ellen Marks and Mark Norton Schatz. Rutherford, New Jersey: Farleigh Dickinson University Press, 1976.

Gragg, Rod. *The Illustrated Confederate Reader*. New York: Harper and Row, 1989.

Gray, Wood. *The Hidden Civil War: The Story of the Copperheads*. New York: Viking, 1942.

Green, Constance McLaughlin. *Washington: Village and Capital, 1800-1878*. Princeton: Princeton University Press, 1962.

Greenhow, Rose O'Neal. *My Imprisonment and the First Year of Abolition Rule in Washington*. London: Robert Bentley, 1863.

Gregory, W. S. "The CSA Signal Corps." *Confederate Veteran* 3 (August 1924).

Hall, James O. "The Mystery of Lincoln's Guard." *Surratt Society News*, May 1982.

_____. *Notes on the John Wilkes Booth Escape Route*. Clinton, Maryland: The Surratt Society, 1980.

Hanchett, William. *The Lincoln Murder Conspiracies*. Urbana and Chicago: University of Illinois Press, 1983.

_____. "Booth's Diary," *Journal of the Illinois State Historical Society* 72 (February 1979).

Headley, John W. *Confederate Operations in Canada and the North*. New York: Neale, 1906.

Hirshson, Stanley P. *Grenville M. Dodge: Soldier, Politician, Railroad Pioneer*. Bloomington: Indiana University Press, 1967.

Hitchcock, Ethan Allen. *Fifty Years of Camp and Field.* Edited by W. Croffut. New York: Putnam, 1909.

Horan, James D. *Confederate Agent.* New York: Crown, 1954.

_____. *The Pinkertons: The Detective Dynasty That Made History.* New York: Crown, 1967.

Hyman, Harold M. *With Malice Toward Some: Scholarship (or Something Less) on the Lincoln Murder.* Springfield, Illinois: Abraham Lincoln Association, 1978.

Johns, George. S. *Philip Henson, The Southern Union Spy.* St. Louis: Nixon-Jones Printing Co., 1887.

Johnson, Angus J. *Virginia Railroads in the Civil War.* Chapel Hill: University of North Carolina Press, 1961.

_____. "Disloyalty on Confederate Railroads in Virginia." *Virginia Magazine of History and Biography* 63 (1955).

Jones, J. B. *A Rebel Clerk's Diary.* New York: Old Hickory Bookshop, 1935.

Jones, J. Wm., comp. "The Kilpatrick-Dahlgren Raid Against Richmond." *Southern Historical Society Papers* 13 (1885).

Jones, Katherine M. *Heroines of Dixie: Confederate Women Tell Their Story of the War.* Indianapolis and New York: Bobbs-Merrill, 1955.

Jones, Thomas A. *J. Wilkes Booth: An Account of His Sojourn in Southern Maryland . . . and His Death in Virginia.* Chicago: Laird & Lee, 1893.

Jones, Virgil Carrington. *The Civil War at Sea.* 3 vols. New York: Holt, Rinehart, and Winston, 1960.

_____. *Eight Hours Before Richmond.* New York, Henry Holt, 1957.

_____. *Gray Ghosts and Rebel Raiders.* New York: Henry Holt, 1956.

Kane, Harnett T. *Spies for the Blue and Gray.* Garden City, N.Y.: Hanover House, 1954.

Kimmel, Stanley. *Mr. Lincoln's Washington.* New York: Bramball House, 1957.

Kirkland, Edward Chase. *The Peacemakers of 1864.* New York: Macmillan, 1927.

Kinchen, Oscar A. *Confederate Operations in Canada and the North.* North Quincy, Mass.: Christopher, 1970.

_____. *Daredevils of the Confederate Army.* Boston: Christopher, 1959.

Klein, Maury. *Edward Porter Alexander.* Athens: University of Georgia Press, 1971.

Lamon, Ward Hill. *Recollections of Abraham Lincoln.* Edited by Dorothy Lamon Teillard. Washington: Teillard, 1895, 1911.

Leech, Margaret. *Reveille in Washington.* New York: Harper, 1941.

Lester, Richard L. *Confederate Finance and Purchasing in Great Britain.* Charlottesville: University of Virginia Press, 1975.

Logan, John A. *The Great Conspiracy.* New York: A. R. Hart & Co., 1886.

Lord, Walter, ed. *The Fremantle Diary: Being the Journal of Lieutenant Colonel Arthur James Lyon Fremantle, Coldstream Guards, on his Three Months in the Southern States.* New York: Capricorn Books, 1960.

McLoughlin, Emmett. *An Inquiry into the Assassination of Abraham Lincoln.* New York: Lyle Stuart, 1963.

Marshall, John A. *American Bastille: A History of the Illegal Arrests and Imprisonment of American Citizens during the Late Civil War.* 23d ed. Philadelphia: Thomas W. Hartley, 1877.

Maynard, Douglas. "Plotting the Escape of the *Alabama.*" *Journal of Southern History,* May 1954.

_____. "Union Efforts to Prevent the Escape of the *Alabama.*" *Mississippi Valley Historical Review,* June 1954.

Miers, Earl Schenck, ed. *Lincoln Day by Day.* 3 vols. Washington: Lincoln Sesquicentennial Commission, 1960.

Miller, Nathan. *The U.S. Navy: An Illustrated History.* Annapolis, Maryland: Naval Institute Press, 1977.

Mitgang, Herbert. "Garibaldi and Lincoln." *American Heritage,* October 1975.

Mogelever, Jacob. *Death to Traitors: The Story of General Lafayette*

C, Baker, *Lincoln's Forgotten Secret Service Chief.* Garden City, N.Y.: Doubleday, 1960.

Montross, Lynn. *The Reluctant Rebels.* New York: Harper & Row, 1950.

Mudd, Samuel A. *The Life of Dr. Samuel A. Mudd.* Edited by Nettie Mudd. New York: Neale, 1906.

Neely, Mark E., Jr. *The Abraham Lincoln Encyclopedia.* New York: McGraw-Hill, 1982.

_____. "Treason in Indiana: A Review Essay," *Lincoln Lore,* February and March 1974.

Official Records of the Union and Confederate Armies. See *War of the Rebellion,* below.

Official Records of the Union and Confederate Navies. 30 vols. Washington: Government Printing Office, 1894–1914.

Otey, W. N. M. "Organizing a Signal Corps." *Confederate Veteran* 7 (December 1899), 8 (March 1900), 9 (August 1900).

Owsley, Frank L. *King Cotton Diplomacy.* Chicago: University of Chicago Press, 1959.

Owsley, Harriet C. "Henry Shelton Sanford and Federal Surveillance Abroad." *Mississippi Valley Historical Review,* September 1961.

Patrick, Marsena R. *Inside Lincoln's Army: The Diary of Marsena R. Patrick.* Edited by David Sparks. New York: Thomas Yoseloff, 1964.

Perry, Milton F. *Infernal Machines: The Story of Confederate Submarine and Mine Warfare.* Baton Rouge: Louisiana State University Press, 1965.

Police Records of Spies, Smugglers, and Rebel Emissaries in Tennessee. Philadelphia: 1863.

Robinson, William M. *Justice in Grey: A History of the Judicial System of the Confederate States of America.* Cambridge: Harvard University Press, 1941.

Roscoe, Theodore. *The Web of Conspiracy: The Complete Story of the Men Who Murdered Lincoln.* Englewood Cliffs, New Jersey: Prentice-Hall, 1959.

Ross, Isabel. *Rebel Rose: The Life of Rose O'Neal Greenhow.* New York: Harper, 1954.

Ruggles, M. B. "Pursuit and Death of John Wilkes Booth: Major Ruggles's Narrative," *Century Magazine* 39 (January 1890).

Salisbury, Allen. *The Civil War and the American System: America's Battle with Britain, 1860–1876.* New York: Campaigner Publications, 1978.

Scheips, Paul. J. "Union Signal Communications: Innovation and Conflict." *Civil War History* 9 (December 1963).

Shelton, Vaughan. *Mask for Treason: The Lincoln Murder Trial.* Harrisburg: Stackpole Books, 1965.

Sherman, William Tecumseh. *Memoirs.* 2 vols. New York: D. Appleton, 1875.

Sloan, Richard E., ed. *The Lincoln Log.* Seaford, New York: Privately printed, 1975–81.

Spencer, Warren F. *The Confederate Navy in Europe.* Tuscaloosa: University of Alabama Press, 1983.

Stern, Philip Van Doren. *The Confederate Navy: A Pictorial History.* Garden City, New York: Doubleday, 1962.

_____. *The Man Who Killed Lincoln.* New York: Literary Guild, 1939.

Stidger, Felix W. *Treason History of the Order of the Sons of Liberty.* Chicago: By the author, 1903.

Stoddard, William O. *Inside the White House in War Times.* New York: Webster, 1890.

Stuart, Meriwether. "Colonel Ulric Dahlgren and Richmond's Union Underground." *Virginia Magazine of History and Biography* 72 (1964).

_____. "Samuel Ruth and General R. E. Lee." *Virginia Magazine of History and Biography* 71 (1963).

[Sweet, Benjamin J.]. "The Chicago Conspiracy," *Atlantic Monthly,* July 1865.

Swett, Leonard. "The Conspiracies of the Rebellion." *North American Review,* February 1887.

Surratt, John H. "Lecture on the Lincoln Conspiracy." *Lincoln Herald* 51 (December 1949).

Tatum, Georgia Lee. *Disloyalty in the Confederacy.* Chapel Hill: University of North Carolina Press, 1934.

Thomas, Benjamin P., and Harold Hyman. *Stanton: The Life and Times of Lincoln's Secretary of War.* New York: Knopf, 1962.

Thomason, John W. *Jeb Stuart.* New York: Scribner's, 1930.

Thompson, George Raynor. "Civil War Signals." *Military Affairs* 8 (Winter 1954).

Townsend, George Alfred. "How Wilkes Booth Crossed the Potomac." *Century Magazine,* April 1884.

Turner, Thomas Reed. *Beware the People Weeping: Public Opinion and the Assassination of Abraham Lincoln.* Baton Rouge and London: Louisiana State University Press, 1982.

War of the Rebellion: A Compilation of the Official Records of the Union and Confederate States Armies. 130 vols. Washington: Government Printing Office, 1880–1901.

Winks, Robin W. *Canada and the United States: The Civil War Years.* Baltimore: Johns Hopkins University Press, 1960.

Woodward, C. Vann, ed. *Mary Chesnut's Civil War.* New Haven and London: Yale University Press, 1981.

Younger, Edward, ed. *Inside the Confederate Government: The Diary of Robert Garlick Hill Kean.* New York: Oxford University Press, 1957.

INDEX